ROCK ART AND
THE PREHISTORY OF ATLANTIC EUROPE

———— •◆• ————

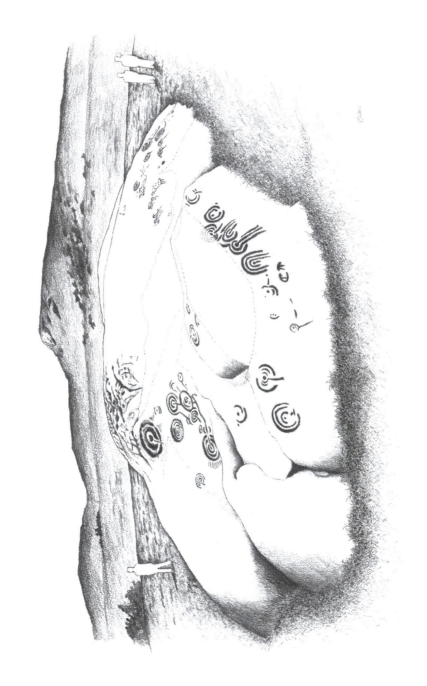

Reconstruction of the carved rock at Roughting Linn (drawing: Aaron Watson)

ROCK ART AND THE PREHISTORY OF ATLANTIC EUROPE

—·◆·—

Signing the Land

Richard Bradley

Richard Bradley (signature)

London and New York

First published 1997
by Routledge
11 New Fetter Lane, London EC4P 4EE

Simultaneously published in the USA and Canada
by Routledge
29 West 35th Street, New York, NY 10001

Typeset in Garamond by
Florencetype Ltd, Stoodleigh, Devon

Printed and bound in Great Britain by
T.J. International Ltd, Padstow, Cornwall

British Library Cataloguing in Publication Data
A catalogue record for this book is available from the British Library

Library of Congress Cataloguing in Publication Data
Bradley, Richard
Rock art and the prehistory of Atlantic Europe: signing the land
Richard Bradley.
Includes bibliographical references and index.
1. Art. Prehistoric – Europe – Atlantic Coast. 2. Petroglyphs –
Europe – Atlantic Coast. 3. Rock paintings – Europe – Atlantic Coast.
4. Atlantic Coast (Europe) – Antiquities. I. Title.
GN803.B66   1997
709′.01′13094 – dc21   96-51119

ISBN 0–415–16535–0
0–415–16536–9 (pbk)

CONTENTS

— ·◆· —

— Contents —

PART III: ROCK ART AND THE LANDSCAPE OF ATLANTIC EUROPE

FIGURES

—— •◆• ——

vii

TABLES

———— •◆• ————

PLATES

———— •◆• ————

For Stan Beckensall and John Coles

PREFACE AND
ACKNOWLEDGEMENTS

—— ·◆· ——

I remember that in 1987 I was asked what I expected to be the important growth areas in prehistoric archaeology. I suggested three fields of study: the deposition of artefacts, the role of monumental architecture and the analysis of ancient art. Perhaps they came to mind because I was already interested in those particular topics, but I did not contemplate writing about them at any length. Little did I know that eight years later I would be completing an informal trilogy concerned with just those issues. *The Passage of Arms* was a study of hoards and votive deposits. *Altering the Earth*, which began life as a series of public lectures, considered the origins of monuments. This book draws on both those projects and takes on the most difficult subject of all three: the interpretation of prehistoric rock art.

I have only been able to write this book through the help of many people and organisations. The main body of the work was carried out whilst I held a British Academy Research Readership in the Humanities; the Academy also contributed generously to the costs of travel and fieldwork. Field surveys here and on the Continent were also funded by grants from the Galician Xunta, the Prehistoric Society, the Society of Antiquaries of London, the Society of Antiquaries of Scotland, the Northumbria National Park and my own university in Reading. Additional travel was funded by Reading University and the British Council.

Much of that fieldwork was undertaken in collaboration with other people. In this country I must thank Tess Durden, Jan Harding, Margaret Mathews, Steve Rippon and Nigel Spenser for all their help and hard work. Full accounts of this research have already been published jointly. The same applies to my fieldwork in Galicia, which was undertaken and published together with Felipe Criado and Ramón Fábregas. This work was carried out with the permission of the Galician Xunta. The book draws on the results of all these projects, but I take sole responsibility for the ways in which they are used here.

In addition, many people have made this project easier and much more enjoyable by showing me their sites, answering my questions, discussing their ideas and commenting on my interpretations. My thanks are due to the following: Gordon Barclay, Antonio Baptista, John Barrett, Martin Bell, Barbara Bender, Jacques Briard, Serge Cassen, Bob Chapman, Christopher Chippindale, Ros Cleal, Angel

Concheiro, Javier Costas, Jeremy Dronfield, Gavin Edwards, Kevin Edwards, George Eogan, Ana Filgueiras, Paul Frodsham, Vince Gaffney, Clive Gamble, Julie Gardiner, Paul Garwood, Lola Gil, Bill Godfrey, Matilde González, John Hedges, Knut Helsgog, Ian Hewitt, Gwylym Hughes, Fausto Infante, Peter Jackson, Susana Jorge, Vitor Jorge, Bob Layton, Tim Laurie, Charles-Tanguy Le Roux, David Lewis-Williams, Joyce Marcus, Fidel Méndez, Roger Mercer, Steve Mithen, Howard Morphy, Muiris O'Sullivan, Antonio de la Peña, Rafael Penedo, Avril Purcell, Pepa Rey, Frances Raymond, Colin Renfrew, Colin Richards, Tomás Rodríguez, Marisa Ruiz-Gálvez, Maria de Jesus Sanches, Manuel Santos, Paula de Mota Santos, Ruth Saunders, Doug Scott, Elizabeth Shee Twohig, Alison Sheridan, Derek Simpson, Jack Stevenson, Julian Thomas, Maarten Van Hoek, Victoria Villoch, Pat Vinnicombe, Helen Watson, Alasdair Whittle and Sonia Yellowlees.

I would like to thank the following publishers for permission to use copyright material: Chatto & Windus for an extract from David Malouf, *An Imaginary Life*; Faber & Faber for an extract from 'The Voyage' by Edwin Muir in Edwin Muir, *Collected Poems*; and Ismail Kadare: lines from *The Palace of Dreams*. First published in Albania in 1981 with the title *Nepunesi i pallatit te endrrave*. First published in Great Britain in 1993 by Harvill. Copyright © Librairie Arthème Fayard, 1990. English translation © HarperCollins Publishers 1993. Reproduced by permission of the Harvill Press.

Lyn Sellwood produced virtually all the figures and did so to a very tight timetable. Aaron Watson is responsible for the reconstruction drawings of Roughting Linn and for three of the photographs; the others are my own. Mark Edmonds, Ramón Fábregas and Martin Henig read all or part of the text and suggested many improvements. Katherine suffered my constant absences from home. I am extremely grateful to them all.

Rock art is one of those fields in which amateurs and professionals have been able to work together successfully. It is only right that I dedicate this book to the two people who have done most to encourage and support me in this work: Stan Beckensall, the most devoted of amateur archaeologists, and John Coles, the consummate professional. Between them they have introduced me to the pleasures of studying rock art. I hope that this book reflects something of that enjoyment.

Richard Bradley
September 1995

PART I

TERMS OF REFERENCE

—— ·◆· ——

How can I give you any notion ... of what earth was in its original bleakness, before we brought to it the order of industry, the terraces, fields, orchards, pastures, the irrigated gardens of the world we are making in our own image?

Do you think of ... [the] land you now inhabit ... as a place given you by the gods ready-made in all its placid beauty? It is not. It is a created place. If the gods are with you there, glowing out of a tree in some pasture or shaking their spirit over the pebbles of a brook in clear sunlight, in wells, in springs, in a stone that marks the edge of your legal right over a hillside; if the gods are there, it is because you have discovered them there, drawn them up out of your soul's need for them and dreamed them into the landscape to make it shine.

David Malouf (1978) *An Imaginary Life*

CHAPTER ONE

NEW DIRECTIONS, NEW POINTS OF VIEW
The experience of prehistoric rock art

———— •◆• ————

INTRODUCTION

As archaeologists, we sometimes wonder how we can know about the past, but members of the public may have a different question in mind, for time and again they ask us where we get our ideas.

Our answers are often rather pretentious, and sometimes they are misleading, for we claim that our research grows directly out of the body of abstract ideas that we talk of as archaeological theory. That is both true and false. It is true that without an explicit range of theories and assumptions we cannot say anything at all about the past, but such a reply is also rather evasive. Archaeologists work in many different ways, but as often as not the cue for a new piece of research is a pattern that is identified by chance and one which has not been predicted. That moment of recognition is first and foremost an experience, but an experience that can only be understood in terms of a theory. We may have some ideas about the significance of that discovery, but from then onwards the experience itself becomes less important. If the initial observation is to be communicated – still more, if it is to be understood – we must work out why it occurred in the first place. We have to retrace the processes by which that experience was formed and, having done so, we must analyse them as strictly as we can. We must find out whether such an imaginative leap was justified by any evidence and we must trace its implications using the theories and methods at our command.

The subject of this book is one which easily provokes such reflections. For years it has attracted the attention of 'alternative archaeologists', nearly all of whom have interpretations of their own. Whilst I was excavating a monument which contains several prehistoric rock carvings, members of the public suggested many reasons why these designs were made. Nearly all those ideas emerged spontaneously from what they saw, and a few were certainly influenced by strong personal beliefs. The sources of such ideas are important to those who suggest them, and they must not be dismissed by archaeologists. The question is whether there is any method by which such interpretations can be assessed.

The late Ronald Morris, who spent many years studying the prehistoric rock carvings of the British Isles, heard many accounts of this phenomenon. In fact he listed more than a hundred separate interpretations of these images, marking them out of ten for plausibility. Applying his professional judgement as a lawyer, he awarded marks of six and above to just 22 per cent of the suggestions; 53 per cent were marked between one and five, and 25 per cent failed entirely, with a mark of nought (Morris 1979, 16–28). Every archaeologist who has studied the same material would add to Morris's list and no doubt they would rank those ideas in their own ways. The important point is not that different people prefer different interpretations, or that many of those ideas are very subjective. It is that such ideas must be discussed in a disciplined manner if they are to inform prehistoric archaeology. One aim of this book is to offer such a discussion.

What is rock art, and what has its study to offer to the well-established discipline of field archaeology? This is where the question of experience is so important. I can best approach those questions by describing my first encounter with rock carvings, for that experience was instrumental in persuading me to study them in detail.

Archaeological field projects tend to flow into one another, and this study of prehistoric rock art, which was carried out at various points between 1990 and 1995, had its origin in an excavation which I conducted during the 1980s. Together with Mark Edmonds, I was excavating the Neolithic axe quarries at Great Langdale in north-west England, and we were coming to realise that our work was producing unexpected results (Bradley and Edmonds 1993, chapters 7 and 10). There was a clear sequence of quarries on these sites, and although the people who had used the later stone sources were making axes more efficiently than their predecessors, it was impossible to study their activities in terms of technology alone. The later quarries were located on perilous ledges, yet to reach these places at all people would have crossed exposures of equally suitable rock which they did not use. They preferred to work, at great inconvenience to themselves, in a spectacular natural setting with an enormous view.

One day we closed the excavation and went on a field trip to West Yorkshire, and here we visited a number of recently published rock carvings on Ilkley Moor. Many of the boulders and outcrops were decorated with abstract motifs (Ilkley Archaeology Group 1986). It was because of our work at Langdale that we were less impressed by these carvings than we were by their natural setting. Some of the most elaborate carved surfaces were located in positions that commanded extensive views over the lower ground (Pl. 1). Once again this was a way of considering the prehistoric landscape that had played little part in the archaeological literature. It was not consistent with the studies of settlement sites that I knew best. Nor were the carved rocks really monuments like so many of the structures built at prominent places in the uplands. That visit to Ilkley Moor set me wondering just how such places had been used.

SOME DEFINITIONS

Having approached my subject obliquely, I must retrace my steps and offer a more formal definition of this material. The term 'rock art' is unsatisfactory, but, as happens with so many technical terms, it is too late to look for an alternative now. It is meant to describe the distinctive practice of painting or carving natural surfaces in the landscape. It is the fact that these motifs were created on stone that has ensured their survival, but we should not suppose that they were limited to this particular medium. Similar motifs might once have extended to other materials; an example is the Australian practice of carving living trees (Rhoads 1992). They may have been found still more widely, for example in body paintings, house decoration, the patterns on clothing or even as the owners' marks on domesticated animals (Layton 1991; Odak 1989).

In fact the distribution of prehistoric rock art may have been drastically reduced. In the area studied in this book many exposed rocks are too friable to retain any evidence of decoration. Some surfaces are being destroyed by acid rain, whilst the prevailing climate between Scotland and northern Spain is far too moist to allow any paintings to survive. These are serious problems, but they are not insuperable, for with few exceptions we can say that the motifs carved on natural surfaces in the landscape are not quite the same as those found on stone-built monuments. To that extent at least we are dealing with a distinctive phenomenon.

The word 'art' poses a further problem. I should make it clear that this is another technical term which has been used for so long that it is difficult to replace it now. A more neutral terminology would refer to 'rock carvings', 'rock drawings', 'rock motifs' or even to 'petroglyphs'. In each case this would be done to avoid any implication that we are studying a purely aesthetic phenomenon. These carvings might have been a medium for creative self-expression, but that is not a claim that we could substantiate today. The subtitle of this book emphasises a different approach. Among other things, the motifs are 'signs'; they are items of information that were inscribed at specific points in the terrain. Taken singly or in combination, those signs would have carried particular meanings for particular people. I shall argue that we will understand this material better if we consider how such a system worked in terms of the broader uses of the landscape.

ROCK ART RESEARCH AND LANDSCAPE ARCHAEOLOGY

I have described my reaction at first seeing the rock carvings on Ilkley Moor. Why did it seem so difficult to interpret these sites according to the methods employed in landscape archaeology? Once again the problem is partly one of definition. Just as we can be misled by contemporary conceptions of 'art', so we can form a false impression of the prehistoric landscape. As we shall see, the rock carvings of Atlantic Europe span the Neolithic and Early Bronze Age periods, but until recently archaeologists studying those phases had placed too much emphasis on the distribution of fixed resources. They tended to think in terms of a stable pattern of settlements, boundaries and fields, not unlike the world that we inhabit today. The distribution of human activity was determined by the requirements of sedentary agriculture (Barker 1985). Consequently, the best way in which to study the landscape was to think in terms of agricultural territories radiating out from permanent settlements.

This way of thinking about the landscape raises a number of problems. First, the importance of cereal agriculture is often assumed rather than demonstrated, with the result that it has been enough to identify the presence of domesticated resources for archaeologists to postulate a pattern of sedentary mixed farming. This does not make enough allowance for the importance of mobility long after the first experiments with agriculture. Second, this approach overlooks a fundamental distinction in the archaeology of many regions where fixed settlements are first found with any regularity in the later second and first millennia BC. Until then the main features of the landscape are specialised monuments devoted to the dead. It is to this period that the rock carvings probably belong.

I mentioned that some of the more striking rock art on Ilkley Moor is located in places with an extensive view over the lower ground. This suggests a very different perception of the landscape. In fact this particular example encapsulates the problem quite effectively, as John Bintliff has taken exactly the same concentration of rock carvings to mark the centre of an agricultural territory and has supported his view by plotting them on a map of the local soils (Bintliff 1988, 129–30). But the siting of some of these carvings at viewpoints makes it at least as probable that they overlooked areas of settlement on the more sheltered land in the valleys. If so, then they were towards the edge of the prehistoric landscape rather than at its centre.

The anthropologist Tim Ingold has commented on a similar distinction. Hunter gatherers, he says, exercise a different form of land tenure from settled farmers. For hunter gatherers (and I would extend his scheme to other mobile peoples) tenure is based on 'sites and paths'. Territories are conceived in terms of the trails running through the landscape and the views across it. Such paths and places may be controlled by specific groups. 'In agricultural societies, on the other hand ... the cultivator appropriates the land in plots, which may be relatively dispersed or consolidated' (1986, 153). It is only in this case that territories can be considered in terms of continuous boundaries.

A rather similar point is made by Peter Wilson:

> The hunter/gatherer pins ideas and emotions onto the world as it exists. ...
> A construction is put upon the landscape rather than the landscape undergoing reconstruction, as is the case among sedentary people, who impose houses, villages and gardens on the landscape, often in the place of natural landmarks.
>
> (1988, 50)

The landscape archaeology of prehistoric Europe is primarily an archaeology of settled communities. Hunter gatherers have been studied effectively for many years, but the same approaches very rarely extend to the archaeology of later populations. It is only recently that more attention has been paid to what Spanish archaeologists have described as the 'archaeology of mobility' (Infante, Vaquero and Criado 1992).

These distinctions are important when we consider the chronological and geographical distribution of European rock art. I am not concerned with the Palaeolithic or Mesolithic periods, but even after those phases the evidence is widely distributed, with major groups of sites in southern France, northern Italy, the Iberian peninsula, Scandinavia, Britain and Ireland. Apart perhaps from northern Italy and south Scandinavia, these regions have certain features in common. Either they are too remotely located to have experienced intensive mixed farming or they are areas in which agriculture was adopted gradually and where it may not have assumed an overriding importance until the Later Bronze Age or Iron Age. A few areas like the northern part of Scandinavia remained beyond the agricultural frontier entirely (Hagen 1990), whilst in most of the others it is difficult to identify a stable pattern of settlement contemporary with the creation of the rock art. Even where cultivation coexisted with hunting and pastoralism, the rock carvings tend to be found in those areas best suited to mobile exploitation.

Still more important, rock art tends to disappear by the period of agricultural intensification during the Later Bronze Age and Iron Age. Again there are exceptions, but for the most part it appears that the establishment of a fully agricultural economy and a network of permanent settlements epitomises a quite different way of seeing the world. I shall discuss the evidence from Atlantic Europe in later chapters, but the point to emphasise here is that over a much wider area rock art seems to be a feature of the period in which mobility remained important and animals, both wild and domesticated, played a significant role in the economy (Bradley 1993, chapter 2). When that way of life changed, rock art generally went out of use.

If this is correct, it means that rock art was more significant in those situations in which Ingold envisages a pattern of land tenure based on paths, places and viewpoints. It lost much of its impact as this was replaced by a territorial system depending on stable mixed farming. As we have seen, only then could territories be conceived in terms of an enclosed area and a continuous boundary. It is this second system that has provided so much of the evidence studied by archaeologists. Perhaps rock art may have a part to play in studies of another kind of landscape.

THE STATUS OF ROCK ART STUDIES IN EUROPEAN ARCHAEOLOGY

If the assumptions of landscape archaeology have their limitations, there are more criticisms to make of the state of rock art research as it affects our understanding of the Neolithic and Bronze Age periods in Europe. In fact the most serious criticism is that in many regions it plays little part in the study of prehistory. It exists as a separate field, with its own institutions and its own publications. Outside Scandinavia and the Iberian peninsula, it is very difficult to connect this kind of research with the dominant concerns of modern archaeology.

To some extent this has come about through an overemphasis on discovery and documentation. Both are laudable aims, but one sometimes feels that they have become an end in themselves. At one extreme there are regions like the British Isles where virtually all the work has been conducted by amateur archaeologists. Their records are of varying quality, although the best of them are excellent. The problem is that not all these people have wished to interpret their findings in a wider context. This is not surprising when so few sites are protected and displayed to the public.

At the other extreme there are groups of sites like those at Valcamonica and Mont Bego where the exceptional quality of the rock art has generated an academic industry (Anati 1994; De Lumley 1995). It has also led to a curiously introverted kind of research, which seems quite out of contact with the main currents in modern archaeology. At its worst it has led to the creation of grandiose interpretations of the imagery based on the literature of comparative religion (Anati 1993). Such projects have an explicit methodology for recording the rock art but seem to lack an equally coherent framework for interpreting it.

In between these two extremes there are many studies which concentrate on the details of the motifs found in prehistoric rock art. Again this is undoubtedly necessary if we are to understand its distribution and chronology, but these results have been won at a price. The carvings, and in some cases the paintings, are detached from the surfaces on which they were created and reproduced on the printed page in exactly the same manner as portable artefacts. As a result publications of this material have an over-familiar air, as if the authors were publishing catalogues of metalwork or pottery. At times this approach breaks up any composition that might be evident on the rockface and divorces the data from all connection with the landscape.

Two examples illustrate this point. In Scandinavia Malmer (1981) has documented the character of prehistoric rock art by dividing its contents into no fewer than 139 separate categories and recording their occurrence in twenty-seven different regions. The same difficulty besets Anati's handbook on the recording and analysis of rock art, based on his work in northern Italy (1976). This recommends the use of three data files. The first, the 'area file', includes twenty-three different fields, yet the only element that extends beyond the rock itself is the provision of a map. The 'file of the rock' includes another twenty-eight fields, but only two of these contain any mention of the topographical position of the carving. The observer is also allowed to note the 'direction faced by the engraved side'. File C, 'classification of the figures', includes 175 variables. Given such a single-minded approach it is small wonder that the study of rock art is often relegated to the margins of modern archaeology.

At this point I should make my own position clear. Rock art research must contribute directly to archaeology if it is to achieve anything of value. It is not a separate discipline, for it is defined by its subject matter and by the techniques that it employs; academic research is identified by its objectives. In this book I shall treat rock art simply as a medium for a wider study of prehistoric society and its occupation of the landscape.

ROCK ART IN THE PREHISTORIC LANDSCAPE

Why should there be a convergence between the areas with prehistoric rock art and those with archaeological evidence of mobile populations? And why was rock art so rarely produced after the agricultural intensification of later prehistory?

I have already drawn attention to Tim Ingold's discussion of land tenure amongst mobile peoples and its implications for the ways in which archaeologists study the pattern of settlement. But its relevance does not end there, for he presents a more detailed discussion of the ways in which those claims are exercised. His argument works from the premise that territoriality is a way of ensuring co-operation between different groups of people who are exploiting the same resources but who are unlikely to meet very often. 'It prevents adjacent groups, ignorant of each other's positions, from traversing the same ground and thereby spoiling the success of their respective ... operations. The same general argument may be applied to the territorial division of grazing grounds in some pastoral societies' (1986, 143). His last point is reinforced in a paper by Michael Casimir (1992), who argues that mobile communities of different kinds are especially concerned to define their territorial rights in areas of above average population or in regions of unusually varied ecology.

How would such a system work in practice? In Ingold's interpretation the process depends on what he calls 'advertisement'. This procedure becomes necessary when different groups of people are not in direct contact with one another. Under those circumstances, 'they must perforce communicate by other means than speech, and must indicate territorial limits by resorting to the "language" of signs. These signs have ... to be "written down" onto the landscape (or seascape) in the form of durable boundary markers ... – notched trees, stone cairns, buoys etc. – whose implicit message can be "read" ... by others' (Ingold 1986, 146–7).

Rock art may have been another medium by which communication of this kind was achieved, but it does not follow that the only function of such a system was to define access to productive resources. There is a broader point at issue here. Why should European rock art be largely restricted to communities who retained an important element of mobility? Although the details would have differed from one area to another, direct communication of any kind would have been unreliable and intermittent. In that case the essential feature would be that rock art provided one means by which different parties, who were not present on the same occasions, could communicate with one another. No doubt it had further functions, but this is one that can be investigated by archaeology.

A promising approach to the analysis of prehistoric rock art is to consider both its content and its audience. Provided it was a means of communication, the two should be connected systematically. We cannot claim to read those messages today, but we can consider the contents of rock art as information of greater or lesser complexity. In the same way, we cannot specify the exact composition of the groups to whom that information was addressed, but we can say something about their likely character by considering where those messages were located in the landscape. Even if the two sides of the equation are difficult to define precisely, the topographical setting in which this exchange occurred will not have altered materially. Some places were probably in the heart of the settled area, and these might have attracted one kind of audience, whilst others were in more remote locations where the audience for the rock art could have been very different.

If this approach is taken, we need to consider each of these elements in more detail. We must address the question of rock art as a source of information before its place in the landscape can be considered. There are two important sources of ideas. In reviewing the first of these issues we can learn from anthropological studies of art in other areas of the world, whilst the second stage in this discussion draws mainly on archaeological research.

ROCK ART AS A SOURCE OF INFORMATION

Perspectives from social anthropology

The main difficulty that archaeologists face in studying prehistoric rock art is that they have no means of knowing what it meant. Perhaps the best course of action is to learn from case studies in which that question can be broached. Although there is little to suggest that individual motifs can be translated directly even today, recent work on the anthropology of art can offer a number of lessons which may have a wider significance.

At an empirical level one point is absolutely crucial. It is quite possible for more than one style of art to exist in the same society (Layton 1992). Such styles may play different roles from one another; they might even be used in quite different contexts. There are ethnographic instances in which one art style is figurative, whilst the other is geometric or abstract. This situation has led to much discussion. There are certainly cases in which the geometric motifs have a more specialised significance. Their apparent simplicity makes them more difficult to understand, and at times these are the images that possess a sacred character (Morphy 1991). Their meanings are protected because they are harder to interpret, and one reason for this emphasis on abstract designs is that they allow a greater amount of ambiguity: any one motif can have several different meanings at the same time (Munn 1973). For this reason the most complex abstract motifs need not have played a more significant role than the simplest ones. The increase in elaboration may have been intended to limit their potential meanings. That is to say, they may have a more precise interpretation than the others because they are less ambiguous.

The distinction between abstract and figurative motifs may be misleading too, for it does not follow that identifiable images are necessarily mundane in character. This mistake has beset many studies of non-western art. Some of these images do not illustrate scenes from everyday life and even the paintings and drawings of animals that play such a prominent part in these compositions can act as metaphors for very complex ideas about the social, natural and supernatural worlds (Morphy 1989). For example, the eland which features so prominently in the art of southern Africa is actually a symbol representing the power of the shaman (Lewis-Williams 1987).

At the same time, it is inappropriate to distinguish too sharply between the sacred and secular properties of rock art. This point has been emphasised by Robert Layton (1992) in his work on Australian rock art. Many of the images are concerned with the deeds of the ancestors and the paths that they followed across the unsettled landscape. This art has a sacred character and yet it also reflects the processes by which native people are linked to particular areas of land. Such a relationship is quite unlike our own ideas of property. It is through their relations to the ancestors and the supernatural that the modern population is able to lay claim to particular resources, yet rock art may be created or renewed in the course of many different activities, from practical tasks like the collection of food to the most specialised ceremonies. In fact the distribution and spacing of ancestral sites proves to be remarkably sensitive to the character of the local ecology (Layton 1986). It would be just as wrong to dismiss the sacred character of the rock art as it would to divorce it entirely from the realities of land use.

Not all rock art need have been equally accessible. Different people might be allowed to visit different places and important distinctions might depend on age, status, gender or ethnic identity. There might also have been limits on the amount of information that would be provided. The meaning of the art might well be influenced by the character of the audience. Howard Morphy (1991) has shown how the meaning of particular designs might only be revealed over a long period of time. The same designs could assume additional layers of significance according to the age and status of the onlooker. Thus any particular symbol need not have a finite meaning at all.

At the same time, a particular motif can also change its meaning according to the contexts in which it is found (Hodder 1992). In our own culture the Christian cross provides an obvious example of this process. It has one set of connotations if it is found in a church, a different meaning if it is on the side of an ambulance and yet another significance if it appears at the mast of a warship. This does not imply that those separate images are entirely unconnected. What it does emphasise is that the meaning of particular images is vitally affected by the contexts in which we encounter them. The same argument applies not only to single motifs but also to entire compositions. Some art styles contain a limited range of motifs, yet the conventions that governed their relations to one another might have changed from region to region. To borrow an analogy from the study of languages, even where the vocabulary seems to be the same, the grammar may be different (Tilley 1991).

It follows from these examples that it would be a futile exercise to try to isolate a single meaning for any motif in prehistoric rock art. It would be equally misguided to suppose that individual panels had one interpretation. The very fact that they survived over such a long period means that there may well have been arguments, even in the past, about the precise significance of the information contained within them, and no doubt those changing interpretations were registered by additions to the carved surface. In certain cases older images might have been renewed as a way of emphasising connections with the past. Each new motif might have qualified the ways in which the others could be understood. This is not surprising, for Paul Tacon (1994) has suggested that the choice of rock as a medium shows that such images were meant to endure.

Perspectives from archaeology

If it is not possible to provide an unequivocal interpretation of ancient art, it might be better to approach the problem from a different direction. Even though the signs can no longer be interpreted, if we can show that they were organised according to certain conventions then they may very well have acted as a source of information.

Ever since the work of Martin Wobst twenty years ago (1977) archaeologists have acknowledged that material culture can serve as a means of communication. His own work was concerned with the ways in which information could be transmitted, and his examples included such basic elements as different styles of dress. He made the crucial point that this process was highly sensitive to the identity of the participants. Thus there might be less information to impart where they came into contact on a regular basis and more would need to be said where they were strangers to one another. The same would apply where the audience was larger or more diverse since each member of that audience would have his or her own expectations and experience. Root (1983) has extended this framework by suggesting that there is an important distinction between 'portable' and 'non-portable' information. It is possible to restrict access to mobile items of material culture through such institutions as sumptuary laws, but it is much easier to control the dissemination of information that remains fixed in one place. One example might be provided by rock carvings, which could not be moved although their locations could be hidden (Hood 1988). Access to these sites might also be restricted by social conventions, as we saw in the case of Australian rock art.

There have already been attempts to extend Wobst's approach from the portable objects described in his original paper to the interpretation of prehistoric art. In this respect four studies have been particularly interesting.

A useful starting point is Clive Gamble's recent account of Palaeolithic art (1991). He compared the exchange of information in the past with the processing of intelligence in the modern world.

> In monitoring radio signals it is obviously impossible to listen in to every conversation or decipher every message. Instead, what is followed is the volume of radio traffic, where a picture based on frequency can be constructed, via a chain of assumptions, into intelligence about the direction and numbers involved in personnel and troop movements. The medium is very much the message and can be quantified and interpreted. In this way complex phenomena can be measured by information flows without precise knowledge of [the content of those messages].
>
> (ibid, 3)

He suggested that the need for artistic communication might have been greater in some periods than in others and that this process would have been influenced by ecological changes and by changes in the pattern of settlement. He illustrates his case by studying the chronology and distribution of Palaeolithic art in Europe.

His approach has recently been extended by Barton, Clark and Cohen (1994) in a more general study of this material. They work from the general proposition that among modern hunter gatherers art is often used to identify 'sacred localities, prominent topographical features, the boundaries of more or less exclusive territories and other . . . landmarks' (ibid, 200). Why is this? They suggest that, where population densities are low, social groups have a flexible composition, and the importance of special places can be transmitted by oral tradition. It is only where population densities are higher and social groups are larger that the situation changes. These features encourage 'the physical demarcation of landmarks near important resources and territorial boundaries' (ibid, 200). This happens 'in order to legitimise group rights to land and resources, and to alert other social groups to these claims'. The authors suggest that such features underlie the regional and chronological distribution of Palaeolithic art in Europe.

Clare Smith (1992), working in two regions of Australia, has taken a comparable approach but on a more limited geographical scale. She has argued that if different motifs had provided a source of information, we might be able to understand the networks in which they were used. In areas with poor resources she suggested that social networks would need to be extensive and information might be shared across a considerable area. Where the local environment was more productive, however, networks should be correspondingly smaller and the distribution of individual motifs should show much less consistency. Both of these ideas were supported by analysis of a large sample of paintings whose history had been recorded.

Smith's study was concerned with items of portable art whose provenance was known. This same applies to Margaret Conkey's analysis of Upper Palaeolithic mobile art at a series of sites in south-west Europe (1980 and 1989). Compared with the objects found at other locations in this region, these were decorated with an unusually wide range of motifs. She suggested that this might be explained because these places had a special role during this period. They were 'aggregation sites' and it was here that people from a wide area around congregated on special occasions. These separate groups identified themselves by their distinctive use of material culture.

These examples operate at quite different geographical scales. Gamble's analysis, like that of Barton and his colleagues, covered an entire continent, whilst Smith's work depended on a systematic comparison between the use of art in two different regions of Australia. Conkey's study operated on the level of the individual site. But all three made particular use of the evidence of portable artefacts. Rock art, on the other hand, is fixed at one place in the landscape. It is this distinctive feature that provides the foundation for a study of rock art in the New World.

Ralph Hartley's work followed the same suggestion that prehistoric art might have provided a source of information (1992). In this case he was working with the records of a large sample of paintings and carvings on the northern Colorado plateau. Although the ethnohistory of this region had already been investigated, he chose not to consider the meanings of these images. In one way this was unfortunate for by doing so he missed the opportunity of interpreting the original significance of the designs. On the other hand, this makes his case study more immediately relevant to the analysis of rock art in western Europe where nothing is known about prehistoric systems of belief. Instead of interpreting the motifs found on the different sites, he developed a purely quantitative measure of the amount of information that they had to convey, based on the number and variety of different images on each rock surface. Lastly, he considered the position of these sites in the wider landscape and offered an interpretation of the prehistoric pattern of land use. On that basis he made a series of predictions about the relationship between the siting of the rock art and the amount of information that it contained. Where rock shelters had been used as occupation sites it seemed reasonable to suppose that access had been restricted to a finite group of people. In this case the art should have provided a limited amount of information. On the other hand, there were instances in which places might be visited by a wider variety of people; the paintings or carvings might also have been created over a long period of time. Such locations could have included sources of permanent water, boulders located along trails, and the bottoms of cliffs or canyons which would have constrained movement across the terrain. Here, Hartley suggested, the rock art might have supplied a greater amount of information.

In the event Hartley discovered that the information imparted by the rock art varied according to its position in the landscape. It was more complex on detached boulders and at the base of cliffs than it was at the rock shelters in his study area. The places which would have been used by the most stable population contained the least differentiated rock art, whilst the parts of the landscape that would have attracted a more diverse group of people contained panels of rock art that communicated a wider range of information.

SUMMING UP

I began this chapter by describing my first encounter with rock art. The carved rocks on Ilkley Moor came as a surprise because they did not seem to fit into accepted interpretations of the prehistoric landscape. I suggested that archaeological research often begins in a similar way. It starts from an experience that does not conform to the expected pattern; with a discovery that seems inconsistent with prevailing views of the past. To that extent academic research runs in parallel with alternative archaeology. But I went on to suggest that what separate these two fields are not necessarily the sources of the ideas but the manner in which those ideas are put to work. In the discussion that followed I tried to define just what it is that is so distinctive about European rock art and the ways in which it upsets accepted notions of landscape history. Instead of treating that experience as something valuable in itself, I sought to account for my own confusion and to work out why such discoveries ran counter to my expectations. That discussion involved some fundamental issues in the analysis of prehistoric rock art, just as they involved some basic concepts in the study of the landscape. Out of the meeting of those two traditions of research there emerged certain possibilities for further work. It is my contention that it is this process of detailed analysis that distinguishes the intuitive interpretations favoured by alternative archaeologists from the perspective adopted by those who take a more orthodox line.

We followed a number of approaches suggested by that first encounter with the prehistoric rock art of Ilkley Moor. Some of these revealed the limitations of a landscape archaeology based on the activities of sedentary farmers. We also reviewed the status of rock art research in Europe. By seeking to link such studies to broader currents in social anthropology, I argued that the two fields of research might profitably be pursued in tandem, and I discussed a number of case studies drawn from both these fields.

Taken together, these studies suggest that it may be possible to investigate the role of rock art on at least four different levels. The first is that of the individual site. Hartley's work revealed the distinctive character of the rock art associated with settlements and the ways in which it might have differed from the art found elsewhere in the landscape. Conkey's research also focused on particular sites, but in this case they had a more specialised function in political and ritual activity. These were not just occupation sites; they were special places that formed the focal point for ceremonial activity among a wider population. Again the distinctive character of the decorated artefacts found at these sites provided vital clues to their original role.

We also examined case studies that extended out into the wider landscape. Hartley's work, for example, revealed a striking contrast between the character of the rock art associated with residential sites and the paintings and carvings distributed across a wider area. The latter included sites associated with paths and also with water sources. The distinctive location of these sites recalls the importance of paths in mobile peoples' experience of the landscape.

There was yet another level at which studies of art could be pursued, as we learned from Smith's careful comparison between her two Australian study areas. This work drew attention to the striking differences in the ways in which art was employed across entire regions with different ecological regimes. In both cases, art styles could be used to trace the extent and character of important social networks. Although these images played many roles in prehistoric society, one of these was undoubtedly related to the practicalities of land use. The two studies of Palaeolithic art extended such patterns still further until they reached across large areas of Europe.

The purpose of this book is to explore many of these methods in studying one particular art style in relation to the settlement history of Atlantic Europe. It is concerned with a period after the first adoption of agriculture and with environments which presented very different opportunities and challenges from those discussed so far. Where this study does have features in common with that work is in the scale of analysis, for once again it will be possible to conduct the enquiry at several different levels. We shall be concerned with the reasons for adopting rock art at a regional scale. We shall discuss the distinctive configuration of prehistoric rock art in relation to settlement and ceremonial sites, and we shall compare both kinds of evidence with the patterns found across the wider landscape. My account will emphasise the contrasts between the evidence found in different regions, but at the same time this will be a study of a style of rock carving that has an international dimension just as much as the styles of mobile art found in the Palaeolithic.

My subject matter will be one of the major groups of rock carvings in prehistoric Europe – the petroglyphs of the Galician–Atlantic style – and my discussion will range along the western seaways for 1,800 km, from the northern limit of this style in Scotland and Ireland to its southern boundary around the border between Portugal and Spain. Above all, this will be an attempt to bring together the two main areas of research considered in this chapter: the study of prehistoric art and investigation of the prehistoric landscape. It seeks to reunite rock art research with the main currents in contemporary archaeology. At the same time it is an attempt to increase our awareness of the symbolic properties of the ancient landscape. In order to do this, we need to know more about the composition of Atlantic rock art and the cultural sequence of which it forms a part. I shall introduce these in the other chapters which make up the first part of this book.

CHAPTER TWO

A CHART OF THE NORTHERN SEAWAYS
An introduction to the prehistory of Atlantic Europe

— ·•· —

INTRODUCTION: THE CONCEPT OF ATLANTIC EUROPE

This book considers the importance of prehistoric rock art in 'Atlantic Europe' and so I must start the chapter by explaining what that term means. Where is Atlantic Europe? To all appearances it should comprise the coastline of the Atlantic Ocean extending from Iberia to Scandinavia. On this definition, it would follow the northern and western limits of the Continent but would exclude the North Sea and the Baltic. But in the archaeological literature the term is normally applied to a smaller area, and I shall follow that convention here. In this sense Atlantic Europe is the coastal region between the Straits of Gibraltar and the Shetland Islands. It includes the west of Portugal, northern and western Spain, the western parts of both France and Britain, and the whole of Ireland.

It is more difficult to decide how much of the European landmass should be considered here, but there is a pragmatic solution to the problem. Following established practice, of which I shall have more to say later, Atlantic Europe is really defined in terms of communications along the coastline. The extent and character of such relationships provide a thread which runs right through this book, with the result that we shall really be concerned with those areas in which prehistoric populations appear to have been linked by sea. In other words, the full extent of 'Atlantic Europe' did not remain constant through time. It changed in relation to the very processes that we need to study. But the period covered in this chapter can be specified more precisely. It is concerned with the entire sequence from the end of the Mesolithic period to the impact of the Phoenician exchange system which linked the Atlantic to the Mediterranean.

Atlantic Europe is sometimes defined as a region, and at other times it is treated more as an analytical concept. It is important to distinguish between these two approaches, for both are coloured by broader perceptions of European prehistory. One emphasises the distinctive character of the Atlantic seaways and stresses the importance of cultural connections along the western limits of the Continent. The other sees the Atlantic as a barrier to developments which began much further to the east. That is why so many writers prefer to talk of an 'Atlantic façade'.

Both approaches are so well entrenched that they incorporate a number of assumptions. Although the Atlantic seaways have played their part in the diffusionist model of prehistory, which saw megalithic tombs as spreading northwards from the Mediterranean, much of this thinking was influenced by the evidence of written sources. There is a surviving account of a voyage from southern France to south-west England undertaken in the sixth century BC, and two centuries later we have the testimony of the Greek explorer Pytheas who travelled even more extensively (Hawkes 1977). In the early post-Roman period there was a well-attested wine trade between Britain, France and North Africa, and it even seems as if entire cargoes were sailing into northern waters from as far afield as Constantinople (Fulford 1989).

Such sources have been supplemented by practical accounts of seafaring in the Atlantic, some of the most valuable of them by historical geographers. This is a tradition of writing that goes back to the work of Fox (1932) and Bowen (1977) and extends to more recent authorities such as Seán McGrail (1993). Now there is a greater concern with the precise routes taken by early sailors and with the problems of navigation in such difficult waters. More attention has been paid to the archaeological evidence of prehistoric boats and harbours (McGrail 1987). The last few years have also seen the underwater investigation of what were probably prehistoric shipwrecks (Muckelroy 1980; Briard 1985).

The other approach is to show how the Atlantic coastline set limits to developments that had started further inland, and that is why so many writers have talked of an 'Atlantic façade'. For the most part this is a rhetorical device without much explanatory power, but in certain cases that criticism would not apply. Thus Colin Renfrew (1976) argues that megalithic tombs developed along the Atlantic coastline because this was where the outward spread of agriculture was checked. That process exerted so much pressure on resources that these monuments might have symbolised the claims of particular groups to agricultural land.

Both approaches converge in supposing that the Atlantic coastline played little part in the mainstream of European prehistory. The very term 'Atlantic façade' implies that major developments had their origins somewhere else, and the Atlantic seaways play a relatively minor part in diffusionist literature. For Gordon Childe they were never as important as the continental landmass. Atlantic Europe is not considered until the closing chapters of *The Dawn of European Civilisation*, and when Childe discusses this area he suggests that innovations had little impact here. A typical statement is his comment that 'the region' (in this case western France) 'remained isolated from the great currents of Bronze Age trade and its population, absorbed in cult practices, *was content to subsist in a Neolithic stage*' (1957, 315; my emphasis).

Similar views can be found in other syntheses of European prehistory, but there have always been dissenting voices. As early as 1940 Christopher Hawkes suggested that more attention should be paid to the Mesolithic hunter gatherers living along the Atlantic coastline (1940, chapter 5). Childe's later work took this argument into account, but it is only recently that this lead has been followed in any detail, so that now the native population have even been credited with the invention of megalithic tombs. Nor is this an isolated instance of such a change of view. Eoin

MacWhite (1951) investigated the cultural connections existing between Ireland and Iberia, and more recent work on the archaeology of the first millennium BC has produced convincing evidence for other links along the Atlantic shoreline, notably the movement of raw materials in the Late Bronze Age. This is not just a question of mapping the movement of goods, for there are claims that such processes may have exercised an influence on the character of local communities. Thus the 'Atlantic Bronze Age' also saw striking convergences in social customs extending from Iberia to Ireland (Coffyn, Gomez and Mohen 1981; Coffyn 1985; Brun 1992).

As we have seen, any review of the archaeological evidence must take into account the geography of the Atlantic coastline. This can be thought of in terms of the major landmasses or the main areas of sea (Fig. 2.1). Both are important if we are to consider communication over long distances. There are three particularly important axes to consider. First, there is the question of communication between the Atlantic and the West Mediterranean through the Straits of Gibraltar. This axis was especially significant because of the difficulty of long-distance movement across the Iberian peninsula. Although some writers have treated the Straits of Gibraltar as an almost impermeable barrier, this was clearly not the case in later prehistory when the network of Phoenician seaports reached to the Atlantic Ocean (Aubet 1993). Second, there has been a tendency to treat European prehistory quite separately from the prehistory of North Africa, and this is also mistaken, for as early as the third millennium BC artefacts were being exchanged between Spain and Morocco (Harrison and Gilman 1977).

The third important axis extends from Galicia in north-west Spain up the Atlantic coastline to Brittany, Britain and Ireland. There are traditional links between these areas evidenced by place names and church dedications, and there was some exchange of population between them during the post-Roman period (Bowen 1977). One indication of the extent of these different networks is found during the early Middle Ages when North Africa and the greater part of the Iberian peninsula belonged to the Islamic world. Only the northern part of Spain was linked to western Christendom and one of the great pilgrimage routes led along the Atlantic to the shrine of St James at Compostela in Galicia (Stopford 1994).

All three routes involved certain hazards, and, as McGrail (1993) has argued, it is profitable to think of them as the seaways leading between certain prominent landmarks: Cape St Vincent in southern Portugal; Cape Finisterre in north-west Spain; the Isle of Ushant off the western tip of Brittany; Land's End in south-west England; and Carnsore Point in south-east Ireland. The most difficult passages would be rounding Cape St Vincent, crossing the Bay of Biscay, and sailing around the Armorican peninsula and through the western approaches of the English Channel. For that reason there were also important land routes. Despite the problems involved in sailing between the Mediterranean and the Atlantic, it would have been almost as difficult to cross the Iberian peninsula. One option was to skirt this area altogether, travelling overland from south-west France to join the Atlantic coast at Bordeaux. It is sometimes suggested that a similar land route developed across the Armorican peninsula. This would have avoided the necessity of following another treacherous coastline, but, if so, that route was no longer used by the Late Iron Age (De Jersey 1993).

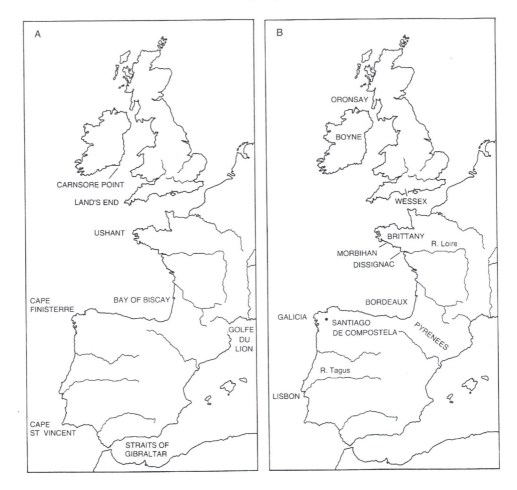

Figure 2.1 Places and regions in Atlantic Europe referred to in the text

Ironically, some of the most difficult passages were in precisely those areas with raw materials that could not be obtained anywhere else. In the Neolithic period there were important stone sources at a number of points around the coastline of western Britain, and the distribution of their products suggests that some of them were transported by sea (Darvill 1989). There were similar sources in Brittany and, further inland, in western France (Le Roux 1990). The Bronze Age saw the use of copper sources in south-west Ireland, south-west England and in southern Spain, whilst the main areas with tin were in Galicia, Brittany and south-west England. Gold was chiefly available in Ireland and north-west Spain. The major source of silver was in south-west Iberia (Tylecote 1987). There is evidence that all these resources were exploited during different periods of prehistory and by the Later Bronze Age the wide distribution of finished metalwork provides compelling evidence for long-distance contacts.

So far I have discussed interaction. At this point I must address a broader theme which is central to the issues discussed in this book. How strong were the links between people along the Atlantic seaways? What was the nature of that inter-action at different points in the sequence? And how far did this process affect the autonomy of local communities?

It is clear that there can be no simple answers to these questions. Interaction took many forms, all of them leaving distinctive traces in the archaeological record, and each would have had a quite different impact on the societies involved. I have already referred to two examples which are entirely different from one another. The exchange networks which constitute the 'Atlantic Bronze Age' were primarily concerned with the provision of raw materials (Northover 1982). There was equally intensive movement in the course of Christian pilgrimage, and this also resulted in the movement of distinctive artefacts over a large area of Europe (Mitchiner 1986). As Colin Renfrew (1993) has stressed, it is no longer sufficient to identify such networks, or even to measure the displacement of artefacts from one region to another. We need to define the character and context of different forms of inter-action, and the social, economic and ideological reasons why travel was taking place. I shall investigate these issues through a review of current research in Atlantic Europe, beginning with the adoption of agriculture and ending with the develop-ment of the Atlantic Bronze Age.

ARCHITECTURE AND IDEOLOGY (6000–3000 BC)

The starting point of this account is perhaps the most controversial topic of all, for it concerns the relationship between three key elements in the archaeology of Atlantic Europe: shell middens, agricultural settlements and megalithic tombs. Virtually every permutation of these features has been studied in recent years.

There are certain points which are well established. From Portugal to Scotland there is evidence of hunter gatherer occupation sites on or near the coast, and in three regions, the Tagus valley, Morbihan and the Irish Sea, there are the remains of shell middens (Morales and Arnaud 1990; Kayser 1986; Mellars 1987). The first two of these groups are also associated with Mesolithic cemeteries, whilst excava-tion on Oronsay in Scotland shows that disarticulated human bones also occur in Mesolithic contexts there. All three regions enjoyed access to marine resources and could have been unusually productive. It is quite possible that settlements were used over longer periods than those in inland areas. This might account for the presence of formal cemeteries. The most intriguing of these sites occur in Brittany where some of the burials were in slab-lined graves.

Nearly all these sites date from the Late Mesolithic period, and this creates some uncertainty, for it is during the same phase that we have the first evidence for the exploitation of domesticated plants and animals, some of which do not seem to have been present in these areas before. Their adoption marks one of the major thresholds in Atlantic prehistory and is supposed to define the transition to a 'Neolithic' way of life. In fact their first appearance is little understood. Some typical finds may be mentioned here. One of the Breton shell middens contained a sheep or goat tooth (Kayser 1986), just as a recently excavated Mesolithic site on the Irish coast included a bone of domesticated *Bos* (Woodman and O'Brien 1993). Similarly, the megalithic tomb at Dissignac in Brittany overlay a Mesolithic flint industry associated with cereal pollen (L'Helgouac'h 1976).

The situation is confusing, but many writers are agreed that this was one part of Europe in which indigenous communities adopted domesticated resources from outside. But there remain a number of complications. The earliest mortuary monuments seem to have been built at the start of this phase, yet in the literature these sites are usually associated with the development of productive agriculture. Certain observations are generally accepted. The first use of domesticates in western Iberia and south-west France appears to be associated with a style of pottery, 'impressed' ware, that originated in the Mediterranean (Scarre 1992), whilst the earliest ceramics in north-west France show the influence of traditions that developed in the Paris Basin and ultimately in the Rhineland (Sherratt 1990). Among the first mortuary monuments in northern and western France were elongated mounds that may very well follow the characteristic form of the long houses found in those areas, although this kind of residential structure had gone out of use by the time that the mounds were built (Boujot and Cassen 1992). By contrast, the first mortuary monuments in the Iberian peninsula seem to have been circular mounds for which there is no outside prototype. For that reason they have a stronger claim to be the invention of the native population (Scarre 1992).

Unfortunately, there are problems with this simple outline. There is an uncertain relationship between the adoption of domesticates and the construction of monuments. There are not enough finds of domesticates to suggest that farming was adopted *before* these mounds were built, but there are sufficient to make it unlikely that monuments were conceived by the native population until their contacts with farmers. In Portugal this period saw a striking change in human nutrition, from a diet that included a high proportion of fish to a regime which placed more emphasis on meat (Lubell et al 1994), yet in Brittany, and most probably in the British Isles, the first convincing evidence of farming on any scale came after the early development of stone monuments (Marguerie 1992; Bradley 1993, chapter 1). Their construction could not have been financed by an agricultural surplus.

Secondly, the two main currents in the Atlantic Neolithic often overlapped. It seems possible that certain areas of Iberia, from the Mediterranean to the Atlantic coast of the Pyrenees, underwent economic changes at practically the same time as one another. In Portugal the sites associated with pottery and domesticated resources seem to avoid the areas with established Mesolithic settlements, and in this case there may be real evidence of colonisation from outside (Zilhão 1993). Even so, that process does not suggest any source of inspiration for the development of megalithic tombs.

In northern and western France there are other complications too, for here it seems as if both continental and Mediterranean elements were combined. The picture is confused, with overlapping styles of pottery and at least two separate traditions of monumental architecture, one of them based on long mounds and the other on circular cairns. The latter type has parallels along the Atlantic seaboard and may have developed out of the stone-lined graves found at cemeteries in Brittany and western France. A number of the mortuary monuments prove to be composite structures whose plans were altered during their period of use, suggesting that the two traditions stood for different ideas about the world. Nowhere is this more apparent than in Brittany where the building of the first long mounds appears to have been accompanied by the erection of decorated monoliths (Sherratt 1990). When the circular cairns were constructed, these were often destroyed, and their fragments were incorporated in the structure of the new monuments (L'Helgouac'h 1983).

The British and Irish evidence is no more straightforward. Neolithic pottery shows links with Atlantic Europe in one direction and with the Rhine–Meuse delta in the other (Whittle 1977). We find the same two groups of mortuary monuments, although in this case the long mounds have more in common with those in Scandinavia, and once again there are a few other sites whose history shows the impact of both traditions.

This evidence seems to suggest two major axes, one of them extending from the West Mediterranean around the coastline of Portugal and Spain and into western France. The other appears to have connected northern France and the British Isles with developments that began in the Rhineland (Fig. 2.2, A). In fact that is an over-simplification, for it seems likely that indigenous communities played a substantial part in all these changes, and this may account for certain features which are widely distributed along the Atlantic coastline, in particular the practice of building circular cairns. The same factors may account for the continued use of microliths from Portugal to Brittany.

These connections can easily be exaggerated. The stone-built monuments resemble one another only at a very general level and all of them include distinctive structural devices of their own. For example, the early passage graves in Brittany had corbelled chambers, but this technique may not have been adopted in the Iberian peninsula for at least another thousand years. Similarly, a number of these tombs were decorated by painting or carving, but in the three areas where this is found (northern France, Ireland and the Iberian peninsula) the earliest art has a largely local character (Shee Twohig 1981 and 1993; Bueno and Balbín 1992). The same applies to the adoption of other traditions of monument building. For example, specialised earthwork enclosures with interrupted ditches were constructed in Britain and Ireland and in northern and western France, but they seem to be entirely absent from Portugal and Spain (Bradley 1993, chapter 4). At this stage there is little to suggest much unity of culture along the Atlantic seaways.

The same point can be illustrated by the distribution of portable artefacts. Several stone sources have been investigated near to the coastline of western Europe, and the distributions of their products have been mapped. The stone axes made in highland Britain were rarely carried across the English Channel, although they were exchanged across the Irish Sea (Bradley and Edmonds 1993). Breton axes are occasionally found in southern England, but their distribution extended in small numbers down the west coast of France, ending at the Pyrenees (Le Roux 1990). The same division is illustrated by the movement of jadeite axes from the Alps (Ricq-de Bouard 1993). These are widely distributed in west and central Europe,

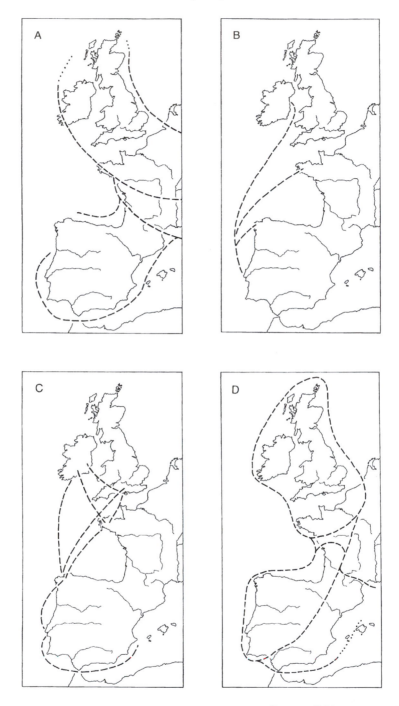

Figure 2.2 Interaction zones in Atlantic Europe. A: Earlier Neolithic; B: Later Neolithic; C: Earlier Bronze Age; D: Later Bronze Age. A incorporates material from Sherratt (1990) and Zilhão (1993), and D is partly based on Brun (1992)

but apart from one small group of finds in south-east Spain they are absent from the Iberian peninsula. They are quite often found in Britain, but with the exception of a major concentration of axes in Brittany and a lesser group in western France, they do not occur elsewhere on the Atlantic seaboard.

The particular connections that *have* been claimed belong to a developed phase in this sequence. These have a most distinctive character. They are almost entirely concerned with the design of chambered tombs and the kinds of specialised artefacts associated with them.

There are some general tendencies in the design of megalithic tombs along the Atlantic coastline. On the whole the oldest monuments were associated with closed chambers; once the covering earthwork had been built, the remains of the dead were no longer accessible. Later constructions departed from this practice. On some sites the chambers were linked to the outside world by a stone-built passage, whilst at others they could be entered directly from the perimeter of the monument. The details of these different designs need not concern us here. What matters is that such tombs contain structural devices that permitted access to the ancestral remains. Many cairns contained more than one chamber, and at some sites even these could be subdivided. At times important divisions of space were emphasised by thresholds, by controlling the movement of light into the monument and by painted or carved decoration (Thomas 1990 and 1992). Such distinctions were occasionally reflected by the ways in which the bones were arranged within these structures (Masset 1993). Indeed the very name 'tomb' may be a misnomer for in some cases it seems as if relics of the dead circulated widely among the living. Some of them may indeed have been taken from these sites.

The most obvious links between different regions of Atlantic Europe concern the 'passage tombs': distinctive circular mounds with entrance passages and corbelled chambers. The funerary ritual was not the same in every area, as some communities emphasised the importance of unfleshed bones, while others practised cremation. Despite the development of local architectural traditions, there do seem to have been certain points in common between separate areas. In Brittany, Ireland and Orkney the passages might be aligned on the rising or setting sun at special times of year (Bradley 1989a). Strikingly similar devices could be employed to emphasise the entrances to those sites, and, as we shall see, in its later phases megalithic art lost something of its local character and specific motifs seem to have been widely shared (Shee Twohig 1981 and 1993). There are also links between some of the artefact types associated with these sites.

The closest connections were between areas that were a considerable distance apart (Fig. 2.2, B). Irish tombs show certain similarities with those in Brittany and also with monuments in Portugal (Eogan 1990). These links extend beyond the details of the architecture to take into account a number of distinctive objects associated with the use of both groups of sites. These include double axes or adzes, maceheads, idols and elaborately decorated pins (Fábregas 1991). There are further links between these idols and finds from passage graves in Galicia, yet in each case there is nothing to suggest similar connections in everyday life.

It is worth summarising this complex sequence. Some of the interconnections evidenced along the Atlantic coastline may have had their roots in the Mesolithic period, but they were profoundly influenced by the adoption of a new ideology which seems to have accompanied the first experiments with domesticates. That ideology is most clearly indicated by the conventions of megalithic architecture. The first adoption of Neolithic material culture reveals two major axes in Atlantic Europe, one linking the southern part of that area to the West Mediterranean and the other forming connections between north-west Europe and regions further to the east (Fig. 2.2, A). With time these broad alignments broke down as regional traditions began to reassert themselves, but with their development there came a series of quite specific links between the monuments and material culture of widely separated areas. These did not extend beyond a limited range of artefacts and a series of architectural devices found in monumental tombs. Whilst they provide some evidence for long-distance connections that transcend the geographical divisions apparent at the start of this period, their restricted scale and specialised character can hardly be overemphasised. Of those links, it is the connections between Ireland, Brittany and western Iberia that may prove to be the most significant (Fig. 2.2, B).

THE INCEPTION OF METALLURGY (3000–1400 BC)

The development of those alignments was to prove very important as different communities adopted metalwork, for here was a resource which by its very nature required the movement of raw materials. For our purposes the key area is Portugal. In the late fourth and earlier third millennia BC there are fresh indications of the importance of the link between the West Mediterranean and the Atlantic coast of the Iberian peninsula. The fortified settlements of south-east Spain have long played a central role in assessments of the diffusionist model (Chapman 1990). Here were major settlement sites associated with corbelled tombs, an array of elaborate grave-goods and evidence for early metallurgy. For a time it seemed as if these developments were the result of colonisation from complex societies further to the east, and the same model was applied, perhaps more tentatively, to similar complexes close to Lisbon, where once again we find a direct association between elaborate fortifications, megaliths and metals (ibid, chapter 10). Less elaborate hilltop enclosures were also created in the north of Portugal during this period (Jorge 1994). The distribution of fortified sites overlaps the distribution of rock art in the Schematic style, which also extends across large parts of the Iberian peninsula (Fig. 2.3).

The traditional framework has suffered a reverse in recent years. It is inconsistent with the radiocarbon chronology of Spain and Portugal, and the supposed imports from the central and eastern Mediterranean have not stood up to scrutiny (Chapman 1990). The presence of a few Mycenaean sherds does nothing to alter the situation, for they belong to a developed stage in the Iberian sequence and their rarity serves only to emphasise the paucity of long-distance links with other areas (Mommsen et al 1990). It seems much more likely that complex societies evolved in comparative isolation within Spain and Portugal and that one of the developments for which they were responsible was the growth of a local metal industry.

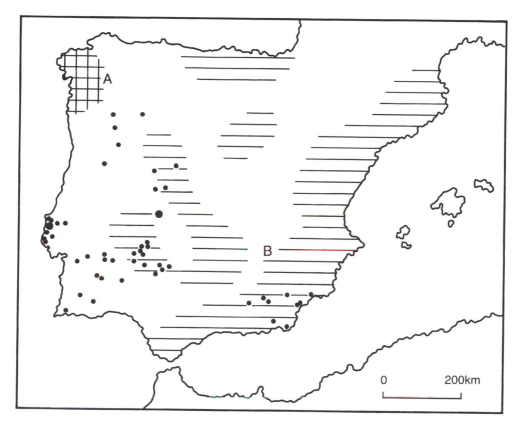

Figure 2.3 The distribution of Galician art (A), Schematic art (B) (after Gómez 1992) and fortified sites in the Iberian peninsula (after Jorge 1994)

It might seem as if these changes have little place in an account of Atlantic Europe, for the closest links were obviously those between Portugal and southeast Spain, but that is rather misleading. We know all too little about the background to developments in Portugal, but among the features that do seem to figure prominently are passage graves and specialised artefacts – precisely the features which were shared with major tombs in Ireland. It is also clear that the later levels in these fortified settlements are associated with Bell Beaker pottery, a ceramic style that has a very wide distribution in Europe (Harrison 1980, chapter 6). Although opinion has moved away from the idea that this was an Iberian invention, its distribution very clearly emphasises the importance of the Atlantic seaways (Diáz-Andreu 1995). In this respect it is no accident that one of its major substyles should be termed the Maritime Beaker (Harrison 1980, chapter 6).

In practice there seem to have been two major axes of contact during the period in which metal came into use, in conventional terms the Copper Age and the Early Bronze Age (Fig. 2.2, C). I have mentioned the first already, and it seems to have involved connections between the West Mediterranean and the Atlantic coast of

Portugal. It also involved movement across the Straits of Gibraltar, as there are African raw materials in southern Iberia and finds of Beakers in Morocco. In addition, there are a few finds of metalwork in North Africa (Harrison and Gilman 1977).

The other major network ran up the Atlantic coastline through northern Spain and western France as far as Britain and Ireland. Galicia, in the north-west corner of Spain, seems to have played an important part in this system, perhaps because it was a source of tin. There are three components of this system to consider here: pottery, metalwork and the rock art which occupies such a prominent place in this book. As in the Neolithic period, we lack much evidence of settlements.

The most informative of the metal finds is probably the Palmella point, so named after its discovery in a cemetery in Portugal. This has a well-documented distribution extending as far up the Atlantic coast as the mouth of the Loire (Harrison 1974; Briard 1991). Another artefact with a still wider distribution is the Maritime Beaker which is found over the same area as well as in Britain and Ireland, although we do not know whether this type was imported or locally produced. There are also distinctive styles of metalwork which were shared between communities along the Atlantic seaboard at this time. Among them there were distinctive styles of axeheads and gold ornaments. As recent research has shown, silver artefacts were also distributed along this axis. These include elaborate copies of the typical Beaker found in western France, as well as a number of metal beads (Briard 1984). Until recently these finds had a restricted distribution, but another silver bead has lately been found on the site of a destroyed burial mound in southern England (S. Needham pers. comm.).

In certain cases there also appear to be links between very specific parts of Atlantic Europe. As we shall see, idols like those found on the fortified sites in Portugal seem to be portrayed in the rock art of Galicia. Among the other elements that have been identified in these drawings are depictions of halberds and daggers (García and Peña 1980, 140–2). Although the actual objects are rarely found in the vicinity of these sites, halberds are another type with a wide distribution along the Atlantic seaboard. Curiously enough, they are found in greatest numbers in Ireland, northern Portugal and south-east Spain but are absent from the major group of burials in Wessex where they are occasionally replaced by copies in miniature.

By contrast, there are close links between the grave-goods found in southern England and those associated with Early Bronze Age burials in Brittany (Briard 1987). These connections also extend to local styles of Bronze Age pottery (Burgess 1987). Ruiz-Gálvez (1978) has suggested that there may be further links between the metalwork associated with rich graves in Wessex and north-west France and the material found in hoards and cist burials in Galicia.

There are two points to emphasise here. First, it would be easy to exaggerate the significance of the Portuguese fortified sites in these wider patterns. Apart from a restricted group of Copper Age enclosures in the Channel Islands (Cunliffe 1992, 49–50), no fortifications have been discovered further up the Atlantic coastline. Of the distinctive range of material culture associated with the Iberian settlements only the Maritime Beaker and the Palmella point are regularly found over a much wider area. Although north-west Spain was important as a source of raw material, Peter Harbison (1967) was probably right when he wrote that during the Early Bronze Age Galicia was located on the edge of two different networks. One led northwards as far as Scotland and Ireland, whilst the other crossed the Portuguese border and extended into the West Mediterranean (Fig. 2.2, C).

The second point to stress is the limited character of these contacts. Once again almost all of them concern specialised artefacts found in graves or hoards. Their deposition often follows established local practices. In fact there is considerable variety among the burials, which vary from collective deposits in reused passage tombs to flat cemeteries composed of individual graves. Maritime Beakers were also associated with the dead, and they rarely appear on domestic sites in Atlantic Europe where the main links are between coarser pottery traditions such as those on either side of the English Channel. In effect the chief connections seem to be between areas either with an exceptionally rich grave-assemblage or with important sources of raw material. The two cannot always be distinguished. For example, the closest connections of all were probably between Brittany and Wessex. Both these areas contain rich graves, but Wessex is entirely without local copper or tin. By contrast, two of the other areas with features in common were Galicia and south-west Ireland, each of which included sources of metal.

Lastly, we should remember that this kind of system was not limited to Atlantic Europe. Just as Bell Beakers were distributed across wide areas of the Continent, the regions with rich burials formed only part of a far larger pattern. It also extended to groups well beyond the Atlantic seaways. Despite the emphasis placed on metal sources, there seems to be little evidence that bronze played a central role in everyday activities. Like so much else, that situation was to change decisively during the Later Bronze Age.

THE GENESIS OF LONG-DISTANCE TRADE (1400–700 BC)

The term 'Later Bronze Age' describes the period which followed this phase of rich burials. Some local sequences distinguish between a Middle and a Late Bronze Age, but in this chapter they are combined. This period can also be subdivided on geographical grounds, and this is especially important. Much of central and western Europe came within the ambit of the so-called Urnfield Cultures and, most especially, the Rhine–Swiss–Eastern French Group (Brun 1988). The western coast of the Continent, however, maintained a sufficiently distinctive identity for commentators to talk in terms of an 'Atlantic Bronze Age' (Brun 1992).

These two geographical units share certain features, however much they diverge in detail. In most areas it was only in the Later Bronze Age that metal was widely used for everyday activities. Until then it had often played a rather specialised role and made little contribution to the subsistence economy. As part of this change the circulation of metalwork probably increased in intensity (Coffyn 1985). New kinds of artefact appear, from socketed axes and saws to helmets and cauldrons, and the repertoire of bronze artefacts emphasises new kinds of activity such as horse-riding and feasting.

The demand for metal extended into more than one domain. In many areas bronze artefacts are found on settlement sites, and it is clear that some of them were actually made there, normally from raw materials that were undergoing recycling. Others were discarded in a much more structured manner; although they were no longer common as grave-goods, they seem to have been deposited in hoards or rivers during this period (Bradley 1990, chapter 3; Ruiz-Gálvez 1995). It is not surprising that greater demands were placed on those areas with local raw materials, although increased experience in working alloys would also have necessitated the long-distance movement of copper, tin and lead. As we have seen, these have a restricted distribution in Atlantic Europe (Northover 1982). One indication of the increasing scale of interaction is provided by finds of Bronze Age shipwrecks (Muckelroy 1980; Briard 1985).

Such changes were not confined to technology, and in most parts of Atlantic Europe this period also provides the first extensive evidence of permanent settlement. Such evidence takes many forms. In the Iberian peninsula it is marked by the development of distinctive hilltop settlements associated with stone-built houses and finds of elaborate metalwork. Many of these sites were defended by walls, but not necessarily at this early stage. The small hillforts in northern Spain and Portugal are known as 'castros'. They provide convincing evidence for cereal agriculture and also for habitation on a scale not previously recognised outside the Chalcolithic fortifications of Portugal. Sedentary settlements were probably established along the Iberian coastline between the tenth and the seventh centuries BC (Ruiz-Gálvez 1991).

At present there is less information from the west coast of France, and it is in Britain that there is more detailed evidence, for here the newly established settlements, with their houses, ponds and storage pits, are directly associated with field systems and land boundaries. Some of those land divisions extend over considerable areas and provide evidence for closer controls over agricultural resources than in any other part of Europe (Darvill 1987, chapter 5). In both Britain and Ireland we also find defended enclosures, some of which were associated with feasting and metal production. It may well have been during the Later Bronze Age that a specifically Atlantic tradition of circular houses became widely established.

There are a number of geographical axes to consider, most of them already prefigured in earlier sections of this chapter (Fig. 2.2, D). The most important division was between the Urnfield sphere of influence and the zone characterised by the Atlantic Bronze Age. Finds of pottery and metalwork belonging to these two traditions show a clearly marked division cutting across northern and western France (Brun 1988 and 1992). The finds with 'Atlantic' associations extend along the coastline into Iberia to the south and Britain and Ireland to the north. In France the border area between these traditions remained more or less stable, whereas southern and eastern Britain were not absorbed into the Atlantic culture area until the very end of the period. Patrice Brun (1993) has argued that it was in the border zone between the French Urnfield and Atlantic traditions that defended sites were first established. It is also in this area that we find most hoards, as well as major deposits of metalwork in rivers.

At the same time, the area subsumed within the Atlantic Bronze Age was by no means uniform. The distribution of some types of artefact extended from

Scotland to Spain, and the same is true of early hillforts and certain types of votive deposit. The distributions of some of these objects suggest the existence of other divisions at a more local scale. The broad expanse of the Atlantic Bronze Age can be divided into two zones of particularly intensive contact. One extended from southern Iberia to the mouth of the Loire, whilst the other ran from the Loire westwards to the Rhine and northwards as far as Scotland (Brun 1992). At the same time, each of those interaction spheres embraced several smaller groups of roughly equal size, best defined by local styles of pottery and metalwork. These regions included Galicia, Brittany and Wales.

There seem to have been two further axes linking the Atlantic to the West Mediterranean. One is suggested by the distribution of bronze artefacts between south-west France and the Gulf of Lion. It seems to provide evidence of a land route skirting the eastern foothills of the Pyrenees (Coffyn 1985). The second route must have entailed navigation between the Atlantic and the Mediterranean, as precisely the same range of artefacts is shared between the Atlantic coastline and sites along the southern shore of Iberia. Still more striking, the same types of material have a distribution that extends eastwards as far as Sardinia, Sicily and the Italian mainland (Coffyn, Gomez and Mohen 1981). The very existence of these links between the central and western Mediterranean contrasts with the virtual autonomy of the Iberian peninsula during the Copper Age and Early Bronze Age.

The scale of long-distance interaction increased sharply during the period of the Atlantic Bronze Age (Ruiz-Gálvez 1987 and 1995). The process began about 1200 BC with an intensification of the links described in the previous part of this chapter. It gathered momentum in the tenth century, but most of the evidence for long-distance relationships belongs to the last 200 years, down to the eighth century BC when Phoenician traders arrived in western Iberia (Aubet 1993).

That development introduces two completely new elements and provides the obvious point at which to bring this account to a close. From this time onwards political relations between more complex societies and their neighbours assume a growing prominence in archaeological writing. The remaining part of the first millennium BC saw the impact of Carthaginians, Greeks and Romans on communities living along the coastline of western Europe. At the same time, the Atlantic axis considered in this chapter lost much of its importance to developments in the Mediterranean and to some extent to the growing significance of overland routes.

SUMMING UP

This chapter has considered a lengthy sequence and an enormous area, but behind the local detail two distinctive patterns stand out. It is clear that throughout Atlantic Europe agriculture was adopted only gradually. For the most part it does not seem to have had a decisive impact until the Later Bronze Age. Before that time settlement sites are difficult to identify and often have a rather ephemeral character. Specialised monuments, including enclosures and tombs, dominate the archaeological record, and all too little is known about the prehistoric landscape.

At the same time, the character of interaction changed steadily throughout this sequence. These patterns are summarised in Fig. 2.2. Quite specific connections were established between different areas from the beginning of the Neolithic. One linked the West Mediterranean to Iberia and south-west France, whilst the other joined north-west France, Britain and Ireland to regions further to the east. By a developed phase of the Neolithic this simple division was breached by striking but significant links between widely scattered regions along the Atlantic seaboard. In time the boundaries shifted and two distinct networks emerge, both of which seem to have been important from the Copper Age into the Early Bronze Age. One linked the Mediterranean with the western part of Iberia, whilst the other extended up the Atlantic coast from north-west Spain to Britain and Ireland. Those two axes were eventually subsumed within the long-distance contacts that characterise the Atlantic Bronze Age. By that time the nature of long-distance relationships was changing, from largely symbolic links that may have placed a premium on knowledge of the remote and access to the exotic, to a much more basic quest for raw materials.

Both developments ran in parallel. The period which saw the closest contacts between north-west Spain and the British Isles was precisely that in which those areas seem to have shared a distinctive style of rock art. It was also the period for which archaeologists have most difficulty in defining the character of the prehistoric landscape. By contrast, the Later Bronze Age saw the development of new alliances along the Atlantic seaboard, and it was then that the landscape began to change its character. As these processes ran their course, rock art lost its importance and thereafter it disappeared. This book seeks to trace its history against this wider background.

CHAPTER THREE

THE CIRCLE AND THE STAG
An introduction to Atlantic rock art

———— •◆• ————

THE CONCEPT OF ATLANTIC ROCK ART

Throughout the Middle Ages one of the great pilgrimage routes led to the shrine of St James at Compostela in Galicia. This was one of the outposts of western Christianity, near to the north-west corner of Spain and some way beyond the area of Moorish conquest. It could be reached overland from the Pyrenees or by sea along the Atlantic coastline. The pilgrims travelled over considerable distances, some of them from as far away as the British Isles (Fig. 3.1).

We can still trace the pilgrims' route through France and the north of Spain, until eventually we enter Santiago de Compostela, following their path into the old city. As we do so, we may be struck by the murals decorating the university School of Education. The traditional signs of the pilgrims were a seashell and a gourd, but here there are images of a very different character, copied from local rock art. These are more abstract motifs, chiefly circular designs, although there are also pictures of human figures and animals. Was it entirely by chance that fragments of one such carving were built into the cathedral steps?

Certain of those motifs might be familiar to British readers, for they can be described more prosaically as 'cup-and-ring marks' (Pl. 2). There are many of them in northern England, Scotland and Ireland, and they occur in much smaller numbers in France, in Portugal and in other parts of Spain. For some people the resemblance between the British and north-west Spanish rock art is so striking that they have talked in terms of a single 'Galician' or 'Atlantic' style, uniting these two regions and resulting from contacts as extensive as any formed by the Christian pilgrims (MacWhite 1946; Simpson and Thawley 1972). This chapter offers an introduction to Atlantic rock art and considers some of the ways in which it has been defined.

The individual components of this style have been known for a long time; it is their wide geographical distribution that has not been appreciated. In Britain and Ireland the first systematic records of open-air rock art go back well over a hundred years, and, perhaps unusually, the earliest studies of this material were among the best. The work of J. Simpson (1867), for example, combines first-class illustrations of the Scottish material with a text that contains many pertinent ideas (Fig. 3.2).

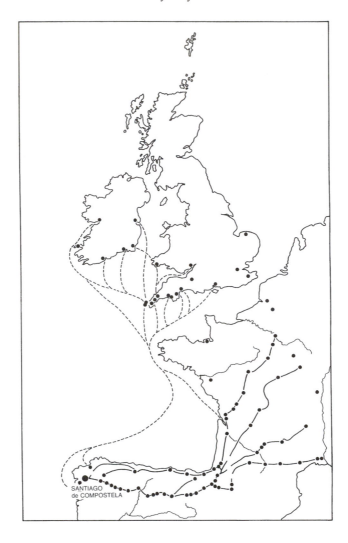

Figure 3.1 Medieval pilgrimage routes to Santiago de Compostela (after Bowen 1977 and Stopford 1994)

To some extent the importance of such nineteenth-century records lies in the fact that the carvings were drawn in detail before they sustained modern damage.

During the early years of the twentieth century research on British rock art seems to have lost its momentum. Many more examples were discovered but they were published piecemeal and soon attracted an increasingly bizarre literature concerned with their interpretation. Pride of place must go to Ludovic MacLellan Mann (1915) who not only interpreted some of the Scottish carvings according to a personal vision of the cosmos (Fig. 3.3) but retouched them with indelible paint so that it is difficult to tell what was actually there (see Morris 1981).

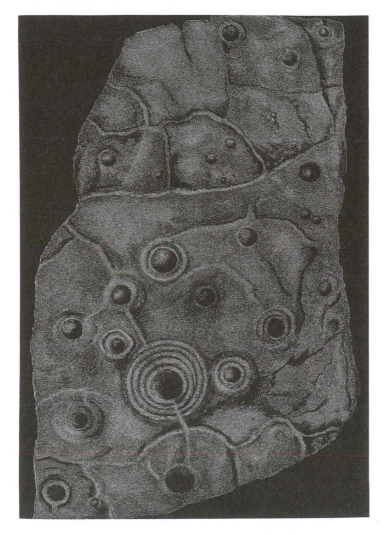

Figure 3.2 Scottish rock art as recorded by Simpson in 1867

It was during the same period that the rock carvings of north-west France commanded most attention. A number of examples were recorded, particularly in Finistère (De Chatellier 1907), and an isolated instance also figures in the first corpus of megalithic art in Brittany (Péquart, Péquart and Le Rouzic 1927, pl. 134), but here again research lost its initial momentum. On the west coast of France still less attention was paid to this material, and its systematic investigation is a recent development. The same applies to the rock art of the Pyrenees, which for the most part concentrates towards the Mediterranean rather than the Atlantic coastline (Bahn 1984, 324–31; Abélanet 1990). In this case too, systematic studies began only recently.

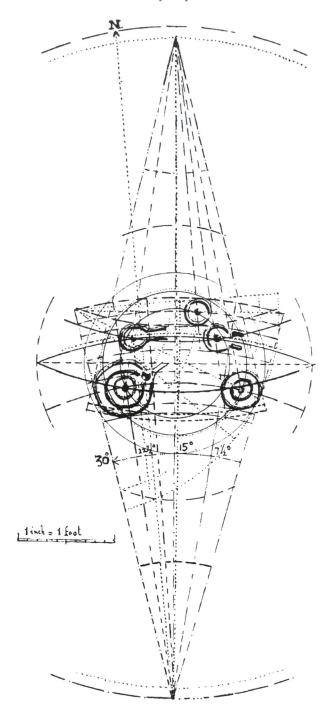

Figure 3.3 Scottish rock art as interpreted by Mann in 1915

By contrast, the study of Iberian rock art has a long history, partly because of the interest created by the discovery of Palaeolithic cave paintings in the north of Spain. It is no coincidence that two of the most influential students of Palaeolithic art during the early years of this century, Obermaier and Breuil, also investigated the later paintings and carvings of Iberia (Obermaier 1925; Breuil 1921). For our purposes one feature is especially important, for this early research drew attention to the distinctive character of the rock carvings found in Galicia. A number of important reviews appeared between 1900 and 1920, but the first definitive account of these sites was not published until 1935. This did not have a wide influence, because the book was issued by a seminary and was written entirely in Latin (Sobrino 1935). Despite this disadvantage, it provided a valuable review of the general character and distribution of rock carvings in Galicia and it remained the basic text until a new phase of research began in the 1970s.

There are several reasons why the study of rock art lost its original impetus. First, it became a victim of the growth of archaeology as a profession, especially in the British Isles. The discovery and recording of rock art was especially attractive to amateur archaeologists. It was not as expensive as excavation and it did not require the participation of specialists or the recruitment of a large team. Still more important, it was not destructive. Rock art could also be recorded by small-scale measured drawings, photographs or rubbings. It did not demand the special skills needed in other kinds of field survey. As a result, like the collection of worked flints, a valuable contribution to archaeology was entirely overlooked by those who had made it their career and very little of this work was published in the major journals.

Such publications as did appear were widely scattered and often difficult to obtain, so it took some time to appreciate the full extent of this phenomenon. Although Breuil had emphasised the wider parallels of Iberian rock art, his comments had little influence. In the event ideas tended to flow in the opposite direction. This came about through a fortunate combination of circumstances. Eóin MacWhite was the son of an Irish diplomat and had learned Spanish as a child. Just after the Second World War he was awarded a travelling scholarship to support his research, and as a citizen of a neutral country he looked to Spain and Portugal which had not been involved in the conflict. Eventually he wrote a monograph on cultural relations along the Atlantic seaboard during the Bronze Age (MacWhite 1951). He soon recognised the potential significance of Galician rock art, and in 1946 he published a paper entitled 'A new view on Irish Bronze Age rock-scribings' in which he drew attention to the close links between the motifs found in Ireland and Spain. On that basis he suggested the existence of a unitary Gallego–Atlantic style of rock carvings. This article has commanded rather more attention among archaeologists working in Britain and Ireland than it has in Galicia.

Language was not the only obstacle to progress, for the agenda in studies of rock art had also changed. After the early phase of research on open-air sites more attention was directed to the study of what became known as megalithic art, the painted and carved decoration found in stone-built tombs extending from Spain to Orkney (Shee Twohig 1981 and 1993; Bueno and Balbín 1992). This change of emphasis had certain obvious attractions. First, because so many of these designs were found inside the monuments there seemed to be a prospect of obtaining dating evidence; and, second, because megalithic tombs played such a central role in the diffusionist model of prehistory the evidence of these paintings and carvings could be linked directly to the main currents in prehistoric research. Open-air rock carvings had neither of these advantages. They did not form part of any monument and they were not associated with artefacts.

It was really Breuil who began the systematic study of the relationship between megalithic art and carvings in the open air. His ideas were presented in a presidential lecture to the Prehistoric Society of East Anglia (Breuil 1934). Breuil is often criticised today for over-interpreting the evidence and sometimes for imagining more than was really there, but for the most part this account was perceptive and soundly researched. It included some ideas which have since fallen from favour – he saw many designs as being drawn from the human face, and he looked for the source of most motifs in the art of Iberia – but his basic approach was more judicious. It was 'to group [the designs] in successive series, classing them either in their technique or their relative positions' (ibid, 289) and it included shrewd observations on the superimposition of different motifs in Irish passage graves. He also sought to establish the relative dates of particular motifs by looking for differences of weathering.

For our purposes the most important element in his paper is the comparisons that he drew between the carvings found in megalithic tombs and those on natural outcrops. He saw them as a continuum and did not distinguish sharply between the two groups. Unfortunately, his interpretation was undoubtedly coloured by his basic thesis that such carvings depicted human features, so that at times he seems to be less concerned to compare these motifs with one another than he is to link them both to an entirely hypothetical prototype (Fig. 3.4).

MacWhite, writing twelve years later, disagreed with Breuil's interpretation. Having defined his Galician style of rock art, he distinguished it from the art found in megalithic tombs (MacWhite 1946). Until recently this was the approach that was favoured by most commentators. Thus Simpson and Thawley (1972) observe the same distinction in their account of the rock carvings associated with single burials in Britain and Ireland and Shee Twohig also emphasises the differences between these two groups (1981, 121–3). Recent accounts of Atlantic rock art perhaps make more allowance for an overlap with megalithic art. To different degrees Hadingham (1974), Burgess (1990) and Johnston (1993) have all expressed doubts about whether those styles were really independent, but the overall objectives of these writers are different. Hadingham is concerned with the origins of open-air rock art, whilst Burgess and Johnston are much more interested in its overall chronology.

All this discussion has been concerned with rock art in Britain and Ireland, but whilst there are certain similarities between open-air carvings at different points along the Atlantic coastline, this does not apply to the decoration of megalithic tombs. Here there is evidence for much greater regional and chronological diversity (Fig. 3.5). For example, there is only a limited overlap between the motifs employed in passage graves in Brittany and those found in Irish tombs. Such links

Figure 3.4 British and Irish rock art represented as versions of the human figure by Breuil in 1934

39

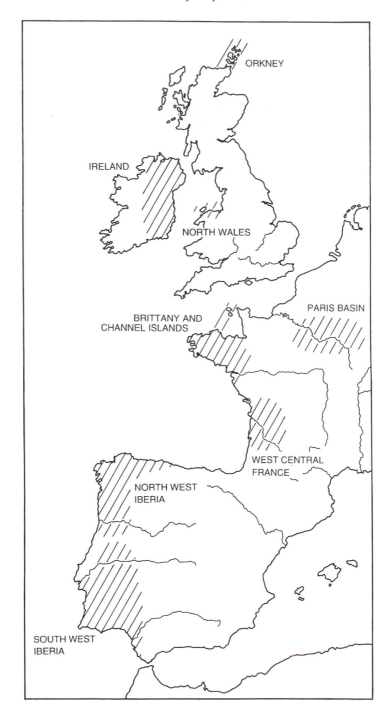

Figure 3.5 Outline distribution of megalithic art (after Shee Twohig 1981 and Bueno and Balbín 1992)

belong to a developed phase in the local sequence in north-west France and most of them concern a few quite exceptional sites (Le Roux 1992). The decoration found in Spanish and Portuguese megaliths has nothing in common with the designs in the tombs of Brittany and Ireland (Bueno and Balbín 1992). This is true although there is other evidence for connections between these areas.

Even if we accept that there are certain similarities between early megalithic art in Ireland and the decoration applied to natural surfaces in the landscape, there are fewer connections of this kind in other areas. Occasional motifs do seem to be shared between these media – depictions of animals in northern Portugal, linear motifs in Galicia – but these particular designs are not among the features that extend along the Atlantic seaboard. Although the two groups of decoration overlap occasionally, they do so at an entirely local level. It follows that, whilst Atlantic rock art shares some features with the decoration found in Irish tombs, that may be the only area in which there is a close relationship between the two groups. The style of the open-air carvings may be more of an international phenomenon than megalithic art.

On the other hand, there is a danger of exaggerating the importance of long-distance connections. This is not so surprising when we understand MacWhite's agenda, for he was concerned with establishing links between different cultural contexts. Elsewhere in his account of Galician–Atlantic rock art he postulates further connections, between north-west Spain, Malta and the East Mediterranean. That was understandable at a time when prehistoric chronologies could not be built in other ways. He placed much greater emphasis on the links between different areas than he did on the points of contrast. As we shall see in Chapter 4, even now rock art remains very difficult to date.

THE COMPONENTS OF ATLANTIC ROCK ART

It is the use of curvilinear motifs that links megalithic art with open-air carvings in Ireland. The angular designs that are also found in passage tombs rarely occur on natural surfaces, and the same applies to more specialised elements in the repertoire of passage-grave art. At the same time, the elements that are shared between these two broad styles are precisely those that link the open-air rock art of Britain and Ireland (Morris 1989) with sites in Portugal and Spain (García and Peña 1980; Peña and Vázquez 1979; Vázquez Varela 1990; Costas and Novoa 1993). But the resemblance is not exact for, whilst almost all the motifs found in British and Irish rock art have close counterparts in Galicia, they are found there with other motifs which are not shared along the Atlantic coastline. The most common are drawings of animals (Pl. 3), although there are also a smaller number of depictions of weapons, idols and human figures.

Galician rock art is by no means uniform. There are two sets of motifs with rather different distributions. The more abstract motifs (Pl. 4) are common to both these groups and are also represented more sparingly in northern Portugal and in the centre and north of Spain. In Galicia they are found on the Atlantic coast and in the foothills of the higher ground further to the east. Simple cup marks (Pl. 5) extend even further inland. Drawings of animals, however, are not so often found in coastal areas and only rarely occur in major concentrations. When they do so they are normally accompanied by curvilinear motifs (Pl. 6). On the higher ground the balance changes and animals play a more prominent role in the rock art, although it is quite unusual for them to appear in isolation. The normal pattern is for the drawings of animals to be combined with geometric designs. Sometimes the two are so closely related that motifs drawn from these two groups merge into one another. Less common motifs – especially weapons and idols – are sometimes found in isolation.

The closest similarities are those observed between sites distributed along the Atlantic coastline between Ireland and Spain, but there are striking variations in the distribution of individual motifs even within Galicia. For example, circular motifs filled with cup marks tend to occur closer to the Portuguese border (Costas 1984), whilst circles with radial lines are often found further to the north. Circles containing crosses feature in the art of inland areas of Galicia, but they are also found in the Pyrenees. There are further variations in the style of animal carvings in Galicia, although these have yet to be explored systematically (Soto and Rey 1994; Concheiro and Gil in press). At a still broader level we can distinguish the Galician art and its counterparts in northern Spain and the north of Portugal from another widely distributed style, which seems to have been current during the same period. Schematic art is the most widely distributed style of rock art in the Iberian peninsula, and in this case the same motifs occur both as paintings and carvings. Again some of them are entirely abstract, whilst many others depict animals and humans. The distribution of Schematic art excludes the north-west corner of Spain and seems to avoid the area with Atlantic rock art (Gómez 1992).

There are well-established typologies for the motifs employed in Atlantic rock art, and at a superficial level there is much in common between the scheme devised by Morris for northern Britain and Peña's classification of the motifs used in Galicia (Morris 1989; García and Peña 1980). There are also a number of studies concerned with individual motifs which drew on evidence from both these areas and sometimes from other countries as well. But there may be problems in taking this approach because the individual motifs are very simple ones. As the term 'cup-and-ring mark' suggests, many are really no more than variations on dots and circles. A purely descriptive analysis is likely to founder because such basic designs are so easy to create. We need a more disciplined procedure if we are to make much progress.

It is really rather unhelpful to compare motifs in isolation. To use a term more familiar from the analysis of portable artefacts, they can only be studied as assemblages. Two examples may help to make the point. Just as we find circular carvings on the Atlantic seaboard, they can also be recognised in the southern foothills of the Alps. For example, at Carschenna in Switzerland there are both cup marks and cups with rings, but they appear together with depictions of the sun and also with drawings of horsemen (Zindel 1970). These are common elements in Alpine rock art and can be identified on many sites at Valcamonica, 100 km away (Anati 1994). Although it is thought that they date from roughly the same period as Atlantic rock art, it is unwise to extract such simple motifs from their local context.

We can see just how misleading a purely formal comparison may be if we also compare the prehistoric rock art of the Canary Islands with the motifs found further up the Atlantic coastline. Here there are some striking abstract carvings which feature a range of concentric circles just like the motifs recorded in Galicia. Yet once again there are problems in making piecemeal comparisons, for it is almost certain that the Canary Islands were not settled until long after the period in which Atlantic rock art went out of use. The earliest radiocarbon date from the islands is about 600 BC and all the others fall in the first millennium AD (Gonzalez and Tejera 1990).

A second requirement is to study not the motifs themselves but the conventions by which they were deployed. This is sometimes described as their 'design grammar' (Friedrich 1970). Although the idea will be considered in more detail in Chapter 5, a simple example will explain what this means. In this case we can begin with the evidence of cup marks, which are virtually ubiquitous. They can be found in many parts of the Atlantic coastline between Scotland and Spain, but they extend further south into Portugal in one direction and into Scandinavia in the other. Such a basic feature is unlikely to have had a short history, nor is there any reason to suppose that it was invented only once. On the other hand, it seems possible that many of the more complex curvilinear designs were elaborations of this simple motif. When we consider the rules according to which whole compositions were created, we shall be better placed to recognise local traditions of rock art.

To illustrate this point, I shall use two examples, one from north-east England and the other from north-west Spain (Fig. 3.6).

The English site is the main rock at Old Bewick on the Fell Sandstone of Northumberland (Beckensall 1991, 60). This is a prominent outcrop with a gently sloping surface on top of which are a range of entirely abstract motifs. The most common element is the cup mark, which, taken in isolation, accounts for ten of the motifs on the upper surface of the rock and for all the twenty motifs extending along its vertical edges. A further twenty-four cup marks are partly or wholly enclosed by circles. Fourteen of these are contained inside a single circle or by a segment of a circle, whilst in another eleven cases they are inside two or more concentric circles or arcs. The two largest motifs comprise cup marks surrounded by six rings and these motifs abut one another, although some attempt has been made to run both of them together. In most cases the cup marks are completely enclosed by single circles, whereas those contained within several different circles tend to be linked to the exterior by radial lines. Sometimes the circles are interrupted and respect the position of these lines, but this is not always the case. In other instances similar lines are attached not to the central cup mark but to the innermost circle, as if the decision to link that design to the surrounding area was taken after the basic motif was already in place. These lines nearly all observe a basic axis running across the contours of the rock and no example links more than two of the circular designs. The longest crosses the surface of the stone joining a pair of circular motifs 1.7 m apart and takes in two isolated cup marks along the way. The simpler circular motifs tend to be linked together, and the same applies to the most complex designs, but though their distributions overlap on the rock-face, the lines running between them ensure that the two groups are usually kept

Figure 3.6 The carved rocks at Old Bewick (A) after Beckensall 1991, and Laxe dos Cebros (B) after García and Peña 1980

apart. Although it is possible that the concentric rings were created over a period of time, the outer ring is often wider than the others and seems to isolate the motif from the remainder of the rock surface. There is no indication that the apparent crowding of motifs is because space was running out. In fact very few of the carvings come near to the edge of the available surface, where almost the only motifs are isolated cup marks. As we have seen, more of these are found on the vertical edges of the outcrop.

One way of understanding this particular group of carvings is to suggest that its composition adhered to some basic rules. The simpler motifs – the isolated cups and those with only one ring – were rarely linked to the other parts of the rock surface. It was only when the circular motifs became more complex that they were normally joined together, and even then there is an obvious gradation by which the most striking designs were interconnected to the exclusion of simpler motifs, which might be linked in a separate network. The two largest circular designs were run together, whereas the smaller motifs are densely distributed but are rarely joined in the same manner. Although there are isolated cup marks across most of the surface of the rock, only two of these were linked to other elements by lines. Whilst the images seem to be densely distributed, there are no cases in which existing cup marks were overlaid by large circular motifs, suggesting a degree of forward planning. In simple terms the circular motifs may have been enlarged by the addition of further rings but this must have been anticipated from the start so that sufficient space was left for it to be achieved.

This is one example of how a complex panel of rock art can be studied not as a collection of motifs but as a system of rules. We can illustrate a similar approach using a major site in Galicia (Fig. 3.6). Laxe dos Cebros is a well-known rock carving which forms part of an important series of petroglyphs around the edge of an upland basin at Fentáns (García and Peña 1980, 54–5). The decorated surface is of roughly the same extent as the main rock at Old Bewick (2.2 m by 1.8 m compared with 2.4 m by 2 m) and all the carvings are on its upper surface. There are six isolated cup marks on this rock and another nine which form the focus for a series of circular motifs. Two of these cup marks are of exceptional size and the larger is in the centre of the most extensive circular motif on the rock. It also occupies the central position on the carved surface as a whole. Four cup marks are enclosed by a single circle or arc and two of these are the only examples without any link to the surrounding area. There are at least ten circular design elements at Laxe dos Cebros and all the others are connected in some way to further motifs on the rockface. In two cases arcs or complete circles abut one another, whilst in the remaining instances the rings are broken to accommodate a radial line extending from the central cup. The majority of these lines follow the same axis.

The central circular motif forms the focus of this composition. It surrounds the largest of the cup marks, and the inner ring is emphasised by a penannular enclosure which occurs in only one other case at this site. It is abutted by an incomplete triple circle which once again is the only feature of its kind. The network of lines extending from this central figure links it to no fewer than seven other circular motifs. At the same time, there is a kind of hierarchy among those parts of the composition, for each of the larger circular designs is directly linked to smaller motifs of a similar kind. Thus the central motif, which is enclosed by three concentric rings, is abutted by a triple arc and then connected to a cup mark with two enclosing rings and another with only one. In a second instance a triple circle is linked to two cup marks described by a single ring.

So far I have commented on the use made of abstract designs at Laxe dos Cebros, but, as its name tells us, this is the 'rock of the deer'. There are no fewer than six drawings of animals on the same site. Four of these are obviously stags with a full set of antlers. They occupy the central space in the carving, whilst towards its edge are two incomplete drawings of animals, both much smaller in size. All the animals are depicted in profile and face in the same direction. Three of the stags are clearly connected with the central circular motif and they abut it on three sides. The front legs of one of the stags are in contact with the outer enclosure and so are the antlers of another. The third stag, which is more difficult to recognise, is even more closely integrated into the composition. It is depicted as overlying one segment of the central circle and part of the triple arc which abuts that feature. Its antlers appear to be linked with another cup and ring. It is quite clear that this is an integrated design and not a case of superimposition: the association between these different elements must have been intended. Nor is there any chance that these motifs were juxtaposed because there was too little room to spread them across a wider area, for once again the entire surface of the rock was never used.

Just as we saw in Northumberland, this is a carving that seems to have been created according to some simple rules. There is an apparent hierarchy among the circular motifs, all of which are based on the simple cup mark. This is expressed both through the network of connections between these different design elements and also through their position on the rock. There is also an obvious relationship between the size of the central cup marks and the complexity of the motifs that enclose them. At the same time, the more elaborate designs are generally linked together in a sequence or 'chain' leading from more complex motifs to simpler ones. The cups with single rings, however, are sometimes left alone.

The animals echo certain of these conventions. The stags occupy the central part of the carving, with the smaller animals at the edge. This relationship recalls the dominant position of the principal abstract motif, and it is no surprise that it should be directly linked to three of the four stags. The association is only strengthened when we consider that one of these animals overlies, or even appears to emerge from, the circular enclosure which dominates the composition. All the animals are drawn from the same viewpoint and they share the same orientation. As at Old Bewick, there is an area which is virtually devoid of carvings around the edges of the rock.

These are only examples of the structuring principles according to which panels of rock art were composed (for further details see Chapters 5 and 12). At this level they do share certain features. The number of rings surrounding each of the cup marks seems to have had an obvious importance and so did the network of lines that joined different motifs together. There is the same preference for level or shallowly sloping surfaces and for the grooves connecting different motifs to follow the same general axis. It is the presence of animals at Laxe dos Cebros that is the main difference between these sites.

But that is still to consider these carvings from a rather narrow perspective. These were not portable artefacts, to be compared for evidence of style, nor can they reduced entirely to two-dimensional images on the printed page. As I argued in Chapter 1, they may also have played a significant role in the pattern of settlement and movement. We shall only be able to compare them on a systematic basis if we also consider their position in the terrain. What really matters is the relationship between three different elements: the motifs that were selected for carving; the conventions by which they were incorporated into the different panels of rock art; and the placing of the carvings in relation to the local topography. Such a study cannot be restricted to isolated instances, for it must consider entire groups of drawings as a unitary system extending across a wider area. The best way of comparing the different components of Atlantic rock art is to consider how they were deployed in the ancient landscape.

Is that possible? In this chapter I have been concerned with the ways in which the study of Atlantic rock art developed and with the early literature on its nature and distribution. The 1980s and 1990s have seen a renewal of interest in this subject. In Britain this has taken the form of detailed local studies that have led to great improvements in our knowledge of the extent and content of prehistoric rock art. These studies have included important accounts of rock carvings in Ireland, southern and western Scotland, and parts of northern England. These will be enumerated in due course. Such work has also reopened the discussion on the chronology and wider significance of these images. Only in Ireland has there been an explicit investigation of the topographical siting of the carvings (Johnston 1991; Purcell 1994), but many of these local studies provide the basic material for such research.

Less work has been carried out in France, although there are already signs of new initiatives. It is in Galicia and northern Portugal that a new phase of research is well established. Again we have the benefit of some extremely thorough studies of the composition and distribution of the rock carvings, together with an entire literature dedicated to their cultural and chronological context. The first studies are now appearing which consider the location of the carvings in relation to the pattern of settlement. These are reinforced by the results of large-scale fieldwork along the commercial pipelines crossing the Galician countryside.

It is these areas that offer the greatest potential for the kinds of research advocated in Chapter 1. There are already large bodies of well-recorded rock carvings, and in each case these can be augmented by the results of current field projects. Galicia and the British Isles have other features in common. As seen in Chapter 2, they have an uncertain settlement history for the very period during which their rock art was created and in both cases we may have underestimated the importance of mobile economies before the economic reorganisation of the Later Bronze and Iron Ages. The disciplined study of prehistoric rock carvings may provide one way of investigating these problems. The issues will no doubt be defined more exactly if this is attempted in more than one region.

But such studies will only realise their full potential provided one more requirement is met. We must be able to show that the different elements that make up the Atlantic style of rock art really were in use over the same period. We also need to consider when and where that style originated. That is my task in the next chapter, for only if those answers are satisfactory, can we move on to our main objective: a comparative study of rock art in the prehistoric landscape of different parts of Atlantic Europe.

CHAPTER FOUR

TIME OUT OF MIND
The origins and chronology of Atlantic rock art

—— ·◆· ——

INTRODUCTION

The title of this chapter indicates the complexity of the problem, for there are two different ways of examining the origins of Atlantic rock art. This account considers them both.

At one level the origins of this style raise the same problems as its chronology. One term refers to the date at which it first appeared, whilst the other traces its currency through to the period in which it lapsed. But the origins of Atlantic rock art raise much wider issues, for they also invite us to consider its essential character. In what circumstances were these images first devised? And what can we say about the sources from which they sprang?

Those questions might seem to involve a protracted discussion of all the interpretations of rock art summarised by Ronald Morris, but in fact very few of those different versions are relevant to this particular issue. I would like to begin the discussion with a much more parsimonious review and shall weigh the claims of just three main approaches. The very nature of prehistoric rock art lays it open to more than one interpretation, in the past as well as in the present, and so these particular perspectives need not be mutually exclusive. We must remember the overlapping levels of meaning found in Australian rock art, in which the same images supply different kinds of information according to the character of the audience.

THE SOURCES OF ATLANTIC ROCK ART

These approaches can be summarised very simply. One conceives the motifs as a reflection of routine experience: as portrayals, however distant, of features seen in everyday life. A second extends this kind of approach to the evidence of specialised monuments: buildings that might be encountered less frequently and perhaps only on certain occasions. And the third sees the images as a reflection of states of altered consciousness, experienced at these monuments among other places and mediated through the human nervous system.

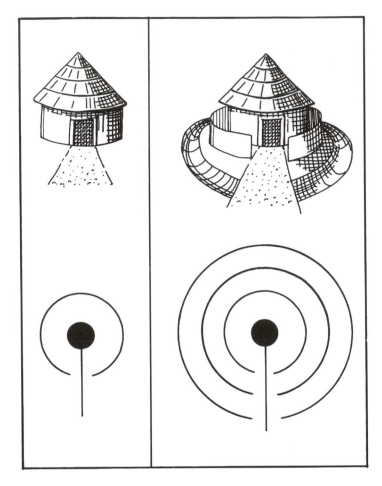

Figure 4.1 Cup-and-ring carvings interpreted as the plans of houses (after Züchner 1989)

The first of these interpretations is perhaps the most vulnerable to criticism. There can be little doubt that certain motifs were always meant to be recognised. They are largely naturalistic portrayals of artefacts and animals. In Britain, almost the only examples are drawings of axes and daggers, but towards the southern limit of Atlantic rock art depictions of weapons are much more common and are combined with representations of human beings, animals, portable artefacts and perhaps some form of vehicle. One problem is that any or all of these motifs could have been understood metaphorically. The red deer, for instance, were not necessarily prey; they might have carried a symbolic significance. As we shall see, the weapons might even have represented deposits of actual artefacts buried in the vicinity of the carvings.

It is revealing, although hardly surprising, that very similar suggestions were made about the meanings of the images in both areas with complex rock art, although in one case this happened before anyone had realised how widely they were distributed. Thus early accounts of the rock carvings of northern England identified the circular motifs as the ground plans of nearby hillforts (Tate 1865). In Spain, Züchner (1989) has claimed to identify the plans of houses and field systems in Galician rock art (Fig. 4.1). At one level these specific suggestions can be countered very simply. The rock carvings in northern England are not contemporary with the hillforts, although there are other circular monuments that most probably were of the same age as these drawings. Nor have any field systems been identified in the prehistoric landscape of Galicia, where there are very few house plans dating from the same period as the rock art. Züchner's case depends on analogy with a popular interpretation of the drawings at Mont Bego and Valcamonica, and even there this interpretation is difficult to substantiate (Delano Smith 1990).

In fact this basic approach raises two fundamental issues. At one level it seems to be weakened by its emphasis on the way in which archaeologists view the world. When Züchner interprets the panels of rock art as maps, his argument is strengthened by the drawings of animals which cross the carved surface along an axis established by other kinds of motif. But when he discusses the evidence of house plans, his illustrations move from the general to the specific and even include rings of post holes taken from excavation reports. This is how archaeologists perceive the world, but it is a technique that they have had to learn. It is a way of seeing which they are unlikely to share with others.

At a second level this approach has rather more to commend it, for mobile peoples certainly do have a very precise understanding of space and may be sensitive to topographical cues that would be missed by anyone else. They have, and they need to have, an acutely developed sense of direction. In certain cultures that extends to a two-dimensional vision of the world akin to aerial perspective. This perhaps reflects the importance of viewpoints in their exploitation of the environment. It is well known that certain supposedly abstract paintings created by native Australians are actually conceived as maps, but as maps that depict the movements of mythical beings and show a landscape in which the supernatural permeates every activity (Morphy 1991).

That might provide one clue to a different interpretation of Atlantic rock art. Perhaps a more appropriate comparison might be between the characteristic layout of the circular motifs shared along the coastline and other phenomena which are found throughout this area. Peter Jackson has emphasised how these motifs portray a circular enclosure with an entrance that allows restricted access to the centre (1995). That is a good description of the structure of a cup-and-ring carving breached by a radial line, but it is also the basic configuration of at least two major types of monument (Fig. 4.2). Throughout Atlantic Europe that is precisely the way in which passage graves are organised, whilst in Britain and Ireland it also describes the structure of a henge.

If we pursue the argument that these motifs played a metaphorical role, this interpretation gains support from another source. At an empirical level, it is certainly true that rather similar images are actually associated with some of the monuments themselves; they form part of the wider phenomenon described as

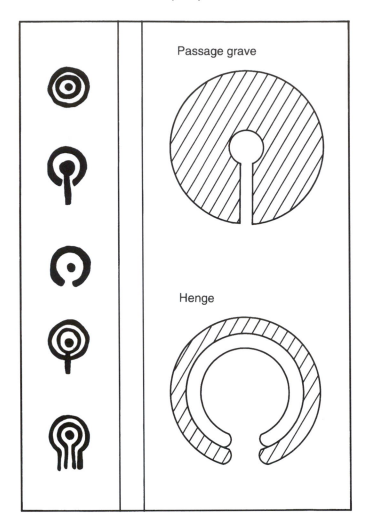

Figure 4.2 The spatial organisation of cup-and-ring carvings, passage graves and henge monuments

megalithic art. At a still deeper level, it may be that such motifs derive from states of altered consciousness and that the very structure of passage tombs would have created the conditions under which these might have been experienced (Lewis-Williams and Dowson 1988 and 1993; Bradley 1989b).

The study of 'entoptic' images presents many problems. The term 'entoptic' is fairly easy to define, for it refers to images generated *within* the eyes: images that are created through disturbance of the optic nerves. Those images are known as 'phosphenes'. Because they are a basic feature of human neuropsychology, the most basic of those images should be found worldwide, although in any one area they will be overlain by others drawn from the local culture. This approach raises two

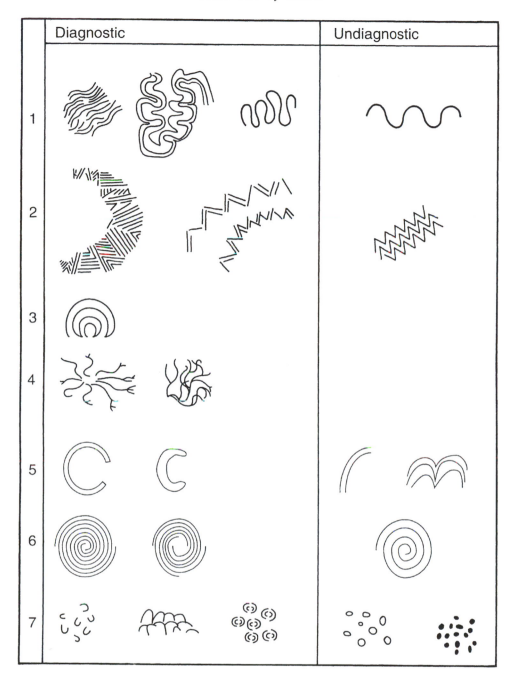

Figure 4.3 Motifs characteristic of entoptic imagery compared with undiagnostic motifs (from an original kindly provided by Jeremy Dronfield)

key issues. First, the images that have been identified as phosphenes are extremely simple ones, derived from ethnographic sources and from the results of clinical experiments (Vázquez Varela 1993). Second, there seems no reason why they should not have been copied widely once their original significance was established.

The first objection has been addressed in a recent study by Dronfield (1995), which compares the content of several different art styles. Some come from societies in which states of altered consciousness were important, whilst a second group derive from cultures in which this is not the case. Some of the motifs originally claimed as phosphenes are found in both these groups, but others are not: they are confined to communities who emphasise the importance of hallucination (Fig. 4.3). Those images are shared between such groups and are not found in the control sample. Although Dronfield's work suggests that there may be fewer entoptic images than was originally supposed, it also demonstrates that they can be identified on a disciplined basis. That is not to deny that in certain cases motifs which are present in both his samples might also evoke states of altered consciousness. It simply means that this may not be their only source.

Certain rock art sites do include these images, particularly the enclosed arc, but phosphenes are more common in megalithic tombs where their distributions seem to focus at particular points in the layout of the monument. These observations provide a helpful clue to the roots of Atlantic rock art, but they also pose another problem. Because they originate in the human nervous system they might be created quite independently in several different areas (Lewis-Williams and Dowson 1993, 61–2). Once again it is not helpful to compare isolated motifs with one another, and certainly not to attempt this over a distance.

The identification of phosphenes does not dispose of a second objection, that once the special significance of a motif has become established it can assume a wider currency, so not every entoptic image need refer to a special kind of experience. Indeed, those motifs might take on additional connotations and could be reinterpreted altogether. An obvious example of this process is the Christian cross, which depicts a Roman method of execution and relates to the central event in a religious narrative. Yet that image can be used in a much more general sense, on a piece of jewellery or a flag, without any attention to the first of these references and with little consciousness of the second.

In fact the main strength of this line of argument comes from the contexts in which the motifs are found. Lewis-Williams and Dowson (1993) have drawn attention to a common feature of ethnographic descriptions of trance. This is the sensation of travelling through a tunnel or vortex. As they say, it is an apt description of the experience of entering a megalithic tomb in which a low passage communicates with the burial area. The chambers of such monuments may be located at a considerable depth beneath the mound or cairn, and at some sites they could only be reached with difficulty, by crawling along the passage in total darkness. All these conditions would increase the sense of being cut off from the world, of entering a place that was occupied by the dead. It is under very much these conditions that the visitors to such sites might undergo sensory deprivation. That is not to deny that other factors would have played a part, as there is evidence for the use of hallucinogens in Neolithic and Bronze Age Europe (Sherratt 1991). What matters is that passage tombs were especially powerful locations, and ones in which people might be particularly prone to experiencing altered states of consciousness. As if to emphasise the importance of tunnel imagery, the entrances of some of these tombs were embellished with curvilinear motifs, whilst the art associated with these monuments includes a range of phosphenes.

The same notion may provide the basis for the curvilinear art of Atlantic Europe. Not only do the main circular motifs echo the characteristic ground plan of the passage grave, they also evoke the sensation of entering the natural rock through a tunnel. Generally speaking, the curvilinear motifs found in passage-grave art take a distinctive form: they are continuous circles or spirals and only a few are interrupted by an entrance. In open-air rock art, on the other hand, the position is reversed and it is extremely common for the circular designs to respect a radial line extending from a central cup mark. At megalithic tombs, where a real passage existed, there would be little reason to symbolise this feature. Where the carvings were created on natural surfaces, however, the radial line emphasised a pathway leading into the rock.

Lewis-Williams and Dowson describe another characteristic of trance experience. Shamans sometimes report the sensation of travelling through the solid rock, entering or leaving it through natural cracks. This can be represented in San rock art by 'lines [which] extend for many metres through a rock shelter ... apparently weaving in and out of the rock face' (Lewis-Williams and Dowson 1990, 5). Sometimes incomplete animals are depicted, as if they were entering the surface of the stone. Again there may be links between this observation and some of the characteristic features of Atlantic rock art. There are certainly sites on which artificial motifs were joined to natural hollows and fissures in the rock and others where motifs were linked by a network of natural cracks. Natural basins or grooves were sometimes enhanced by pecking, and quite often the circular motifs were joined by a complex network of lines that had been created for the purpose. In certain cases these also emphasised the positions of features of geological origin.

More important, this relationship extends to the depictions of animals found in the rock art of Galicia. Peña (1976) has published a study of the relationship between the carvings of animals, circles and spirals. It is very revealing that in this area animals are more likely to be linked with concentric circles than they are with single rings. These animals can be portrayed directly overlapping the curvilinear motifs but in most cases Peña concludes that both sets of images were created at the same time. Animals appear to be emerging from circles and spirals and in several cases their bodies are obviously incomplete (Fig. 4.4). As we have seen, this feature is also recorded in the rock art of southern Africa.

I must end this section by emphasising a point made earlier. This discussion has been concerned with the *sources* of the images found in Atlantic rock art. It has not addressed the equally important issue of how they were deployed over time. There is no reason to suppose that, once certain images had been recognised as socially significant, their meanings were immutable. Since those designs were fixed on the surface of the land, they would have been seen by communities who had no direct knowledge of their creation, and their significance could very well have changed. If we accept that certain motifs became important because they

Figure 4.4 The relationship between circular motifs and drawings of animals in Galicia (after Peña 1976)

were associated with states of altered consciousness, there is no reason to suppose that they retained that specific significance for later generations. Their changing roles in prehistoric society can only be investigated by archaeology. The first requirement is a clearer understanding of the place of Atlantic rock art in the sequence of settlement.

THE CHRONOLOGY OF ATLANTIC ROCK ART

I began by investigating the origins of Atlantic rock art through a discussion of the possible sources of the imagery. We can also consider its origins using a more conventional approach. When was it first created in different areas? And when did it go out of use?

These questions once again raise the difficult problem of relating rock art to the decoration found in megalithic tombs, but those monuments do not provide the only relevant material. Although it is often supposed that open-air carvings are undatable, that is not quite true. In the account which follows I shall attempt to work around some of the areas of ambiguity by starting the discussion with sites that are found in apparent isolation. I shall treat the most prolific groups of carvings separately, as one objective of this review is to decide whether those in northern Britain were really contemporary with the sites in northern Spain.

Two kinds of clue are vital here. There are the indications provided by drawings of artefacts of known age, and occasionally there are direct associations between rock carvings and datable objects. I shall begin with the first group as it provides some of the clearest outlines.

There are very few naturalistic drawings in the rock art of the British Isles, and nearly all of these are associated with monuments, although not with megalithic tombs. Four of these sites are Early Bronze Age barrows or cairns, and the fifth is Stonehenge. Between them they include a number of depictions of identifiable daggers and axeheads (Simpson and Thawley 1972). The daggers portrayed in the carvings are largely undiagnostic but other drawings appear to depict flat axes which date from the early part of this period. Apart from cup marks, none of these images is found in direct association with other components of British rock art, and at Nether Largie in Argyll the carvings of axes appear to be superimposed on an existing arrangement of cups (Bradley 1993, 91–3). Strictly speaking, they provide a minimum age for those motifs. Apart from depictions of metalwork, there are a few representations of animals in Britain, but in no case is their date assured. The best examples are three drawings found amidst an array of curvilinear motifs at Ballochmyle in western Scotland, comparable with some of the motifs found in north-west Spain (Stevenson 1993); indeed, one of them, a drawing of a deer, overlaps a circular carving in the way that Peña describes in his study of Galician rock art.

In Galicia there are more drawings of metalwork, and the range of artefact types is rather wider. There are no convincing axeheads but there are drawings of daggers and halberds. Some of these motifs include enough detail for a more thorough account of their chronology. Those depicted in Galician rock art resemble a type recorded in the north of Portugal (Peña 1980). It is a form that is closely related to similar weapons in Ireland and Britain, and that comparison is certainly strengthened by the evidence of the daggers. A number of these seem to belong to the Beaker horizon, or the beginning of the Early Bronze Age (Vázquez Varela 1990), but others are assigned to a later stage in the development of these artefacts. In Pena's opinion those at Castriño de Conxo, outside Santiago de Compostela, are most like types found in the Wessex Culture (Peña 1979). Those may be among the last rock carvings in Galicia as none of the drawings of weapons date from the Later Bronze Age.

The second important group of naturalistic images in north-west Spain are the drawings described as 'idols'. These are rather unusual and represent objects which seem to have been cylindrical in form, with parallel grooves or even a human face at one end. These are clearly depictions of artefacts of a type which is known in south-east Spain and the south of Portugal where they can be found both in settlement sites and also in megalithic tombs (Almagro 1973; Aparicio 1986). They are conventionally dated to the Late Neolithic or Copper Age. The earliest examples of these objects are associated with radiocarbon dates in the late fourth or early third millennia BC. Related examples have been discovered in Brittany and in megalithic tombs in the Boyne valley where there is similar dating evidence (Eogan 1990; Fábregas 1991).

Most of the direct associations between rock art and dated material come from the British Isles. This is because fragments of already carved rock were often incorporated in funerary monuments; indeed, the decorated stone in the burial cist at Nether Largie may originally have been a menhir (Bradley 1993, 91–3). In some cases carved stones were used in constructing Early Bronze Age cists. The cultural significance of this practice will be considered in Chapter 9. For the moment it is treated as a source of dating evidence. A number of writers have observed that the decorated pieces used on these sites were already old. The decoration seems to have undergone weathering in the open air and some of the motifs were truncated when the stones were trimmed to allow their reuse (Fig. 4.5; Simpson and Thawley 1972; Burgess 1990). That is not to say that these pieces had lost their significance by this stage, for there seem to have been certain conventions governing the selection of carved stones at these sites. The more complex motifs are over-represented compared with those found in the open air, and this evidence suggests that such motifs still retained their significance at a time when Beakers and Food Vessels were being deposited with the dead. That could take the use of abstract carvings into the early second millennium BC.

Two exceptions may prove the rule. Another decorated cist has been found at Knappers near Glasgow, but in this case the decoration seems to have been created when the site was built. This is revealing as the only artefact from this cist is not of Early Bronze Age origin at all. It was a specialised form of flint axe which dates from the Late Neolithic period (Ritchie and Adamson 1981, 189–92 and 198–9). The second site, at Lilburn in Northumberland, poses more problems, for it is only known from an account published in the late nineteenth century (Moffatt 1885). It consisted of a rectangular trench containing two layers of cremated bone, with a decorated stone at one end. The cross-section of this feature suggests that

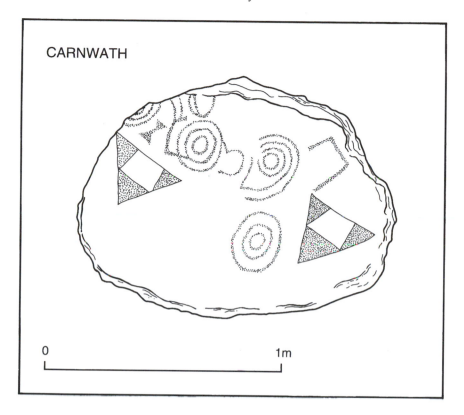

CARNWATH

0   1m

Figure 4.5 A decorated cist cover from Wester Yardhouses, Carnwath, Lanarkshire

it might once have held some kind of wooden structure. This is important because trench burials very much of this type are recorded from a series of Neolithic burial mounds in northern England. These include both long barrows and round barrows, and they are commonly associated with cremations (Vyner 1984, 188–92). They have radiocarbon dates extending down to 3300 BC. The ends of these mortuary structures are often marked by upright posts, but in this case it seems possible that a carved stone fulfilled the same purpose. In view of these arguments for an early origin it is particularly interesting that the decoration should include a spiral, which is one of the motifs found on passage graves during the same period.

There is much less information about the contexts of decorated stones in other parts of Atlantic Europe, although what evidence there is does take a similar form. Simple abstract designs, principally cup marks, are associated with a series of massive burial cists found in Finistère and dated to the Early Bronze Age. Most of the sites were investigated many years ago and there is little to show whether the carvings were created for the purpose or whether they were being reused (De Chatellier 1907). One Galician cist does seem to have contained a reused carving (R. Fábregas pers. comm.), whilst another motif associated with cist burials in that region is also found in open-air rock art, lending weight to the argument that it was of some importance during the period of the first metalwork in north-west Iberia (Fábregas and Penedo 1994).

There are even fewer examples of direct associations between rock carvings and datable artefacts. The tip of a flint arrowhead was found during excavation at Greenland near Dumbarton, but too little survives for it to be dated (A. Sheridan pers. comm.). There is more promising evidence from Ilkley Moor in northern England where two concentrations of Late Neolithic artefacts have been excavated amidst a concentration of rock carvings (Edwards and Bradley in press). These are associated with an assemblage of flintwork of quite exceptional quality including finished artefacts and raw material introduced from the North Sea coast 90 km away. A number of these objects would normally be found in burials or close to specialised monuments where they might be buried with some formality in pits. The same is often true of the style of decorated pottery – Grooved Ware – associated with the artefacts on Ilkley Moor. There are indications that both these collections of artefacts may have been specialised deposits and there certainly seems to have been a higher proportion of finished objects towards one of the decorated rocks. The centre of the other concentration of material may have been marked by an undecorated stone. There are two radiocarbon dates from this site which indicate an age range of 2900–2600 BC.

In Galicia there are only two finds that may be relevant. One is a copper flat axe found in a major group of carvings at Lombo da Costa, but its context is uncertain (Monteagudo 1977, 57). The site itself includes many geometric motifs and drawings of animals, but in this case none of the petroglyphs portrays metal artefacts. By contrast, an important rock carving at Leiro includes drawings of both halberds and daggers (Calo and González 1980). A hoard containing the same types of objects has been discovered in the vicinity, but its position is not known in any detail (Meijide 1989). This is the only halberd hoard in north-west Spain, and its discovery at Leiro can hardly be a coincidence (Fig. 4.6). Perhaps the rock art was intended to record the deposition of these weapons, but, even if that were true, it would do nothing to elucidate the wider chronology of the art.

There are broad similarities between the motifs employed in Atlantic rock art and those found in two other media: megalithic art and decorated pottery. We must consider just how the open-air carvings are related to those found in stone-built tombs. Most of the relevant evidence comes from Britain and Ireland, although there are occasional areas of overlap in other regions. In Iberia cup marks are regularly found in these monuments, but circular motifs are rare and hardly ever occur in isolation (Bueno and Balbín 1992). Animals may also be portrayed in Iberian megalithic tombs, but they are rather different from those portrayed in Atlantic rock art and tend to occur with designs known in Schematic art. In fact there are very few cases in which Galician rock art has elements in common with the decoration of passage tombs, and where it does happen the motif in question, a simple rectilinear design, is rarely found in either medium (Fábregas and Penedo 1994). The same point can be made with regard to the megalithic art of western France. Circles and cup marks can be found occasionally but they were not a major feature of the decorated monuments (Shee Twohig 1981). The best-dated examples come

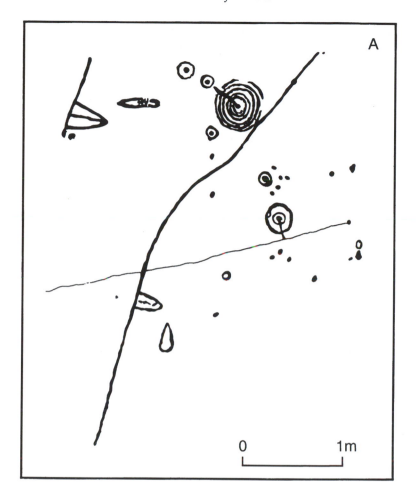

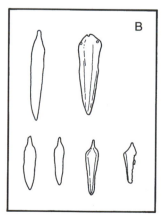

Figure 4.6 A: the decorated rock surface at Leiro, Galicia (after Calo and González 1980) and B: the contents of the nearby weapon hoard (after Meijide 1989)

from Table des Marchand in the Morbihan where cup marks and a cup and ring can be no later than the construction of the well-known passage grave (S. Cassen pers. comm.). This is likely to date to the earlier fourth millennium BC.

It is more appropriate to compare Atlantic rock art with the decoration of tombs in Britain and Ireland, although it is necessary to proceed warily. Here, discussion normally begins with a cup-marked stone found in a timber mortuary structure beneath Dalladies long barrow in Scotland (Piggott 1972). The radiocarbon dates from this site actually span several hundred years, but two of them are in close agreement and seem to show that at least these simple motifs were being created by the later fourth millennium BC. In fact there are other reasons for taking this view, for an early form of megalithic monument known as the portal dolmen is also associated with these motifs (Burgess 1990, 160). This connection is found on both sides of the Irish Sea. Although it is usually supposed that the carvings were added during a later period, this does not seem likely simply because this form of embellishment was virtually confined to one type of tomb. The classification of megalithic chambers may be second nature to the archaeologist, but it is unreasonable to suppose that people in the past were exercising similar skills. It is far simpler to see the cup marks as an original feature of these sites. If so, then they should date from the earlier fourth millennium BC (Lynch 1976).

Apart from portal dolmens, there are cup marks on the entrance to a megalithic tomb at Tregiffian in Cornwall. This monument is normally dated to the Late Neolithic period and the carvings were certainly hidden from view when the site was reconstructed during the Early Bronze Age (ApSimon 1973). Otherwise nearly all the decorated tombs are passage graves, and these carry a far more varied range of motifs. Most of these are in Ireland but there are small groups in Orkney and north-west Wales (Shee Twohig 1981). Unfortunately, their chronology is poorly understood. There seems little doubt that passage tombs had a lengthy history within Britain and Ireland yet only the later of the sites provide any dating evidence for megalithic art. That may be because this style developed late in the history of these monuments. Irish megalithic art has nothing in common with the first phase of tomb carving in Brittany, and its closest relations are with a subsequent phase (ibid). Alternatively, such a short chronology could be entirely misleading, and may result from the concentration of research at monuments in the Boyne valley.

Alison Sheridan (1987) has studied the development of passage tombs in Ireland. She proposes a date a little after 3700 BC for the start of this sequence, which incudes some of the monuments at Carrowmore. Many of the monuments at Loughcrew were built between 3500 and 3250 BC, and the great tombs of the Boyne – those with the main concentrations of art – she dates between about 3100 and 3000 BC.

All these sites include decorated surfaces. The discovery of a carved motif at Carrowmore is a recent development (Curran-Mulligan 1994), but the other monuments have been well known for many years. The rock carvings at Loughcrew have always seemed rather different from those associated with the major tombs at Newgrange, Knowth and Dowth, but it was not long ago that the full significance of this contrast became apparent. When Breuil was writing about megalithic art in the 1930s it was known that the largest tombs in the Boyne valley had undergone more than one phase of carving; some motifs were superimposed on one another and in certain cases the designs were entirely inaccessible and must have been created before the tombs were finished. M. O'Sullivan has taken this argument further (1986 and 1989). He has shown that the apparently early motifs are created in a distinctive style. They are formed by shallow pecked lines and seem to be distributed haphazardly across the available surface. Many of these elements must have been created before the stones reached their present positions. These early drawings comprise his 'Depictive Style'. The later art, on the other hand, was undoubtedly created in situ and there are many cases in which it overlies these simple designs. The carvings are deeper and have a sculptural quality. They form extensive compositions moulded to the contours of the rock. This is O'Sullivan's 'Plastic Style'. The comparison is particularly revealing because the decoration at Loughcrew shares so many features with the *earlier* style in the Boyne.

Why is this so important for our studies of the chronology of rock art? It is because the motifs found in the open air have more in common with those in the Depictive Style than they do with the designs that characterise the Plastic Style. It would be wrong to exaggerate the overlap between these two groups, but both of them include cup marks, cups and rings, curvilinear enclosures, simple spirals and rosettes, as well as more specialised motifs that are found only occasionally in either tradition. This provides prima facie evidence that the roots of Atlantic rock art may go back at least as far as the mid-fourth millennium BC and that they may very well precede the final flowering of tomb decoration in the Boyne valley.

Even so, such similarities must not be given too much weight, for there are many differences. Individual motifs appear in quite different proportions between Atlantic rock art and O'Sullivan's Depictive Style. The carved surfaces were built up according to distinct conventions, and there are other, more complex motifs that are not found outside megalithic tombs. Equally important, there is a vital difference of technique. The simple pecked lines that characterise the Depictive Style have no equivalent on open-air sites, where the method of carving is more like that used in the later art of the Boyne valley. Yet the outcome was by no means the same, for it is uncommon for British and Irish rock carvings to pay much attention to the contours of the rock. That is not the case in Galicia.

Lastly, it is important to remember that megalithic art would have owed much of its formality to the fact that it was located within an extremely rigid architectural setting. There were certain thresholds within these buildings that it was normal to emphasise by the use of panels of decorated stone: the kerb, the entrance, the passage and the burial chamber (Thomas 1992). There seems to have been no obvious equivalent among the carvings in the open air. But there is one site at which we can see how the components of Atlantic rock art could have played exactly the same roles, and in the same type of building. Like some of the tombs in Ireland, the two passage graves at Balnuaran of Clava in northern Scotland were both built using already carved stones. The corbelled chambers of both these tombs were constructed from slabs that had previously been decorated with cup marks, and where one of the passages entered the chamber there was further decoration. In Ireland we might have expected to find an elaborate composition at this point, but at Clava the decoration was of the simpler variety that we also see in the local landscape, and one of the uprights was embellished with cups and rings. The carvings extend below the floor of the chamber and cannot be a later addition to the monument (Pl. 7; fieldwork by the writer, 1994). Here we may have one of the vital links in the chain of connections that flows from one style of art to another. The Clava passage graves are ringed by circles of monoliths which find their best parallels at Newgrange; their kerbs are emphasised by low platforms like those found at passage tombs in Orkney, and they are decorated with the characteristic motifs of Atlantic rock art. But the logic according to which such motifs were located was inspired by megalithic art in Ireland.

The second topic to consider is the relationship between rock art and decorated ceramics. In this case the evidence is limited entirely to the British Isles and mainly concerns one style of pottery: Grooved Ware. It was material in this tradition that was found among the carved rocks on Ilkley Moor. There is also a more limited overlap with a northern British variety of Peterborough Ware.

Most authorities are agreed that there is a certain overlap between Grooved Ware and the motifs found in Irish megalithic art (Wainwright and Longworth 1971, 246; Shee Twohig 1981, 125–8) but they have not realised that the same is true of open-air rock carvings. In both cases it is the curvilinear motifs on the pottery that are important. There are three of these: the cup and ring, the rosette, and the spiral. The rosette appears at only one site – the Grooved Ware settlement at Barnhouse in Orkney, which is dated between 3200 and 3000 BC (C. Richards pers. comm.). It also contains sherds decorated with cups and rings, although similar motifs are found on sites in Wessex which were built over 500 years later, suggesting that this particular design was very long-lived (Wainwright and Longworth 1971, 71). The same applies to the spiral. There is a sherd with this motif from an early phase at Skara Brae, and this should be broadly contemporary with the finds from Barnhouse (C. Richards pers. comm.). At the same time it also occurs in what is probably the latest secure context for Grooved Ware of any kind, a pit at Radley in Oxfordshire which has a date in the second half of the third millennium BC (R. Cleal pers. comm.).

The overlap with Peterborough Ware is limited to two vessels from an uncertain context near to Ford in Northumberland (Kinnes and Longworth 1985, 135). The rims of both pots are decorated with a series of concentric semicircles which recall the rock carvings found in the same area. There is no direct dating evidence, but at Meldon Bridge in southern Scotland vessels of exactly the same form come from contexts with radiocarbon dates between 2900 and 2500 BC (Burgess 1976, 173–6).

There are two other indications that British rock art has a lengthy chronology. The first is the discovery of a carved stone ball in the Earlier Neolithic settlement of Eilean Domhnuill on North Uist (Armit 1996, fig. 14.10). The decoration seems to include a cup surrounded by two concentric rings. This motif is approached by a radial line. Such objects are usually dated to the Later Neolithic period and share certain forms of decoration with Grooved Ware or megalithic art. This find may suggest an earlier origin for this particular design. The second piece of evidence comes from Achnabreck in Mid Argyll, where differences of weathering suggest that the motifs were created in two different phases (RCAHMS 1988, 87–99). According to that interpretation, the early motifs are concentric circles which lack a central cup mark, and a series of double spirals best paralleled in the passage-grave art of Orkney. The later motifs at Achnabreck consist mainly of cups and rings, many of them breached by a radial line. These elements are much more common in open-air rock carvings and are found throughout its distribution.

Taken together, these arguments suggest that the abstract motifs in British rock art might have been used over a considerably longer period than their equivalents in megalithic tombs. At the same time all these dates are earlier than those ascribed to the types of metalwork depicted on sites in Wessex and Mid Argyll. Open-air rock art was obviously very long-lived. In Britain and Ireland it could have originated as early as 3300 BC and may have remained important into the early years of the second millennium BC. Although the evidence is much slighter, this does seem to coincide with the currency of similar rock art on the Continent.

There is also some consensus over the later history of these sites. In Britain, it seems likely that rock carvings had gone out of use by the agricultural intensification of later prehistory. Individual carvings on Ilkley Moor are overlain by field walls (Ilkley Archaeology Group 1986) whilst another carved surface on Dod Law in Northumberland was covered by the rampart of a hillfort (C. Smith 1989). The same pattern is seen in the Peak District where a substantial piece of carved rock was reused in the rampart of another defended site (Stanley 1954) and at Eston Nab in Cleveland where cup-marked boulders were used as packing stones in a palisaded enclosure and in the defences of the hillfort that replaced it (Vyner 1988a). All these sites seem to date from the Late Bronze Age or Iron Age.

The Iberian evidence is very similar. There is no clear evidence that any of the metalwork depicted in the rock carvings remained in use in the Middle or Late Bronze Ages, and once again panels of carved rock came to be buried beneath the ramparts of early hillforts (García and Peña 1980, 64–5; Costas 1988). The same process is illustrated by the reuse of already carved rocks in the construction of their ramparts (Martin 1983). As in the British Isles, this provides a minimum age for the Atlantic style of rock art.

SUMMING UP

The argument has been lengthy and it is time to summarise its conclusions. Because certain of these images might have originated in the human nervous system, it is possible that they developed independently in different areas, but that does not seem likely. Chapter 3 showed how similar motifs were organised in much the same ways from northern England to Galicia. Now it appears that those designs also shared much the same chronology. Whether or not it had its roots in altered states of consciousness, Atlantic rock art first appeared by the late fourth millennium BC. It ran in parallel with the development of megalithic art in Ireland, with which it shares a range of circular motifs, and it was still in use in the Early Bronze Age when a series of distinctive weapons were portrayed in the carvings. Nowhere does it seem to have survived into the first millennium BC.

There are also significant contrasts. Open-air rock carvings overlap with mega-lithic art in Ireland, but they have little in common with the motifs found in the passage graves of France and Iberia, and it may well be that the original source of inspiration was in the north. At the same time, they include occasional references to the importance of long-distance contacts extending along the Atlantic coastline. Thus Galician art contains carvings of idols of a kind evidenced in Portugal and apparently related to those in north-west Spain, Brittany and Ireland. It also contains drawings of weapon types which have their closest counterparts in the British Isles. It is because of such long-distance links that we are entitled to consider 'Atlantic' rock art as a unitary phenomenon. Its later history is important too, and again it took much the same course in different areas. Galician rock art became redundant as the character of settlement changed during later prehistory, and insular rock art did the same. The parallels between these two sequences are more than a coincidence. Now that the basic framework has been established, I can continue by considering the role of rock art in the prehistoric landscape.

PART II

ROCK ART AND THE LANDSCAPE OF BRITAIN AND IRELAND

———— •◆• ————

'You may be wondering how you'll ever learn to manage the techniques. Don't worry, my boy – you will learn and quite quickly too. . . . The work in Interpretation is above all creative. It mustn't carry the analysis of images and symbols too far. The main thing, as in algebra, is to arrive at certain principles. And even they mustn't be applied too rigidly, or else the true point of the work could be missed. The higher form of interpretation begins where routine ends. What you must concentrate on are permutations and combinations of symbols. One last tip: all the work that's done [here] is highly secret, but Interpretation is top secret. Don't forget it. And now off you go and start your new job.'

Ismail Kadare (1981) *The Palace of Dreams*

CHAPTER FIVE

THE RULES OF ENGAGEMENT
The character of British
rock art

— ·•· —

INTRODUCTION

I began this book by describing my first encounter with rock art, and explained how I had attempted to understand that experience by considering the role that petroglyphs play in other areas of the world. This led me to discuss a variety of approaches drawn from recent research. Many of these will appear again in this and succeeding chapters. But like any account of an experience that took place some time ago, the outlines command more attention than the details. It is to the details that I must turn my attention now.

That visit to Ilkley Moor was only the first of many. Where I had originally been struck by the siting of rock carvings at viewpoints, I came to realise that such a characterisation was too crude. Some carvings certainly were located on the edge of Wharfedale and commanded a view right along the valley, but others did not do so. As I visited more of the carvings, I came to recognise an important distinction. The more complicated carvings were among those with the widest views, but some of the simpler carvings were located in a different way.

That perception raised two questions where there had been only one before. I had started by considering the physical setting of the rock art, but now I was obliged to think about the principles behind its composition. Again it was necessary to account for perceptions that at first were entirely intuitive. Why did certain carvings appear more complex than others? Could that distinction be captured by a more formal analysis? And would similar distinctions be recognisable to other people? Behind all these questions there was a still more fundamental uncertainty. Would the distinctions that I seemed to recognise on the ground have been apparent to people in the past? In Chapter 1 I sought to account for my first reactions to the siting of rock art on Ilkley Moor by drawing on a body of theoretical writing. We can follow a similar process in looking at the contents of those carvings.

This required a fairly simple programme of research. Could any rules be identified determining the form that these carvings should take and the kinds of places where those images should be made? Still more important, if both kinds of analysis did produce fruitful results, how would the two systems have been related to one another? If we could distinguish between simple and complex rock art in a purely

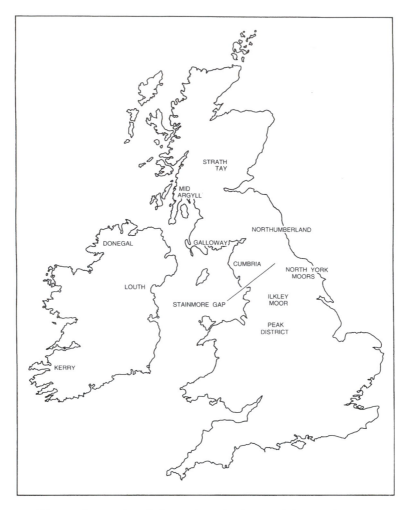

Figure 5.1 The regions of Britain and Ireland containing major groups of rock carvings

formal analysis, could we recognise the same distinction in their placing on the ground?

These questions were easy to ask, but they were by no means easy to answer. Formal analysis depends on the availability of records of good quality, and these were not available in every area. They required accurate transcriptions of the petroglyphs, and the quality of those records had to be assessed by visiting a large number of sites in the field. The rock carvings found in those regions also needed to be typical of the range of compositions found across Britain and Ireland as a whole. The samples needed to be large ones too, but there were plenty of regions to consider (Figs 5.1 and 5.2). In Ireland the main concentrations of rock art were

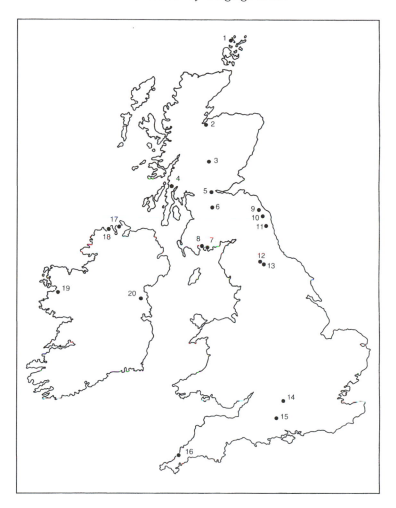

Figure 5.2 The locations of British and Irish sites or groups of sites illustrated in the plates and figures. Key: 1. Pierowall; 2. Balnuaran of Clava; 3. Strath Tay complex (including Loch Tay and Aberfeldy); 4. Kilmartin complex (including Achnabreck, Baluacraig and Temple Wood); 5. Castleton; 6. Carnwath; 7. Kirkcudbright complex (including High Banks); 8. Cairnholy; 9. Milfield complex (including Buttony, Cuddy's Cave, Dod Law, Fowberry, Gled Law, Roughting Linn and Weetwood Moor); 10. Old Bewick; 11. Millstone Burn; 12. Barningham Moor; 13. Gayles Moor; 14. Barrow Hills; 15. Stonehenge; 16. Trethellan Farm; 17. Doagh Island; 18. Mevagh; 19. Boheh Stone; and 20. Boyne valley complex (including Newgrange and Knowth)

in three areas of the country, in County Kerry to the south-west (Cuppage 1986, 56–65; O'Sullivan and Sheehan 1993; Purcell 1994), County Donegal to the north-west (Van Hoek 1987 and 1988) and in County Louth in the north-east, close to the modern border between Ulster and Eire (Clarke 1982; Buckley and Sweetman 1991, 82–7). The distribution of Scottish sites was just as wide, extending from the English border as far north as Sutherland, with major concentrations in Mid Argyll to the west (Morris 1977; RCAHMS 1988, 85–126), in Galloway to the south-west (Morris 1979; Van Hoek 1995) and in Strath Tay in the southern highlands (Stewart 1958). Rock art was rare in Wales and the south-west but it occurred throughout northern England, with the main groups of finds in the Peak District (Barnatt and Reeder 1982), West Yorkshire (Ilkley Archaeology Group 1986), Cleveland (Spratt 1993, 84–6), Northumberland (Beckensall 1991 and 1992a), Cumbria (Beckensall 1992b) and the borderland of North Yorkshire and County Durham (Laurie 1985). In the event just three of these regions seemed to be well suited to a pilot study: Mid Argyll and Galloway in Scotland, and Northumberland in England. Both areas of Scotland had been studied by Ronald Morris (1977 and 1979), although his work in Mid Argyll had been supplemented by more recent surveys of the prehistoric archaeology of both areas (RCAHMS 1988; Van Hoek 1995). The rock art of Northumberland had been investigated over many years by Stan Beckensall (1991 and 1992a), who often worked with us in the field.

THE CARVINGS ON THE ROCK

In my account of Atlantic rock art in Chapter 3 I argued that piecemeal comparisons are unhelpful: that it is not especially informative to compare individual motifs between different regions. What is needed is a more basic analysis of how those different design elements were drawn together in a single composition. I attempted to illustrate this point by comparing two well-known carvings, one in North-umberland and the other in Galicia. Although they had certain features in common, it is the analysis of the English site at Old Bewick that will be considered now.

Three particular points stood out even from a first superficial study. The different design elements were not equally represented, and circular motifs tended to be linked to one another in a specific sequence. That is to say, few motifs were joined to all the others. Instead circular designs might be linked to just one or two similar motifs and these links established axes or 'chains' running across the rockface. At the same time, it was quite clear that the more prominent motifs – those with the largest number of concentric circles – were more likely to be drawn into a wider composition than the isolated cup marks or cups with a single ring.

It is basic features like these that first attract attention when we look at British rock carvings, and such elements quite clearly account for any superficial impression that some compositions are more complex than others (Pls 8–12). But is it possible to place such comparisons on a more disciplined basis? The first point is to consider the representation of the main design elements. Were the simpler designs more common than the more elaborate motifs, and was there any order in their distribution?

Table 1   The distribution of circular motifs in six areas of Britain and Ireland

	1	*2*	*3*	*4*	*5*	*6*	*7*	*8 rings*
Northumberland	56	26	10	4	2	0.8	0.6	0.6%
Galloway	51	21	14	7	4	2	0.5	0.5%
Mid Argyll	43	24	14	12	4	2	0.5	0.5%
Donegal	50	27	17	3	3	–	–	– %
Dingle	67	23	9	1	–	–	–	– %
West Yorkshire	80	14	4	2	–	–	–	– %

Table 2   Regions of Britain and Ireland with similar distributions of circular motifs

	1	*2*	*3*	*4*	*5*	*6*	*7*	*8 rings*
West Yorkshire	80	94	98	100	–	–	–	– %
Dingle	75	91	98	99	100	–	–	– %
Donegal	50	77	94	97	100	–	–	– %
Galloway	51	72	86	93	97	99	99.5	100%
Northumberland	56	82	90	96	98	98.8	99.4	100%
Mid Argyll	43	67	81	93	97	99	99.5	100%

In every area where adequate drawings are available we find a similar pattern. The cup marks with single rings are the most frequent circular motifs and the designs with the greatest number of concentric rings are the least common of all. In Table 1 the evidence from different areas is summarised by the percentage of each type of motif. In every case there is an orderly relationship between the complexity of the different motifs and their representation in the art. All these figures come from well-defined regional groups of rock carvings. The order in which they appear reflects the range of motifs in each of these groups. The following sources are used: Northumberland: Beckensall 1991 and 1992a; Galloway: Van Hoek 1995; Mid Argyll: RCAHMS 1988; Donegal: Van Hoek 1987 and 1988; Dingle: Cuppage 1986; and West Yorkshire: Ilkley Archaeology Group 1986.

We can also consider the distribution of these distinctive motifs by organising the material according to cumulative percentages. In Table 2 the different areas are grouped according to the shape of the distributions.

How were these different motifs employed on the carved surface? A useful analogy is provided by the decoration of pots. Some years ago Margaret Friedrich (1970) introduced a useful method for comparing the design of different vessels. She sought to reconstruct the hierarchy of decisions that the potter would need to make at different stages in production. For example, a pot might be left undecorated, or its surface could be divided up into different zones; those zones might be embellished or they could be left entirely plain; and the decorated zones could be broken into smaller panels or could be treated in the same way throughout. Each decision involves a further level of complexity in the decoration of the vessel.

Table 3 The relationship between different design elements in Mid Argyll

Relationship	Correlation coefficient
Mean number of rings per site:	
percentage of design elements other than cup marks	.822
Mean ring spacing per site:	
mean ring diameter	.734
Mean ring diameter per site:	
percentage of rock surface carved	.804

It should be possible to identify a similar hierarchy of decisions in the creation of British rock art. The evidence from Mid Argyll was particularly well suited to this kind of study, as the transcriptions of the petroglyphs are of very high quality and are published at a common scale (RCAHMS 1988). When we visit those sites, certain features certainly stand out, and these provide one starting point for the analysis.

For example, the eye immediately distinguishes between the most basic motifs – the isolated cup marks – and similar cups surrounded by a series of concentric rings. The contrast is certainly one of size, but it is more than that: multiple circles are visually more arresting than single rings. Those motifs have less impact where they are run together, and they stand out especially clearly when they are spaced across the surface of the rock. The same applies where they are connected up by lines.

At a purely descriptive level these distinctions are obviously real ones. There is an inverse relationship between the number of isolated cup marks in any panel of rock art and the mean number of rings found on the same site: the more cup marks there are, the simpler the circular designs, and vice versa. It seems likely that this did not occur by accident, for regression analysis shows that there is an equally strong relationship between the size of those circular motifs and their spacing across the carved surface – it was clearly important that they could be told apart. The study used those sites in the area with seventy or more separate motifs, except for analysis of the space available for carvings which considered all those with suitable scale drawings (RCAHMS 1971 and 1988) (Table 3).

These simple patterns have important implications. It is often suggested that individual motifs may have grown by accretion as further rings were carved on different occasions. No doubt this could have happened, and we have already seen how at Old Bewick some of the radial lines did not extend to the centre of these designs, as if the decision to incorporate them into the composition was not taken until the first ring had been carved. But this process must have been governed by rules even if the compositions were built up over time. It is very rare for the outer rings to be superimposed on any other motifs, which is what would have happened if the drawings had developed haphazardly. Nor would that explain the remarkably regular relationship between the final size of the circular motifs and their spacing across the carved surface.

Table 4 The number of linked design elements in Mid Argyll and Northumberland in relation to the number of separate motifs

Number of separate motifs	0–4	5–9	Over 10
Percentage of linked design elements per site (Mid Argyll)	–	16	23
Percentage of linked design elements per site (Northumberland)	–	26	35

There is a further feature of many of these sites which was highlighted in my account of Old Bewick. It is not common for the drawings to cover the entire surface of the stone. In Mid Argyll there is a regular relationship between the extent of the carved area and the size of the rock itself, but in this case only 45 per cent of the available space was decorated. It is quite common for the edges of the carved surface to remain empty, as if to 'frame' the composition. That is not to say that the process of carving need have followed a pre-ordained pattern. The individual motifs would have weathered in the British climate, and the repetitive character of the rock art might be explained because particular motifs were renewed as others became obscured. A freshly carved design would have a quite different colour from the natural surface.

So far this study has been concerned with the opposite extremes in the ordering of the rock art: with cup marks, on the one hand, and with multiple circles on the other. That approach is too schematic, for it does not come close to the more subtle patterning that seemed to be apparent at Old Bewick. There the major contrast was between the larger and smaller circular motifs. To quote my original account,

> the simpler motifs – the isolated cups and those with only one ring – were rarely linked to other parts of the rock surface. It was only when the circular motifs became more complex that they were normally joined together, and even then there is an obvious gradation by which the most striking designs were connected to one another to the exclusion of simpler motifs, which might be linked in a separate network.

A broadly similar pattern could be recognised in all three study areas, although detailed differences in the local repertoire of motifs meant that the analysis took different forms. In Mid Argyll there is a wide variety of individual motifs, including some which overlap with those in megalithic art. In this case it is clear that it is on the surfaces with the widest variety of separate designs that motifs are more likely to be joined together. The same applies to the rock art of Northumberland (Beckensall 1991 and 1992a), although in this case such connections seem to be more common (Table 4).

Much of this variety is created by the different number of rings surrounding individual cup marks, but if they were created over a long period this may be a little misleading. Perhaps only the newest motifs had any special significance.

Table 5 The distribution of passage-grave motifs in Mid Argyll in relation to the maximum number of rings on the same carved surface

Maximum number of rings	1	2	3	4	5	6	7	8
Passage-grave motifs	–	–	–	X	X	X	–	X

Table 6 The number of linked motifs on sites in Galloway in relation to the maximum number of rings on the same carved surface

Maximum number of rings	Surfaces with linked motifs	Surfaces without linked motifs
1–3	24	28
4–6	30	8

Table 7 The distribution of passage-grave motifs in Galloway in relation to the maximum number of rings on the same carved surface

Maximum number of rings	1	2	3	4	5	6	7	8
Number of surfaces with passage-grave motifs	2	1	2	6	5	2	–	1

Another way of studying these sites was to record the maximum number of rings found on any one surface. This exercise was carried out in Argyll where we can compare the number of rings on any one carving with the distribution of motifs shared with passage-grave art. Again it seems as if the less common sites with four or more rings were the very ones with these specialised designs (Table 5).

Galloway is another part of Scotland in which these different features were closely related to one another, but in this case as the number of concentric rings increased, it also became more likely that the motifs would be linked together (Morris 1977; Van Hoek 1995). The sample of carvings with seven or more rings continues this trend but is too small to be tested for statistical significance (Table 6).

There is only one chance in a hundred that this pattern could have arisen fortuitously. Again it is the rock carvings with most concentric rings that include more of the specialised motifs shared with passage-grave art (the remainder are found on their own) (Table 7).

The carved rocks in Galloway are very fractured and so there are limitations to this kind of exercise. But in Northumberland larger areas of carved rock are exposed, and here a more elaborate analysis is justified, although passage-grave motifs are so unusual that they do not feature in this study. Again it is clear that the greater the maximum number of rings surrounding any one cup mark, the greater the likelihood that the different design elements would be joined together.

Table 8 The distinction between 'simple' and 'complex' rock carvings in Northumberland

	Maximum number of rings	*Number of sites without linked motifs*	*Number of sites with linked motifs*
'Simple' carvings	1	18	3
	2	5	3
'Complex' carvings	3	7	15
	4	1	9
	5	1	8

Table 9 The orientations of the rock carvings in five selected regions

	Easterly orientations (0–180 degrees)	*Westerly orientations (181–359 degrees)*
Ireland	57%	43%
Galloway	76%	24%
Northumberland	66%	34%
Ilkley Moor	65%	35%
Mid Argyll	92%	8%

	Southerly orientations (90–270 degrees)	*Northerly orientations (271–89 degrees)*
Ilkley Moor	33%	67%
Northumberland	54%	46%
Ireland	56%	44%
Galloway	77%	23%
Mid Argyll	92%	8%

There was only a 5 per cent chance that this relationship could have happened by accident. Sites with no more than one or two rings rarely show any signs of a more elaborate composition; those with three or more concentric rings are much more likely to form part of a broader design. Although there is clearly a continuous range of variation, this provides a more formal way of distinguishing between what I shall call 'simple' and 'complex' carvings (Table 8).

Except in Galloway where many of the rocks slope towards the north, the lines extending from the central cup marks normally run downhill, although not necessarily at right angles to the contours; Susan Johnston's work shows that the alignments of these motifs are not determined entirely by the gradient of the rock (1989, chapter 3). In other cases the carved surface is horizontal, but even here these lines are usually orientated to the east rather than the west and, with one exception (Ilkley Moor), towards the south rather than the north (Ilkley Archaeology Group

1986) – the exact orientations vary widely within and between separate regional groups. The only common feature is that many of the carvings would have faced into the sun at different times of day. We can illustrate the general characteristics of these sites using the evidence of published drawings. The percentages are calculated by individual motifs for all illustrations which contain a north point; for Galloway they are those provided by Van Hoek (1995, table IV), and those for Ireland, which do not include the south-west of the country, are taken from Johnston's dissertation and are based on her original fieldwork (1989, chapter 3) (Table 9).

To sum up, although there are many local variations, the simpler carvings normally involve a smaller range of motifs, including cup marks and cups surrounded by a limited number of rings. These motifs are rarely linked together and there is little overlap with the repertoire of megalithic art. The more complex carvings, however, include a wider range of motifs and may share a few of these with Irish passage graves. The circular motifs are larger and involve more concentric rings, and in the complex carvings it is quite common for different design elements to be joined to one another by lines. These are more likely to extend to the south or east than in other directions.

Chapter 1 suggested that even though we cannot recover the original meanings of these compositions, it is still possible to treat each carved surface as a source of information of greater or lesser complexity. The more elaborate panels of rock art may have provided more complex or varied information, or they may simply have been the ones where any potential ambiguity had been eliminated. In either case they might have been directed to a larger or more diverse audience. At the same time, the wide distribution of cup-and-ring carvings must have ensured that the basic elements in these compositions could be understood across a large area; it was the organisation of these components that provided the crucial information. The simpler rock art, on the other hand, might have played a rather different role, and here the audience might have been smaller or more homogeneous. Perhaps there was less information to impart because more was already known. Alternatively, these carvings were directed towards a smaller and more specific audience because only they would have been able to understand them. What seem simple images to us may have had a restricted, even sacred character.

If any of these distinctions are valid, they should be reflected in the positioning of rock art in the landscape. We can study this at two different levels. On a local level we might expect the simpler rock art to be distributed differently from the more complex carvings. That is because a local audience would have been able to locate it easily, whilst strangers would only be able to read the messages if they knew how to find them in the first place. On that basis complex rock art should be placed in more conspicuous positions than the rest.

The same distinction applies at a much larger scale. Rock art could only have functioned as a medium of communication if it had been distributed on a predictable basis. That applies to both the simple and the complex carvings. If these had been located haphazardly, such a system would not have worked. Thus a second level of analysis is vitally important if we are to decide whether the rules influencing the form of the compositions also extended to their positioning in the terrain. At this point we can no longer work with scale drawings of the art; these questions can only be addressed through fieldwork.

THE ROCK IN THE TERRAIN

Again it was important to select suitable areas for study, but in this case there was an additional complication. There are some regions of Britain in which the rock has been destroyed by modern development and there are others in which it has been concealed by the growth of vegetation since its original discovery. Any attempt to assess its place in the topography must take account of these features. In some cases it would have been possible to compensate for these biases by using a Geographical Information System which can recreate the locational characteristics of different carvings on a three-dimensional model of the terrain, but unfortunately this would not be able to tell us where the viewer would have stood in order to see the designs or even whether a particular rock was visible from the surrounding area (Gaffney, Stancic and Watson 1995). These qualifications were important, but they were not fatal to the research design. Their main effect was to ensure that a large sample of sites was studied on the ground. Unless this happened it would not have been possible to test any interpretations for statistical significance. In the account that follows, most of the examples are drawn from work in Northumberland and Galloway, although this is supplemented by more limited information from published work in Mid Argyll and Strath Tay.

The simplest analysis builds on an observation made by Margaret Stewart in her account of the prehistoric rock art of Strath Tay (1958, 76). Cup marks, she said, were normally found on boulders, whilst more complex carvings were located on outcrops. Her own records are not sufficiently detailed to put this idea to the test, but fortunately similar information has been recorded in the published account of the prehistoric rock art of Mid Argyll (RCAHMS 1988). Here it is only possible to distinguish between cup marks and cup-and-ring carvings, but in this case they do seem to be found on different kinds of rock. In the dense distribution of rock art in Mid Argyll there is very much the pattern that Stewart described, although the situation is complicated by large sheets of exposed rock which form an additional category. There is only a 1 per cent likelihood that these contrasts could have arisen by chance. We have already seen that the carvings in this area did not fill the available surface, so this cannot be explained by saying that the larger carvings were on the larger rocks (Table 10).

In Northumberland the same information had to be acquired by fieldwork. In the largest concentration of carvings in north Northumberland, those between Ford and Old Bewick (Beckensall 1991), we considered the setting of no fewer than sixty-four separate sites, but in this case we were able to build on the results of our earlier work in distinguishing between simple and complex rock carvings. Once again there was a striking contrast between the settings of these two groups. The simple carvings were mainly on boulders or sheets of rock, whilst the more complex carvings were normally created on outcrops. In this case there was only a 10 per cent likelihood that this pattern had arisen by chance (Table 11).

Table 10 The rock surfaces selected for carving in Mid Argyll

	Boulder	*Outcrop*	*Other*
Cup marks	28	19	9
Cup-and-ring carvings	9	23	24

Table 11 The rock surfaces selected for carving in Northumberland

	Boulder or rock sheet	*Outcrop*
Simple carvings	14	13
Complex carvings	11	26

Table 12 The visibility of the carved rocks in Galloway

Visibility of carved rocks from 50 m	*Simple carvings*	*Complex carvings*
Visible	30	25
Invisible	15	1

Table 13 The visibility of the carved rocks in Northumberland

50 m radius	*Simple*	*Complex*
Narrow (visible from up to 90° of the surrounding area)	12	6
Medium (visible from 91° to 180° of the surrounding area)	15	7
Wide (visible from 181° to 360° of the surrounding area)	44	26
100 m radius		
Narrow visibility	17	6
Medium visibility	27	7
Wide visibility	26	26

This work also highlighted a problem. Generally speaking, British petroglyphs tend to favour flat or shallowly sloping surfaces. This means that very often the carvings themselves cannot be identified from a distance, although the rock on which they are found may be plainly visible. At the same time, some of the boulders were quite conspicuous, whilst a number of outcrops were difficult to recognise from far away. For that reason we also considered the local setting of each of the carvings in Galloway and north Northumberland.

Galloway was another area in which it was possible to distinguish between 'simple' and 'complex' carvings (Morris 1977; Van Hoek 1995). In this case we asked whether the rock itself could be recognised from a distance of 50 m. Among the rocks that we could classify, almost all those with complex carvings could be identified, but this applied to only half the rocks with simpler designs. Because the fieldwork was carried out before Van Hoek's work became available, the sample is smaller and we cannot test the results for statistical significance (Table 12).

There were more sites to study in north Northumberland (Beckensall 1991), where we adopted a more complicated procedure. In this case we investigated the visibility of the carved rocks from 50 m and 100 m away and also asked whether they could be seen from all or only part of the surrounding area. The two groups showed exactly the same characteristics at a distance of 50 m, but at 100 m from the same sites it was clear that the rocks with the complex carvings could be seen from much more of the surrounding area than the other group. There was only a 5 per cent chance that this could have happened by accident (Table 13).

To sum up, there does seem to be some evidence that the two groups of carvings defined in the earlier part of this chapter were associated with different features of the terrain. Generally speaking, the simpler carvings tended to be found on boulders, whilst the more complex panels of rock art were associated with outcrops. In both groups there was normally enough space for a more extensive composition had anyone wanted to create one. The rocks with the more complex carvings would also have been easier to find than the others and could sometimes be identified across more of the surrounding area. Again this is consistent with the idea that the more complex designs might have played a different role from the other petroglyphs and may even have been addressed to a different audience.

THE WIDER SETTING OF THE ROCK CARVINGS

So far this discussion has been concerned with the local setting of individual carved rocks. But if the different designs provided a source of information, they should also have been located on a predictable basis within the landscape as a whole. The remainder of this chapter will address that question.

Because British rock carvings are so rarely considered in relation to the topography, there have been few suggestions concerning the location of these features. There are just two ideas to consider. Ronald Morris (1979) suggested that these sites are normally found at viewpoints, an observation which would certainly be consistent with my first impressions of the rock art on Ilkley Moor. Less clearly formulated ideas have linked the positions of the rock carvings with paths or trails running across the landscape (Walker 1977; Van Hoek 1995).

Neither suggestion is at all easy to assess. The recognition of ancient roads or trackways is notoriously subjective and all too often it turns out to be based on a circular argument. Nor is the identification of viewpoints as simple as it might appear, since this approach betrays the influence of contemporary conceptions of the landscape. All too often the view is considered in terms of modern aesthetic qualities, when what is really needed is a more precise definition. Were the carved rocks normally located at vantage points and, if so, how much of the surrounding country did they command? Susan Johnston considered this question in her study of Irish prehistoric rock art (1991), but otherwise the basic information has never been collected. In any case the character of such locations would have been strongly influenced by the composition of the local vegetation. This is a point to which I shall return in the next chapter.

That is not to say that such suggestions are entirely unhelpful, but they cannot be taken at face value. They must be subjected to detailed investigation on the ground. Is it possible to show that the areas selected for carving had different kinds of view from those in the surrounding region? Even if ancient paths have left no trace today, do the carvings appear in particular kinds of topographical situation? Do they share a common axis along the apparent line of such paths? And are the carvings supposedly located on the course of such routes in fact visible from one another? In each case these questions form part of a wider agenda, for if rock art had provided a source of information, however specialised or difficult to understand, it must have been possible to find it in the first place.

The idea that rock carvings were located at viewpoints is one of the major themes of Ronald Morris's study of the prehistoric sites of Galloway (1979), but for it to provide a useful starting point for the present review we must be able to show that the views which can be seen from these particular locations are significantly different from those available from other points in the vicinity. Unless this can be established, there is no chance of taking the argument any further. Fortunately, this is a kind of question that has been asked before in archaeology, and a well-established methodology already exists for investigating this issue. In a study concerned with the alignment of megalithic tombs in Orkney, David Fraser (1988) had compared the extent and direction of view from those sites with similar measurements taken from a series of other locations selected by random sampling. A similar procedure had also been used in studying the stone rows on Mull (Ruggles, Martlew and Hinge 1991). The method works by measuring the extent of visibility at a series of different distances from the point of observation: usually 250 m, 500 m and 5 km. The width of the view in each category is recorded by compass bearings from the monument and compared with similar measurements from the locations chosen by random sampling.

In this case we were not concerned with astronomical alignments, but the principle was much the same, and the field methods employed in Galloway were similar to those developed by Fraser. We selected two different control samples, one of them reflecting the entire topography of the area being studied and the other representing the immediate surroundings of each carved rock. The first group of locations was chosen by random sampling and consisted of 15-kilometre squares based on the National Grid (Fig. 5.3). Taken together these represented 3 per cent of the area studied in most detail. Each of these units was subdivided into nine sampling sites, arranged at 250 m intervals along two transects crossing in the centre of the grid square. The views from all these locations were recorded unless visibility was impeded by features such as houses or trees. The random sample extended across the entire distribution of the rock art and was not weighted towards those areas in which it was most abundant.

The second control sample was based on the positions of the carved rocks themselves. Again it consisted of two transects, but in this case the sampling points were located at 100 m intervals. They crossed at the carved rock, with one transect running along the contours and the other offset from it at right angles.

Plate 1 The view from one of the carved outcrops on Ilkley Moor

Plate 2 Cup-and-ring carvings at Castleton near Falkirk

Plate 3   An animal carving at Campo Lameiro, Galicia

Plate 4 Circular motifs at Chan de Lagoa near Campo Lameiro, Galicia

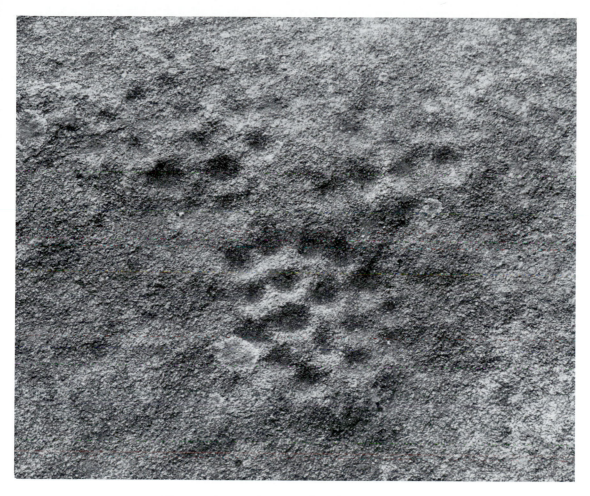

Plate 5 Cup marks near Chan de Lagoa, Galicia

Plate 6 Carvings of animals and circular motifs at Chan de Lagoa, Galicia

Plate 7 Cup-and-ring carvings in the chamber of the south-west cairn at Balnuaran of Clava near Inverness (photograph: Aaron Watson)

Plate 8   A cup-marked rock on Ilkley Moor

Plate 9 Cup marks, a basin and circular motifs on Gayles Moor near Barnard Castle

Plate 10 Curvilinear carvings at Cairnbaan, Mid Argyll

Plate 11 The rock carving at Achnabreck, Mid Argyll, after heavy rain

Plate 12 A carved rock in its setting on Gled Law near Wooler

Plate 13   General view over Barningham Moor near Barnard Castle

Plate 14 View over a valley 'territory' near Cairnholy, Galloway

Plate 15 The main carved rock at High Banks near Kirkcudbright

Plate 16 Detail of the main carved rock at High Banks

Plate 17 A carved surface overlooking the east end of Loch Tay
(photograph: Aaron Watson)

Plate 18 Part of the area investigated by field walking near to Aberfeldy in Strath Tay
(photograph: Aaron Watson)

Plate 19 The carved rock at Roughting Linn near Wooler, emphasising the circular carvings around its edge

Plate 20 Angular and curvilinear motifs in the kerb at Newgrange

Plate 21 The carved surface at Achnabreck, Mid Argyll. Note the horned spiral in the foreground

Plate 22   Rock carvings on the summit of Dod Law near Wooler

Plate 23 The rock shelter at Cuddy's Cave near Wooler. Rock carvings were recorded here in the nineteenth century

Plate 24 The decorated stone known as Pancake Rock on the edge of Ilkley Moor

Plate 25   View along the sea channel leading from the rock carvings at Mevagh,
County Donegal

Plate 26 The mountains of County Donegal seen from the rock carvings on Doagh Island

Plate 27   Part of the frieze of rock carvings at Buttony near Wooler

Plate 28   A possible cist quarry at Fowberry near Wooler

Plate 29 A reconstructed cairn on Weetwood Moor near Wooler. Note that the decoration on the kerbstone originally faced inwards

Plate 30   The upland landscape of Galicia near Fentáns

Plate 31 General view of the braña above San Francisco near Muros, Galicia

Plate 32 Laxe das Rodas near Muros, Galicia

Plate 33 General view over part of the study area at Muros

Plate 34 Drawing of a stag at Rianxo, Galicia

Plate 35 The braña at Fentáns, Galicia

Plate 36 Drawing of a horse and rider at Paredes, Galicia

Plate 37 Drawing of a stag with prominent antlers at Fentáns, Galicia

Plate 38 Drawing of deer ascending the mountainside above Porto do Son, Galicia

Plate 39 Dagger carvings at O Ramallal, Galicia

Plate 40 Carvings of weapons and circular motifs at Caneda, Galicia

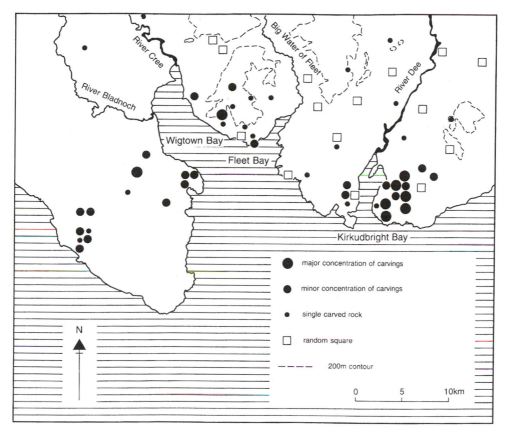

Figure 5.3 The distribution of rock art in Galloway and the positions of the randomly chosen control samples recorded during fieldwork

In most cases this meant that the samples were taken both above and below the level of the petroglyphs.

Each method showed that there were striking contrasts between the views available from the two samples (Bradley, Harding and Mathews 1993). In the two nearest distance bands, those at 500 m and 500 m to 5 km, the rock carvings commanded a much wider area than the random sample. There was only a 1 per cent chance that these differences were fortuitous. Beyond 5 km, however, the contrast was no longer apparent. That is very revealing, but part of the explanation may be that most of the carved rocks are found near to the coastline, whilst the random sample extended into a dissected terrain further from the sea. For that reason the second control sample may be more informative, for this consisted of locations in the immediate vicinity of the petroglyphs themselves. In fact it produced almost the same results as the first exercise. In each distance band the views from the carved rocks were between 1.2 and 1.3 times the width of those in the control samples. At 500 m there is only a 1 per cent chance that this contrast could have

Table 14 The extent of the views from the carved rocks in Galloway

	Mean width of view
500 m distance band:	
Carved rocks	113±69°
100 m control sample	101±65°
200 m control sample	103±62°
500 m – 5 km:	
Carved rocks	176±76°
100 m control sample	147±77°
200 m control sample	138±77°
5 km and above:	
Carved rocks	61±44°
100 m control sample	51±47°
200 m control sample	54±65°

come about by accident. At 5 km the chances of this happening increase to 5 per cent and beyond that threshold the differences disappear. In each study it seems as if the carvings were commanding a view over the nearer ground and that their location was not so sensitive to the extent of the far horizon. The much smaller number of standing stones in the study area exhibit the same basic pattern (Table 14).

This was not the only method for assessing Morris's hypothesis. It was well suited to fieldwork in the small fields of Galloway, but in north Northumberland some of the rock carvings are found in large areas of open moorland. Here a different method was appropriate. Again this approach had already proved its worth in another area. In 1983 Barnatt and Pierpoint had published a study of the siting of prehistoric monuments at Machrie Moor on Arran. Like Fraser, they were particularly interested in the possibility that these sites had incorporated astronomical alignments, but once again they compared the evidence from those sites with observations from a control sample of points in the surrounding area. They mapped a large tract of moorland on a grid and isolated the areas from which such observations would have been possible. These were closely related to the positions of the monuments.

Our study took the same approach to the distribution of exposed rocks suitable for carving (Bradley, Harding, Mathews and Rippon 1993). Two large areas of open ground were examined on a 100 m grid and wherever a suitable rock was discovered close to the grid intersections the view was recorded by the methods that we had already used in Galloway; locations in which the natural outcrops had been damaged by quarrying were not considered in this exercise. Exactly the same observations were made from each of the petroglyphs and results from the two samples were compared with one another. In the first study area, on Dod Law near to Wooler, it soon became apparent that the carved rocks avoided the places with little or no view (Beckensall 1991, 14–32; Bradley, Harding, Mathews and Rippon 1993, 133–4). Instead they clustered in the parts which commanded large areas of

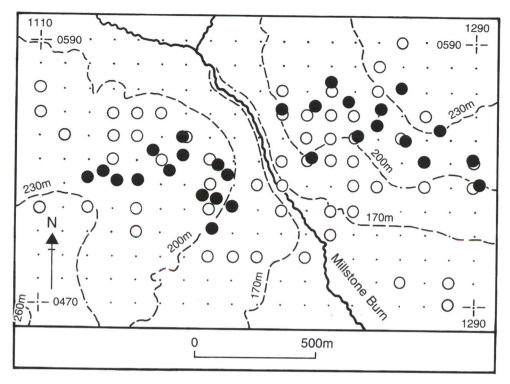

Figure 5.4 The distribution of rock art at Millstone Burn, Northumberland (closed symbols), and the positions of the control samples recorded during fieldwork (open symbols)

the surrounding lowlands (Pl. 12). In this case the sample was too small to be tested for statistical significance.

A second study took place at Millstone Burn, 30 km to the south, and incorporated a denser distribution of rock carvings, and here we followed exactly the same procedure in the field (Beckensall 1992a, 41–51; Bradley, Harding, Mathews and Rippon 1993, 133–42). The only difference was that because the samples were so much larger they could be analysed in more detail (Fig. 5.4). The width of view was much the same at 500 m but it steadily diverged at greater distances. Between 500 m and 5 km the views from the carvings became wider than those from the control sample and this difference was accentuated in the farthest distance band. Between 500 m and 5 km there was a 10 per cent chance that these differences could have arisen fortuitously, but at a greater distance the figure fell to 1 per cent (Table 15).

The contrast between the two case studies has interesting implications. In Galloway the carvings commanded wider views then the control sample but only within a range of 5 km. At Millstone Burn, on the other hand, the opposite occurred, and the greatest difference between the two samples was towards the farther limits of the view. This can probably be explained in terms of the local

Table 15 The extent of the views in the study area at Millstone Burn

Width of view	500 m		500 m – 5 km		Over 5 km	
	Carvings	Control sample	Carvings	Control sample	Carvings	Control sample
(degrees)						
0–30	–	10	–	6	–	13
31–60	1	6	–	1	–	8
61–90	8	6	1	1	6	11
91–120	5	7	1	6	10	11
121–150	3	6	1	6	8	3
151–180	1	12	5	13	2	–
181–210	2	2	8	6	1	–
211–240	2	2	5	7	–	–
241–270	1	2	2	8	–	–
271–300	–	–	2	–	–	–
301–330	–	–	–	–	–	–
331–360	–	–	1	–	–	–

Table 16 The direction of view in the study area at Millstone Burn

	Views in one direction	Views in two directions
Carvings	11	17
Control sample	36	13

topography. As we shall see, most of the carvings in Galloway are situated in or around shallow valleys near to the coast. These are the areas where the modern farms are found and it seems quite likely that many of these carvings were located on or close to land that was settled at the time. The main exceptions were a few more complex petroglyphs which were located on higher ground.

By contrast, the rock art at Millstone Burn is located at the junction of an extensive area of high ground and the Northumberland coastal plain. The principal route between these two areas follows the valley where most of the carvings are located, and the same route was also selected for a Roman road. The valley provides one of the obvious paths between the lowlands and the Northumberland hills, and today there is no similar route into the high ground for 7 km to the north-east and 6 km to the south-west. The area closest to the carvings is extremely exposed and the modern soils are poorly drained. It may be that the petroglyphs were located in relation to a major routeway rather than to an area of prehistoric settlement.

It is certainly true that the views from the petroglyphs at Millstone Burn focus on the opening of the valley, rather than the surrounding area, and, as we have seen, they differ from the control sample in terms of long-distance visibility. They

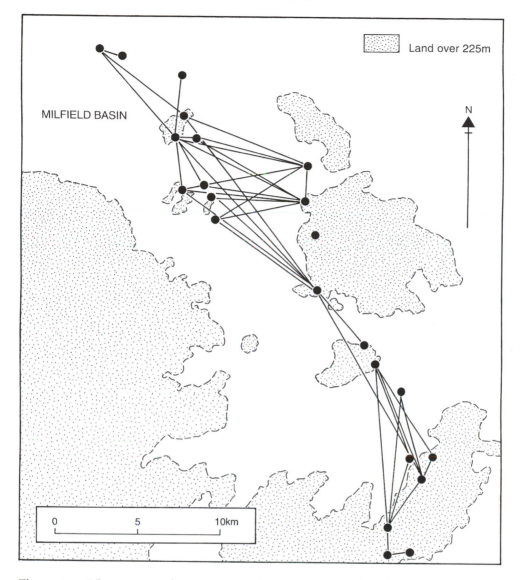

Figure 5.5 The pattern of intervisibility between groups of rock carvings in north Northumberland (based on fieldwork by Ruth Saunders)

have one other characteristic which might also be consistent with their siting beside a prehistoric routeway, for, unlike those in the control sample, the most distant views from the rock carvings extend in two directions along the axis of the valley. There is only a 1 per cent probability that this could have happened by chance (Table 16).

This observation may shed light on another striking characteristic of the rock art of north Northumberland, for it is apparent that the main locations with rock carvings can be seen from one another, even over distances of 6 km or more. Not all the sites are intervisible by any means. Rather each major complex may be linked to only one or two other locations with rock carvings, forming a network of connections along the major valley system, which extends from south-east to north-west. The rocks themselves cannot be picked out over such long distances, but it is certainly possible to identify the natural locations where they are found. Some of these patterns can be identified by analysing contour maps, but the scheme illustrated in Fig. 5.5 amplifies my original outline and is the work of Ruth Saunders who has checked these connections on the ground. She has also considered a series of alternative locations in the area selected by random sampling. Her control sample does not reveal the same evidence for long-distance visibility. Although the individual motifs do not follow these axes running across the landscape (the radial lines usually extend to the east rather than the north), it is hard to reject such striking relationships as fortuitous. As we shall see in Chapter 7, some of the major rock carvings of Mid Argyll exhibit a similar pattern, although in this case the modern landscape is so heavily wooded that parts of the interpretation are based on computer analysis. Again this evidence lends some support to an association between rock carvings and routes across the landscape.

CONCLUSIONS

Like Chapter 1, this chapter has been an attempt to move from an intuitive reaction to prehistoric rock art towards a more analytical approach to its interpretation. Any attempt to make use of this material in studies of the prehistoric landscape can only be attempted if the art was originally structured in a coherent way. I have argued that in fact this was the case. The details may seem tiresome and the statistics may suggest a misplaced quest for precision, yet behind these minutiae it is possible to discern some patterns. The designs on individual rocks were not laid out capriciously; they adhered to a few general rules, and although those rules might have been developed in different ways in different areas they do seem to have followed similar principles in many parts of the British Isles. Moreover the existence of those rules is powerfully reinforced in the local setting of the rock art. There are striking differences in the character of those rocks with simple and complex designs, and these correspond to more basic distinctions affecting their local setting in the landscape. I have suggested that some of these distinctions also reflect the audiences to whom these symbols were originally addressed.

Such an argument is only sustainable if it also operates at the broader regional level, and in the closing section of this chapter I reviewed two of the commonest interpretations of the siting of British rock art. Again the field methodology may seem over-elaborate, but this is an area in which intuitive interpretations have remained unquestioned for too long. Fieldwork in Northumberland and Galloway, however demanding it may have been in terms of time and energy, has suggested that once again the carvings were not located at random. They were sited at local vantage points and quite possibly some of them were distributed along paths or trails. The two interpretations are not exclusive of one another. Important thresh-

olds along the routes leading across country might have been marked by petroglyphs, and these would have had the greatest impact if they were located in places
where the vista changed. In Northumberland it even seems possible that some of
the main sites were intervisible over long distances and may have marked important stages in the passage through the country.

Such regularities are there for those who try to find them, but their recognition
is not an end in itself. They remind us that we should consider British rock art
as a system and not merely as a series of disconnected 'sites'. But if we are to
understand the roles that those rock carvings might once have played in prehistoric life, we must shed some of the abstraction that has coloured the argument
so far. We need to pay careful attention to the ways in which it seems to have
been used in individual landscapes. Otherwise we can easily lose sight of its distinctive character.

In their different ways the next four chapters move from the general to the
particular as they attempt to follow that programme.

CHAPTER SIX

THE SHEPHERD
ON THE ROCK
Rock art in the British landscape

——— ·◆· ———

There is more than one way of studying rock art, and each affects the scale at which it is viewed. For those who analysed the motifs as if they were portable artefacts, small-scale distribution maps were quite sufficient, as these would be enough to chart the connections between different areas. Those who undertook regional surveys were more concerned with the placing of these sites in relation to other aspects of the local pattern of settlement, including the character of the soils and the siting of prehistoric monuments. In the last chapter much of the discussion was conducted at still more detailed level and concerned itself with the immediate setting of individual rock carvings. If we are to understand the importance of rock art in the prehistoric landscape, our approach will have to be flexible, and the scale of analysis must be sensitive to the kinds of questions being asked. This chapter involves a progressive sharpening of focus from patterns which can be recognised on a regional scale to small-scale studies of the character of individual landscapes.

I have already described the overall distribution of rock art in Britain and Ireland, and now I must consider it again, but from a different perspective. We may know roughly where it is found, but we also need to know why it is there and not some-where else. Despite a century of research, rock art has not been discovered in some of the areas where it might have been expected. It is virtually absent from upland areas well outside the settled landscape, and the same applies to several regions with the same evidence of prehistoric occupation as those containing petroglyphs. They include a similar range of stone and earthwork monuments and, most impor-tant, they contain exposed rocks of the same lithology as those selected for carving. In some cases the empty areas are even located alongside the regions which provide most evidence of rock art. For example, the distribution of Northumbrian rock art runs out towards the northern limit of the Fell Sandstone even though the area has been intensively surveyed (Beckensall 1991 and 1992a). Similarly, the rock art of West Yorkshire is rather tightly confined and does not seem to extend far into the Pennines (Ilkley Archaeology Group 1986). In fact it is quite unusual for the distribution of carvings to cover the full extent of the parent rock. This is a problem that needs to be explained.

Susan Johnston (1991) has explored some of these questions in a paper on the distribution of prehistoric rock art in Ireland. She presents some useful statistics

Table 17 The distribution of Irish rock art in relationship to potential land use

County	Percentage of land suitable for tillage or pasture	Percentage of Irish rock art sites
Meath	88%	2%
Louth	83%	11%
Carlow	78%	6%
Cork	63%	8%
Donegal	21%	17%
Kerry	20%	37%

on the relationship between the carvings in different regions of the country and the amount of land suitable for tillage or pasture. At first sight the relationship is a close one – the carvings are usually found on or near the better soils – but in fact two of the three areas with the highest density of petroglyphs contain the lowest proportion of productive land. In the third area, County Louth, the high density of rock art may reflect the proximity of a major group of ceremonial monuments (this question will be discussed in Chapter 7). With that exception, there appears to be an inverse relationship between the frequency of rock carvings and the extent of fertile land; there seem to have been more petroglyphs in those areas in which resources were restricted. In Table 17 counties with fewer than five rock art sites have been omitted.

Johnston also notes that Irish rock carvings 'are typically located on hill slopes [which are not] topographically advantageous for cultivation. However, these hill slopes frequently overlook fertile valleys or are adjacent to flatter land which would have been easier to cultivate' (1991, 93). That is to say, they are not always situated on the most productive land but at or beyond its limits.

Taken together, these two observations may help to explain the wider distribution of rock art. At one level it is certainly true that petroglyphs seem to be found in areas with fertile soils, and in most cases they overlook them from rather higher ground. Those carvings seem to be most abundant where the best soils are of limited extent and are often found towards the outer edges of especially favoured areas where the possibilities of sustained land use might have been curtailed. Here there would have been fewer opportunities for expansion.

Some examples may help to make this point. In north Northumberland the rock carvings are generally found around the edges of fertile valleys and basins, restricted by the Fell Sandstone to the east and the Cheviots to the west. To the north, where there is more open land of similar quality rock art is no longer found (Beckensall 1991). Similarly, the rock carvings of south-west Scotland are confined to a restricted zone between the Solway Firth and the Galloway hills (Van Hoek 1995), whilst those in Strath Tay are found as the areas of productive soil become more limited towards the head of the valley (Stewart 1958). That is also the pattern around the entrance to the Stainmore Pass in north-east England (Laurie 1985) and again in West Yorkshire where the areas of fertile soil in Wharfedale and Airedale decrease as the valleys reach into the high ground of the Pennines (Ilkley Archaeology Group 1986). Other examples of this pattern are not difficult to identify. The rock art of Mid Argyll was also created around the limits of a restricted area of unusually productive land (RCAHMS 1988). In the Peak District most of the rock carvings are found to the west of the River Derwent, close to the junction between the moorland and the fertile soils on the limestone plateau. They are much less common in the large tract of sandstone east of the river, and here the majority are associated not with natural outcrops but with Bronze Age burials (Barnatt and Reeder 1982).

It would have been in just such areas that resources might have come under pressure, and, following the argument put forward in Chapter 1, this is exactly where we might have expected territorial arrangements to have been defined more explicitly. Where productive land was freely available, there would have been less reason to mark particular places in this way. Similarly, on the high ground further from the distribution of those lowland soils, conflicts of interest would have been less likely to arise.

Such distinctions are probably echoed in the character of the rock art itself. In some cases the designs are more varied where resources may have been most restricted. Thus in Kintyre cup marks are found in isolation in the main areas with lowland soils, and cup-and-ring carvings are located where those resources are more restricted (RCAHMS 1971; Morris 1977). On the border of North Yorkshire and County Durham Tim Laurie has identified a rather different pattern (pers. comm.). Many of the carvings overlook productive areas of lower ground or may be distributed along trails leading through the uplands. In this case the more complex carvings are found near to extensive tracts of lowland soils, while simpler carvings are generally associated with valleys containing areas of less productive land.

We must now attempt to integrate these observations with other kinds of evidence, and at this point the scale of the enquiry changes.

How do these interpretations compare with the results of pollen analysis? At first sight these should provide a clear indication of the usefulness of this approach, but in fact the two sources of information are difficult to use together. At a broad level the results of environmental archaeology certainly are consistent with the approach suggested here. There is evidence for the opening of upland landscapes during the period in which the rock art was created, and this is found in some of the areas in which petroglyphs are most abundant. There are Late Neolithic and Early Bronze Age clearance horizons in south-west Scotland (Moar 1969; Birks 1975), north Northumberland (Davis and Turner 1979; Tipping 1992) and the Pennines (Spratt ed 1993, chapter 2; Coggins 1986; Hicks 1972; Faull and Moorhouse eds 1981, chapter 3), but there is little to suggest the extensive cultivation of cereals. The human impact on the landscape is sufficiently limited to indicate a pattern of short-lived, possibly intermittent activity. It was only in subsequent phases, normally during the Middle and Late Bronze Ages, that the same areas sustained a more substantial impact on the natural environment (D. Wilson 1983; Fenton-Thomas 1992).

It is difficult to relate the two approaches on a local level, for it is in the nature of pollen analysis that its results reflect the vegetation over a substantial catchment. Similarly it is hard to work out the character of the prehistoric environment across a smaller area. This is only possible through the expensive and time-consuming practice of three-dimensional pollen analysis and, to a smaller extent, through studies of buried soils. Such information does not exist in the immediate vicinity of the rock carvings. For that reason we must depend on detailed analysis of the sites themselves. If we can show that they commanded different kinds of views from control samples located within the same landscape, and if those contrasts prove to be statistically significant, it may not be necessary to compare these results directly with those of pollen analysis. Such evidence is inconsistent with a completely closed environment, although some of the 'linear' views commanded by these carvings might have been directed along trackways through a largely wooded landscape. Fieldwork of the kind described in the previous chapter provides results that can be considered as 'environmental evidence' in their own right (I am grateful to Kevin Edwards for discussion on this point). It may never be possible to 'test' the results of such studies against those of pollen analysis, but this is simply because the two methods provide information at quite different scales. We can show that the rock carvings were first created during a period which saw increased activity in the uplands, but it is unreasonable to expect a closer correlation.

A more appropriate procedure is comparing the distribution of rock carvings with the distribution of artefacts. Again the available material has many limitations. With the sole exception of two sites described in Chapter 4, no British rock carvings have been found in direct association with artefacts and very few occur in areas with a tradition of surface collection. That is because so many of the major sites are located in areas of pasture or moorland, where there are few exposures of the subsoil. Unfortunately, there are not many carved rocks in ploughed fields, perhaps because they have been removed as obstacles to cultivation.

There remain a few vital clues as to the broader pattern of activity. In several areas there is a distribution of simple rock carvings, often cup marks, along the edges of the lower ground. It is in such areas that we may also find a concentration of polished stone axes. This is of particular interest because these artefacts only rarely extend outside the same areas. The best example of this pattern is in the valleys of north-east Yorkshire (Spratt ed 1993, chapter 4), and in the same region there are important finds of Neolithic and Early Bronze Age pottery. In this case there is a second series of findspots on the higher land. The artefacts here consist mainly of flint arrowheads, discovered in small numbers on the sites of Mesolithic settlements. The association is a regular one and is unlikely to be coincidental. This does not mean that the two groups of artefact need have been used simultaneously. Rather, these sites were ideally located for use during hunting expeditions and it seems likely that this activity continued long after the Mesolithic period. The pollen evidence indicates that these sites were usually located in open country which had originally been cleared and maintained by burning; they are on the some of highest ground on the North York Moors and are situated well beyond the distribution of the rock art. Although some of the carvings may have been moved from their original positions, they would seem to mark the upper limit of the areas that were capable of sustaining year-round settlement. They may have divided those areas from remoter regions that were used less regularly, for hunting and perhaps for pasturing domesticated livestock (Fig. 6.1).

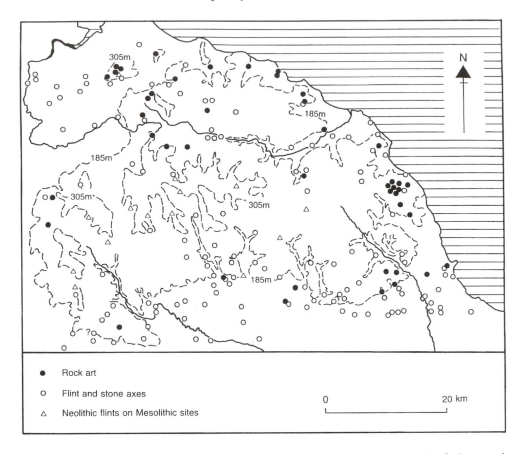

Figure 6.1 Distribution of rock carvings in north-east Yorkshire showing the findspots of polished axes and discoveries of Neolithic arrowheads on Mesolithic sites (information from Spratt ed 1993)

Around Barningham Moor in County Durham there are indications of a still more complicated relationship between rock carvings and finds of lithic artefacts (Pl. 13). Fieldwork by Tim Laurie suggests that this may be an area like Strath Tay in which the character of the rock art changes in relation to the local topography (Laurie 1985 and pers. comm.). We can distinguish between two broad zones, on the lower and upper moor respectively. Both include large areas of open land which are partly buried by peat. Where the surface cover is broken there are numerous finds of worked stone. With certain exceptions, the cup-marked rocks are mainly found on the more sheltered ground of the lower moor, which is also where stone-built settlements were established by the Roman period. More complex rock carvings tend to be found at a greater elevation, although another important focus was a pass providing access through the moorland to a tributary valley of Swaledale. There is an isolated stone circle beside this path, but there are no indications of permanent occupation sites of any period.

These gradations in the distribution of the rock art are matched by changes in the composition of the lithic industries. The densest concentration of finds is in the Tees valley, well below the surviving distribution of the petroglyphs, but in the same area as the cup-marked rocks on the lower moor Tim Laurie has found scatters of artefacts containing scrapers and barbed and tanged arrowheads. These do not extend further uphill and similar material is lacking from the area in which the more complex carvings are located. On the high ground, however, there were a number of major Mesolithic sites and once again they are associated with finds of arrowheads. These include leaf-shaped arrowheads, dated to the Earlier Neolithic period, as well as later forms. In this case it seems as if the distinctions observed on the North York Moors have gained an added dimension, with more balanced flint industries among the cup-marked rocks and isolated collections of arrowheads from the sites of Mesolithic hunting camps on the higher ground. In between the two was a distribution of complex rock carvings. These sites commanded views over the lower ground and also focused on an important route leading into the uplands, but they do not seem to have been associated with any artefacts.

In this case the distribution of later stone-built settlements provides a useful clue to the likely pattern of occupation and may help us to distinguish between the upper edges of the areas suited to sustained land use and remoter regions that were used only occasionally. If so, then it seems as if the more complex carvings were ranged along the upper edge of the prehistoric landscape. This evidence is particularly useful as very similar settlement sites are found among the prehistoric rock art on Ilkley Moor, where individual field walls actually overlie some of the carvings. Again the location of these settlement sites provides an insight into the ways in which this area might have been used.

The northern slopes of Ilkley Moor are divided into a series of steps, and parts of the lower terraces can be surprisingly sheltered. As at Barningham Moor, this is where a series of stone-built settlements were established. It is also where we find one of the densest distributions of rock carvings in West Yorkshire (Ilkley Archaeology Group 1986). Inside one of these enclosures, provisionally dated to the Late Bronze Age, were the deposits of Neolithic artefacts described in Chapter 4. Although these may well have been associated with the rock carvings on the same site, the distribution of lithic artefacts extends across a very much wider area (Cowling 1946; Faull and Moorhouse eds 1981, chapters 6–8). By no means all of this material has been accurately provenanced, but the distribution of Mesolithic artefacts across the moorland provides a kind of control sample: it seems unlikely that Neolithic material was overlooked in those areas in which microliths have been collected.

In this case there is very little evidence for significant contrasts in the height distributions of simple and complex rock art. The main distinction seems to have been one of micro-topography. The main concentrations of the simpler designs are found in the more sheltered areas in which later settlements were established. The more complex carvings are generally less clustered and tend to occur in more exposed locations, including a number of rocks which command extensive views over the lower ground. For the most part the two groups of carvings have different distributions.

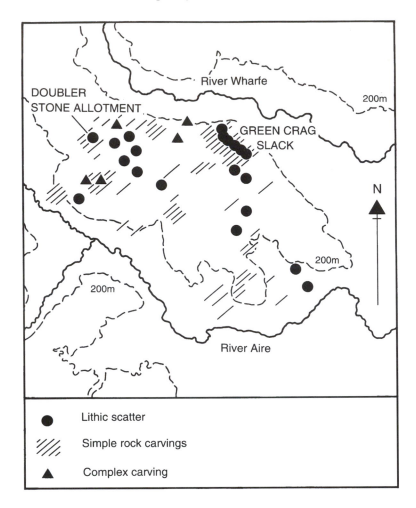

Figure 6.2 The distribution of flint scatters and carved rocks on Ilkley Moor (information from Cowling 1946, Faull and Moorhouse eds 1981 and Ilkley Archaeology Group 1986)

The same broad distinction is reflected in the distribution of surface finds from this area (Fig. 6.2). One major concentration occurs around the later settlement sites on Ewe Crag Slack, and here most of the carvings are of cup marks or of cups with only one ring. The other main group of findspots is near Doubler Stone Allotment where the art has an almost equally straightforward character, with a number of cup-marked rocks and two nearby sites each featuring a cup with two concentric rings. By contrast, some of the rock carvings with three or more rings avoid the distribution of Neolithic or Early Bronze Age flint scatters, although they do occur in areas with Mesolithic finds. Current fieldwork has shown that the distribution of rock carvings extends to the facing slopes of Wharfedale, and at present the same distinctions seem to be in evidence there (B. Godfrey pers. comm.).

This last example is a little different from the others, for it places a greater emphasis on the details of the local topography, where my earlier studies concentrated on the height distributions of different kinds of rock carving. This approach helps to document some of the key elements in the system of petroglyphs but it may do so by suppressing too much local variety. The same criticism applies to the more abstract studies of the views that can be seen from these carvings. By measuring the extent of those views, and by comparing the results with those from a sample of uncarved rocks, we can demonstrate that these sites were not located at random, but it is hard for such a rigid procedure to capture the full complexity of the landscapes in which they were made.

In the remainder of this chapter I shall describe two studies which have attempted to bring a greater flexibility to our understanding of rock carvings in the landscape. The first took place in Galloway and suggested a number of approaches to the interpretation of these sites. The second was in another region which has often featured in this account. In Strath Tay we attempted to employ the insights gained during work in Galloway in a more rounded study of the relationship between rock carvings and the prehistoric pattern of settlement. Where the Galloway survey was based entirely on the setting of the rock art, in Strath Tay the work included a programme of field walking and sample excavation.

The rock art of Galloway is the subject of a book by the late Ronald Morris, but he has little to say about its place in the prehistoric landscape:

> [The motifs] were nearly always carved on fairly smooth and nearly horizontal surfaces. Sedimentary rock was usually used, probably because it is easier to carve. The carved outcrops are nearly always situated where they can be seen from quite long distances all around, or – perhaps one should say – where the sun can reach them for most of the day. Copper has been worked and streams have been panned for gold in the past, only in the parts of Galloway where these carvings are found, and a little further eastwards. ... Nearly all [the carvings] are within a very few kilometres of the sea. ... Only three sites ... are over 330 metres [above sea level].
>
> (1979, 14)

For the most part he limits himself to comments on specific sites, many of which, he says, were located in places with views.

There is an inevitable tension between his cautious observations on the distribution of metal sources and his comments on the topography of individual sites. Elsewhere he tells us that:

> Many archaeologists have suggested that these carvings were made by the early prospectors searching for copper ores and for gold. In Galloway ... this is supported by the fact that every carving except two is within 12 km of a place where copper ore has been worked at some time, or is within $1\frac{1}{2}$ km of streams where gold has been panned. ... 12 km seems a reasonable search area.
>
> (ibid, 16–17)

It is difficult to see how such a system would have worked if these markers could have been created at any point within 12 km (two hours' walk) of a copper source. This is particularly improbable since elsewhere in the same book Morris explains that 'in searching for such small, inconspicuous objects as these carvings, to have a map reference to within ten metres as opposed to the hundred metres of accuracy for the more usual six-figure reference, is a very real help' (ibid, 29).

Again the problem is partly one of scale. Should we discuss the rock art of Galloway as a single entity or should we capitalise on the detailed topographical studies which Morris himself pioneered? In fact the study area is not at all homogeneous. The distribution of rock art follows the south-west coastline of Scotland for 40 km and extends inland for 15 km (Fig. 5.3). This area comprises four separate peninsulas, divided from one another by the estuaries of major rivers leading into the Galloway hills. Each of the estuaries is a major source of fish and the remains of salmon fences can still be seen towards the mouth of the River Cree. For the most part the coastal area is unusually fertile and today it is mainly used as pasture. The modern farms are generally located in or alongside shallow, well-drained valleys leading down to the sea. Although cliffs do occur on this coastline, for the most part the shore is easily accessible. Towards the west of the study area there is a well-preserved raised beach.

Towards the head of the valleys leading inland from the coast the character of the topography changes. Where the gradient is more abrupt, as it is around the megalithic tombs at Cairnholy, there are large expanses of open moorland, whilst in other areas we encounter an extensive plateau broken by a series of poorly drained basins and divided up by dykes and outcrops of rock. It is an area with few natural boundaries. In this dissected terrain there are a number of small lakes and pools.

For the most part the higher ground runs parallel to the coast and does not contain many rock carvings, but there are a few quite steep hills in the intermediate zone between here and the coast. These command especially wide views over the surrounding area and also out to sea. Those isolated hills provide the sites for some of the round cairns in this area, although earlier, megalithic tombs are more commonly associated with the lower ground on the coast.

These basic divisions in the landscape are reflected by the distribution of the rock art. The simpler motifs tend to be found near the sea. They command wide views along and across the valleys running down to the shore, but they rarely focus on more distant features of the landscape. They are often found in concentrations around the limits of individual valleys and, in particular, those with direct access to the water's edge (Fig. 6.3; Pl. 14). As we have seen, these are just the areas where the modern farms are found, and they include some of the most intensively worked land in the study area. It is tempting to suggest that the same regions formed the major focus of settlement when the petroglyphs were created, but in fact this is difficult to show. Pollen analysis from the Moss of Cree certainly suggests that part of the coastline was open heathland from the period of the Elm Decline (Moar 1969), but finds of lithic artefacts are rare. There is a notable concentration of polished axes from the estuary of the River Dee near Kirkcudbright, where many of the rock carvings are found (Williams 1970), whilst there are reports

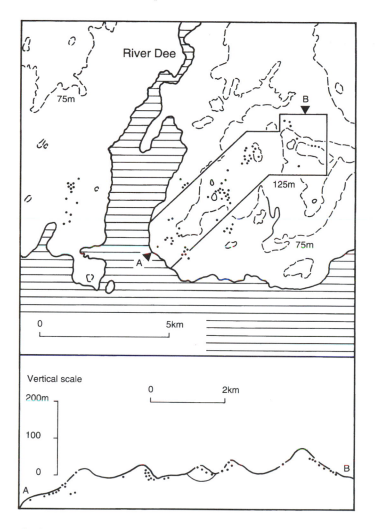

Figure 6.3 The location of prehistoric rock carvings near Kirkcudbright, together with a topographical section showing their positioning in the terrain (modified from Van Hoek 1995)

of flint scatters near to the coast, some of them from the raised beaches. In this case the most diagnostic material is Mesolithic and it is uncertain whether it could have been mixed with artefacts of later date (Coles 1964).

The main exceptions to this general pattern are found on higher ground overlooking the coast where there is a tendency for more complex carvings to appear. These can command more extensive views than the others. Sometimes they overlook coastal landing places, like that at Knock, or they seem to command the mouth of a major estuary, as happens at Knockshinnie. This small group of sites includes a number of spirals with their counterparts in megalithic art.

Such carvings are not common and, with some exceptions, the more complex compositions tend to be found away from the sea. For the most part these carvings are beyond the fertile valleys and in areas which are less productive today. Although the sites of some of the more complex carvings command extensive views across the lower ground, this does not happen in every case. For instance, the spiral-decorated stone on Cambret Moor may command a pass leading through the hills, whilst the best-known site in Galloway, that at High Banks, has no view at all (Pls 15 and 16). Sometimes this happens because the petroglyphs were originally near sources of water. Complex rock carvings, like those at Torrs and Blairbuie, share this distinctive feature. They are within sight of lakes or smaller pools, and the most elaborate of the carvings at High Banks are on the edge of a drained waterhole. It is unfortunate that no artefacts are recorded from this area. Nor is there any information on the prehistoric environment.

Although we know so little about the distribution of artefacts in Galloway, there does seem to be a consistent relationship between the character of the rock art and the nature of the local topography. The simplest carvings are found in the areas that were best suited to year-round settlement. These were the most fertile parts of the study area and they were also the best drained. It seems as if these petroglyphs marked the outer limits of a series of valley territories leading down to the sea.

That contrasts sharply with the situation elsewhere in the study area, where more complex rock carvings occur. These are distributed on a less consistent basis, although some of them are located on higher ground. A number are sited on conspicuous hills with extensive views, but others are located on cliffs overlooking the sea. One site commands a pass leading through the hills whilst others overlook the mouths of major estuaries. There are also complex carvings on the more dissected ground above the limits of the coastal valleys and here they may be associated with natural basins or waterholes. Only rarely is there an obvious link between the placing of these images and a well-defined area of land. In that respect they contrast with the simpler carvings near the coast.

In some respects this evidence resembles the other studies described in this chapter. The simpler carvings appear to be mainly in settlement areas, whilst some of the complex rock art is located on higher ground. But because this discussion has considered the micro-topography, other kinds of pattern have come to light. There are carvings that appear to overlook the sea, and there is another site which commands a small harbour on the coast. One of the most complex carvings is situated in a pass, whilst others are found near natural pools. It would be quite impossible to suggest one explanation that accounts for all these examples. Some of these areas might have been used for hunting and others for seasonal grazing, whilst certain sites may not have played a role in food production at all. They could well have been in places with a specialised role in ritual and ceremonial.

The complex carvings have only two features in common. Many were placed at the edges of the settlement pattern where they might have attracted a more varied audience than the other petroglyphs. If some of them had been on a boundary, then they would have been seen by strangers. If they were placed in summer pasture or even on hunting land they might have been encountered by people who

...me argument would apply to any
...ding places on the coast. Those
...been among the most visited of
...vious focal point for people and

...ough. The interpretation involves
...tions of the settlement sites, nor
...ex art on the higher ground was
...scape. We cannot tell whether the
...etween the area with the simpler
...found in other places. To answer
...ce of information, which was why
... Tay.

...ay is fairly simple. This is one of
... Scotland, but almost all the rock
...20 km long, between its confluence
...Loch Tay (Stewart 1958). There are
...n the valley, where rock carvings
...ive soil along the shores of the lake
...ailed. Most of the carved rocks are
...occur alongside areas of fertile land
...och.

...nost entirely through its monuments,
...ange from the Neolithic round mound
...he timber and stone settings at Croft
...ring cairn at Sketewan (Mercer 1988)
...ingall and Carse (Burl 1988, 149, 169
...a non-megalithic long barrow and a
...ll these sites are found on the terraces
...onuments of similar date on the higher
...e so much fieldwork in the area, only
...red: a group of Late Neolithic pits over-
...mpson 1990). There are very few records

...t of Strath Tay has a very simple distri-
...d mainly on the river terraces and the
...lusively on the higher ground. Figures
...sion show that there is only a 1 per cent
...ro distributions could be fortuitous (Table

...s is very similar to that of the stone and
...w the river terraces, although other exam-
...floodplain. As so often, the more complex
...gher ground. They generally appear in one
...ated part way up the hillside or they are
...es of shallow basins located on the upper

[Overlaid leaflet text:]

...its equipment for the period of hire.

23 Your young children and dogs are your responsibility.
We cannot be held responsible if they are killed, injured,
or cause an accident on the Houstry Road or on the A9,
which is easily accessible from the caravan park.

24 Musical instruments, TVs, radios, CD players etc and all
motor vehicles must not be used to cause a nuisance to
others, especially between the hours of 10.30pm and 8am.

25 A copy of these rules is available in the Caravan. All visitors
are expected to read and respect the rules during their stay.
Payment of a deposit constitutes an acceptance of these
responsibilities for all members of your party.

26 Left belongings can be returned by arrangement and

before the arrival date. If the balance has not been
received by the due date, your booking may be cancelled
and the caravan offered for hire without notification. For
bookings made within the 28 days prior to the holiday start
date, you will be required to pay the full hire charge at the
time of booking.

11. All prices may be varied to include any extra charges we may
incur if you pay in a foreign currency, or if we have to
represent a cheque.

12. If you cancel, the deposit will not be refunded. If
cancellation is made before the balance is due, we will
relieve you of all responsibility to pay the balance and will
refund to you the balance should this have been paid. If
cancellation is made after the balance due date you forfeit

Table 18   The height distribution of rock art in Strath Tay

	200 m and below	*Over 200 m*
Cup marks	39	39
Cups and rings	5	21

edge of the valley. These are places in which sheep farms have been established, and they lie well above the modern limits of cultivation (Pl. 17). Two of these groups of rock carvings, at Remony and at Urlar, are located some distance above the heads of gorges with a series of dramatic waterfalls, and, as if to reflect their unusual setting, these are among the only places on the high ground which also include stone circles (Stewart 1958; Coles and Simpson 1965).

Much of the valley is very fertile and is used for cereal growing. In fact it is the one extensive area of arable land where prehistoric rock art is found in northern Britain. As such it provided a rare opportunity to test some of the ideas suggested by fieldwork in Galloway. There were three important questions to ask: Were the simpler rock carvings associated with any evidence of settlement? Did the pattern of activity change on the upper slopes of the valley? And were the more complex carvings associated with a distinctive range of activities, or were they located on the edges of the prehistoric landscape? Two transects, close to Aberfeldy, were examined by field walking on a 20 m grid, supplemented by a programme of test pitting where the ploughsoil had not been weathered (Bradley 1995). One transect extended along the river terraces where the cup-marked rocks are found, whilst the other climbed the valley side and cut across the distribution of the more complex art (Pl. 18). We wished to record three particular features. Was the distribution of worked stone clustered or diffuse? How did its density change as the sample transect extended up the slope? And was the choice of raw material (in this area it was normally quartz) consistent with a sustained period of use or had it been worked on the spot and then discarded?

The results of this exercise were quite unambiguous (ibid). The only clusters of worked stone were on the river terraces, in the same topographical setting as the stone and earthwork monuments. These locations were very close to those of the cup-marked stones, although the latter were sometimes found a short distance upslope. The raw material used in these clusters of worked stone was among the best anywhere in the study area and some of it had probably been introduced for the purpose (Fig. 6.4). These concentrations are not at all easy to date, but their positions are very different from those of crop-mark settlements probably of Iron Age origin.

There were no other clusters of artefacts in the study area, but worked quartz was widely scattered. Apart from one concentration where the study area crossed a source of raw material, the density of finds decreased steadily with height above the valley floor and reached a minimum where the sample transect crossed the distribution of cup-and-ring carvings. At the same time, the raw material selected for use was of progressively poorer quality, even when more suitable pieces were

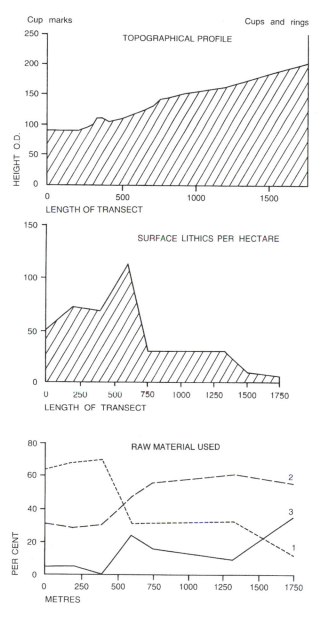

Figure 6.4 The positioning of prehistoric rock art in relation to the topography of Strath Tay. The drawing also summarises the distribution and character of the worked quartz found by field walking in the same area. The quantity of lithic artefacts decreases along a transect leading up the valley side, whilst the proportion of high-quality (grade 1) quartz also falls. The representation of poorer raw material (grade 2) increases, and towards the distribution of cup-and-ring carvings pieces of even less suitable quartz (grade 3) were worked in growing numbers. The peak of artefacts 500 m along the transect is where the study area crossed a source of raw material

available on the spot (Fig. 6.4). It seems as if the intensity of prehistoric activity diminished and that its character changed. On the river terraces raw material was selected for a prolonged period of use, but on the higher ground this was no longer the case. The evidence suggests that this area was used over a shorter period and probably in a different way.

Taken together, the results of this exercise add substance to some of the suggestions made elsewhere in this chapter. The simpler rock carvings, in this case the cup-marked stones, were most probably in settlement areas, and these were the only part of the study area in which we can talk of a distribution of 'sites'. By contrast, the more complex carvings were found where the density of worked stone reached its lowest point. There is evidence for very ephemeral activity in this area, and it seems likely that these carvings were actually located on the outer limits of the prehistoric landscape. The very low density of finds suggests that in this case the area around the petroglyphs had been very little used.

Of course that cannot be the whole story, and work in Strath Tay and in Galloway revealed enough anomalies to suggest a whole range of additional issues that would have to be investigated. A piece of pure crystal quartz was found at the foot of one of the complex carvings in Strath Tay and had probably been placed there deliberately. I found a second fragment beside the Lundin stone circle (Stewart 1966), whilst excavation at Croft Moraig has shown that the entire site had been covered with quartz (Piggott and Simpson 1971). It may be no accident that this is the largest monument on the lower ground and the only one to be associated with cup-and-ring carvings. In Galloway too the distribution of rock art overlaps with that of stone circles, and above the estuary of the Dee there were between one and three of these monuments. Again the local rock art has a most individual character. Groups of complex carvings occur not far from these sites and among the motifs that are found there is a series of unusual designs that have features in common with megalithic art (Van Hoek 1995).

These anomalies are troubling but slight, yet they raise important issues that have yet to be addressed. How far were the simple patterns described here modified in areas with more elaborate monuments? In one sense these studies may provide a deceptively simple impression of the organisation of British rock art, for the monuments found both in Galloway and Strath Tay are widely scattered and were built on a modest scale. Would the same pattern be found in an area with a major ceremonial centre? That is a more difficult question to answer. It forms the subject matter of Chapter 7.

CHAPTER SEVEN

READING ROUGHTING LINN
Rock art and ritual
monuments

—— ·◆· ——

INTRODUCTION

Roughting Linn (Pl. 19) is the largest carved rock in northern England and one of the very few which is displayed to the public. The site is located just outside the Milfield basin in Northumberland, a region which contains a particularly dense concentration of henge monuments (Harding 1981). The carvings were first recognised by Canon Greenwell in the mid-nineteenth century when part of the outcrop had already been destroyed by quarrying (Tate 1865). Some of the designs were exposed at the time but others were revealed by removing the turf (Shee Twohig 1988; Beckensall 1991, 6–12). Even now it is uncertain whether all the motifs have been found.

The outcrop is large and conspicuous, although at present it is difficult to recognise from a distance because of trees. It is very roughly oval in plan, 20 m long and 12 m wide, and stands well above the surrounding area. As much as half of its surface has been destroyed, and other parts are still obscured by vegetation. It is undoubtedly an impressive site to visit, particularly in the evening when the low sun highlights the positions of the carvings, but that is not why it plays such a central role in this chapter. The evidence from Roughting Linn raises a number of issues that are fundamental to any discussion of the relationship between rock art and major monuments.

That is partly because the site itself looks so like a monument. Not only does it occupy a particularly striking outcrop; the carvings are laid out in a rather unusual fashion. For the most part the simpler motifs are on the upper surface of the rock, where they might be expected to occur. These are difficult to recognise from below. The most prominent designs, however, are on the steep flanks of the outcrop and form a kind of frieze around its edges. Originally it would have looked like a cairn with a decorated kerb (Fig. 7.1 and frontispiece).

The resemblance is all the more striking when we consider the character of those carvings. The motifs on top of the rock are mostly small and simple, and they can be paralleled on other sites in north Northumberland. But those found on its edges have a very different character. They are considerably larger than the others and they had been carved more deeply to create a three-dimensional effect. The

Figure 7.1 Reconstruction of the rock carving at Roughting Linn, Northumberland (drawing: Aaron Watson)

technique by which these designs were created is not unlike that used in O'Sullivan's 'Plastic Style' of megalithic art (1986). The resemblance is even stronger when we realise that two of the designs at Roughting Linn echo those in Ireland. The arrangement of horseshoe motifs towards the south-east limit of the rock resembles a motif found at Loughcrew, whilst the same applies to a nearby cup-and-ring carving with a series of parallel rays emphasising part of its perimeter (Shee Twohig 1981, 205–20). The motifs on this area of the rock are rather eroded and some of the designs, especially the rayed circle, might be older than the others. They appear to have been respected by the large circles on the sloping face of the rock, which are generally well preserved. There may be many reasons why this happened, but one possibility is that the circular designs were conceived as a border around the limits of the outcrop but respected the positions of the carvings that were already there. In any event the location of large circular motifs on the steeper edges of the rock echoes the layout of the designs on the kerbs at Newgrange and Knowth. That is not to deny that most of the motifs at Roughting Linn resemble others found in the surrounding area. It is their organisation on the carved surface that is their most striking characteristic.

In order to investigate this situation, we must reconsider the connections between megalithic art and the carvings found in the open air.

FROM PASSAGE GRAVES TO HENGE MONUMENTS

As we saw earlier, there are few ways of dating British rock art directly and purely stylistic comparisons between open-air carvings and megalithic art do little to ease the confusion. The unusual layout of the designs at Roughting Linn illustrates this point. One way of taking the argument further is to consider the use of passage-grave motifs on portable artefacts, for, unlike rock carvings, some of these appear in well-dated contexts.

Pottery is very important here. Most authorities are agreed that there is a certain overlap between the motifs found in Irish megalithic art and those used to decorate Grooved Ware ceramics (Wainwright and Longworth 1971, 71; Shee Twohig 1981, 125–8), but the history of these connections has not been considered in detail. Whereas some of the links between open-air rock art and megalithic art are found in O'Sullivan's Depictive Style, it is the later art of his Plastic Style that has more features in common with ceramic decoration (O'Sullivan 1986). But not all the motifs found in Irish megaliths have their counterparts on Neolithic pottery. Curvilinear motifs, though often discussed, are actually very rare, and the most convincing links are with lozenges and triangles. Those connections are especially revealing as they do not extend to all the substyles of Grooved Ware. In particular, they are found in the Clacton style, but not in the Woodlands style which seems to have developed later (Garwood in press). These arguments have important implications: the closest links are between the later carvings in the megalithic tombs and the earlier development of the decorated pottery.

This conclusion is important in another way, for it surely implies that, even if their meanings had changed, certain of these motifs retained a special importance when passage graves were no longer being built. In the Boyne valley Grooved Ware appears to be secondary to the creation of the passage tombs (Eogan and Roche 1994), whilst few of these monuments in Orkney contain pottery in this style, despite the fact that Grooved Ware may have originated locally. The sequence at Quanterness illustrates the complexity of the situation, for the sherds from this particular tomb may have been introduced some time after its original construction (Renfrew 1979, 65–79). They seemed to form a compact group, and many of them refitted between different levels in the burial deposit. Five of these were analysed by thermoluminescence, and, with one exception, the dates corresponded to calibrated radiocarbon dates of about 2400 BC from the uppermost layers in the central chamber (two further sherds gave dates which are much too late for this style of pottery).

At other sites artefacts bearing individual motifs similar to those in passage-grave art are also associated with radiocarbon dates, and, as I argued in Chapter 4, these suggest that such designs had a long history after the currency of those monuments. Their chronology extends from about 3000 BC for at least 500 years. A chalk plaque decorated with lozenges in the same manner as those on megalithic tombs also has radiocarbon dates in the first half of the third millennium BC (Cleal, Cooper and Williams 1994). These are considerably later than the period around 3100 BC when the last decorated passage graves were built in Orkney and the Boyne valley (Sheridan 1987).

What was the context for these developments? This question has been considered by a number of writers. Eogan and Roche (1994) believe that the Grooved Ware found in the Boyne valley was associated with activities outside the megalithic monuments, including the construction of timber settings of various sizes, some of them closely related to the features found with British henges. Circular embanked enclosures may also have been created in the vicinity (Stout 1991). Sharples (1985) suggests a rather similar sequence in Orkney where passage graves were apparently replaced by open platforms or even by earthwork enclosures and circles of upright stones. The decorated passage tomb at Pierowall seems to have been levelled in order to construct one of these platforms, and Derek Simpson argues that an episode of deliberate destruction also took place at Newgrange during this phase (1988, 35). At all events, there seems to have been a significant change from closed monuments that could accommodate a very small number of people to larger open arenas that might have been used by a different kind of audience.

The art of Newgrange and Knowth can be divided between 'public' and 'private' imagery. The 'public' imagery was displayed at the entrance and on the kerbstones and could be viewed without entering the tomb. These designs were mainly curvilinear. The 'private' imagery, on the other hand, was found inside the monument, in the passage or in various parts of the chamber. Although there are some curvilinear motifs here, most of these designs are angular (Eogan 1986, chapters 7 and 8).

That very broad distinction is echoed in a number of ways during the succeeding phase. For the most part the angular designs are taken up in pottery decoration. They are very rare in later forms of monuments and hardly ever appear in open-air rock carvings. As we have seen, curvilinear motifs are not at all common on

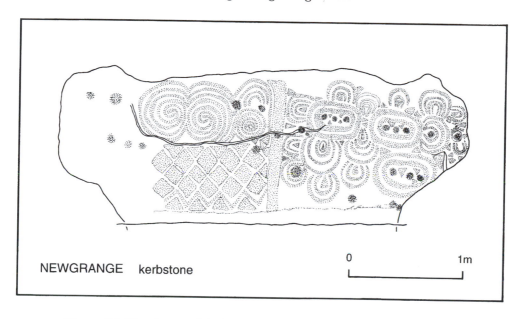

Figure 7.2 The decorated kerbstone opposite the entrance to Newgrange

pottery, but in a somewhat different form they account for a large element in open-air rock art. It is not clear whether this happened because circular motifs were already being carved in the wider landscape, or whether the designs associated with the 'public' art of the tombs provided the prototype for later developments.

There is one famous carving in the kerb at Newgrange which encapsulates many of these relationships (Fig. 7.2; Pl. 20). This is located directly in line with the passage and the chamber, and at one time it seemed likely that it marked the entrance to another tomb, but this has been disproved by excavation (O'Kelly 1982, chapter 7). The stone is divided into two panels by a vertical line. On its left are three spirals and a series of concentric arcs. A horizontal crack divides these from a remarkably regular frieze of lozenges, separated from a row of triangles by a zigzag line. These are exactly the elements that were transferred from tomb art to pottery, although the motifs appear in different proportions on these vessels. To the right of the vertical line there is a very different pattern. This includes three oval enclosures, each containing three cup marks and some small triangular motifs. There are also fifteen curvilinear enclosures on this part of the stone, all of them apparently broken by an entrance. Two were left entirely empty, nine contain small triangular designs, whilst three more include central cup marks or a larger basin. The comparison is not exact, but this emphasis on open enclosures, some of them containing cup marks, is quite unlike the designs on Neolithic pottery. On the other hand, it shows the same basic structure as open-air rock art.

The motifs found on the left-hand side of the stone are those primarily adopted in Orkney where they appear in a variety of media. There are a small number of

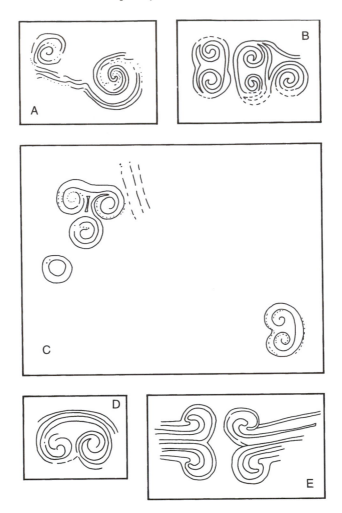

Figure 7.3 The representation of horned spirals in various contexts during the Late Neolithic. A: Temple Wood (stone circle); B: Pierowall (passage grave); C: Achnabrack (open-air rock carving); D: Knowth (macehead); E: Barrow Hills (Grooved Ware). Information from Scott (1989), Davidson and Henshall (1989), RCAHMS (1988), Eogan (1986), Alastair Barclay and Ros Cleal

decorated passage tombs (Davidson and Henshall 1989, 82–3), but these motifs played an even greater role in other contexts, quite possibly after all these monuments had been built (Fig. 7.3). The angular designs assume a growing significance on pottery in Scotland and England but they were also used to emphasise important thresholds in the layout of Skara Brae. Here they focus on the position of House 7 which is rather different from the other structures and may have played a specialised role in the life of the settlement (Richards 1991). The door of this building could only be sealed from the exterior, and inside the structure were a number of specialised deposits, including a bull's skull and a human burial. This was the oldest house on the site and when the settlement was abandoned it was the only one that was left with its contents intact.

By contrast, the spirals which are such a feature of the Boyne valley are distributed quite widely in northern Britain, where they are mainly found towards the west coast (Van Hoek 1993; Fig. 7.3). They can occur on natural surfaces, as we saw in Galloway, but they are also associated with a series of stone-built enclosures including Temple Wood in Mid Argyll (Scott 1989), and Long Meg, Little Meg, Glassonby and Castlerigg, all in Cumbria (Beckensall 1992b, 10–19; P. Frodsham pers. comm.). There are other links between the latter region and Neolithic Ireland. For example, the megalithic tomb at Millin Bay in Ulster (Collins and Waterman 1955) shares a range of idiosyncratic motifs with a now destroyed site at Kirkoswald in Cumbria (Ferguson 1895), and the embanked henge monument of Mayburgh, only 10 km from Kirkoswald, is remarkably similar to those found in Ireland (Burl 1976, 59; Topping 1992). Further links have been suggested between the early stone circles on both sides of the Irish Sea. There are difficulties in dating any of these sites, but that may be less important than another observation, for it was in the areas that seem to have had such strong links with Ireland that open-air rock art is particularly abundant. If ceramic decoration drew on one group of designs on that kerbstone at Newgrange, rock art in the northern landscape utilised the other one.

In a few cases the connection is even more direct, for among the small group of decorated monuments in Scotland and northern England there are several examples in which the carved motifs were confined to the entrance, to the kerbstones or even to an outlying monolith; as at Knowth, curvilinear designs are very much a feature of the exterior. In the Eden valley in Cumbria such decoration included elaborately carved spirals (Beckensall 1992b), but there are other sites where much simpler motifs were employed instead. These include monuments such as Croft Moraig where the outer kerb carried a cup-and-ring carving (Piggott and Simpson 1971), the stone circle at Monzie where an outlying monolith was embellished with a complex circular design (Mitchell and Young 1939) and the recumbent stone circles of north-east Scotland whose entrances contain a notable concentration of cup marks (Burl 1976, 167–90). Almost all the motifs were on the limits of these sites, facing into the surrounding area. Only the spirals are unusual; otherwise the important element in every case is that a precisely similar range of motifs was to be found on natural surfaces in the vicinity.

I have emphasised the way in which the siting of some of these carvings involves a reference back to the 'public' art of the Boyne valley. The pottery of the same period refers to images taken from the 'private' art of the tomb where similar motifs were used to define important thresholds within the structure of these sites (Thomas 1991, 97–8). Both groups of images are important because of their connections with distant places, yet each was used in the new kinds of monument that developed after the currency of passage graves in Britain and Ireland. The essential feature of these sites is that they could have been used in large assemblies. In England and Scotland such monuments were generally provided with an external

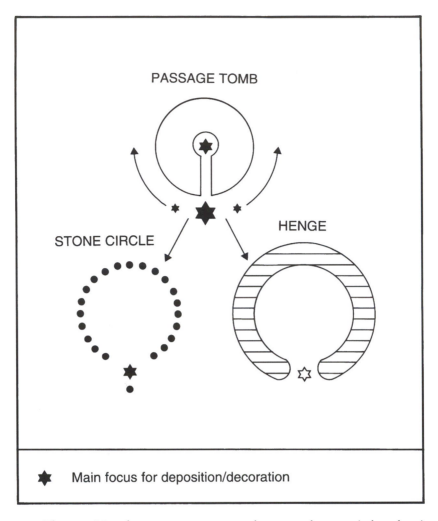

Figure 7.4 The transition from passage graves to henges and stone circles, showing the focal areas for decoration and the deposition of artefacts

bank which could accommodate a large number of spectators whilst excluding them from the central area. In Ireland the same might be achieved by the use of embanked enclosures, whilst the platforms added to some of the Orkney tombs would have had a rather similar effect. The entrance remained a major focal point and occasionally it was associated with deposits of pottery including the rare circular or spiral motifs whose ultimate inspiration was in megalithic art (Fig. 7.4; Cleal 1991, 141–4). Such monument complexes have two other features which may be relevant to the interpretation of open-air rock art. They extend across large areas of the landscape and individual monuments may even be aligned on natural features of the terrain (Harding 1981). At the same time, these sites often appear in groups which may be located considerable distances apart, suggesting that they must have

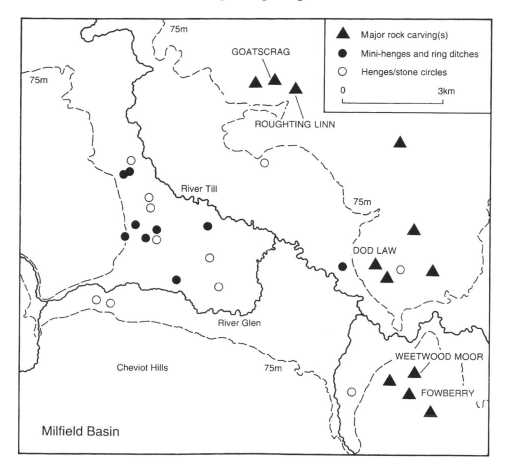

Figure 7.5 The distribution of rock carvings and earthwork monuments in the Milfield basin, Northumberland (partly based on Beckensall 1991 and Burgess 1992)

been visited by people from a wider area. Thus the edges of those landscapes could assume a particular importance. And that takes us back to Roughting Linn.

ROCK ART AND MONUMENT COMPLEXES

Roughting Linn is located on the upper edge of a fertile basin, flanked by sandstone hills to the east which include an unusual number of complex carvings (Fig. 7.5). As we shall see, these sites stand out sharply from northern rock art as a whole. The same area has one other distinctive feature, for it contains nearly all the henge monuments recorded in Northumberland. There may be as many as nine

Table 19 The relationship between rock carvings and the position of the Milfield basin

	Distance to the nearest edge of the Milfield basin			
	0–10 km	11–20 km	21–30 km	31–40 km
Maximum number of rings	4.4	4.0	2.4	2.5

Table 20 The distribution of simple and complex rock carvings in relation to the Milfield basin

	Distance to the nearest edge of the Milfield basin	
	0–20 km	Over 20 km
Complex carvings	22	6
Simple carvings	5	8

of these sites, and their distribution comes within 5 km of Roughting Linn (Burgess 1992). The sites have been investigated by excavation and were first built during the Late Neolithic period. A cup-marked stone had been buried in the centre of one of these monuments (Harding 1981). There are also a number of stone circles in the vicinity of the rock carvings, but their chronology remains uncertain.

Was this link coincidental, or was there a more systematic relationship between the siting of major groups of monuments and the character of the prehistoric rock art found in the same areas of the landscape? If so, did the significance of those monuments lead to certain departures from the simple patterns described in Chapter 6?

In that chapter I discussed a number of areas in which complex rock art tended to occur on the higher ground whilst simple carvings were more frequent lower down, in areas that might have sustained year-round occupation. But two regions with exceptional bodies of rock art do not conform to this scheme. One of them is north Northumberland (Beckensall 1991 and 1992a) and the other Mid Argyll (Morris 1977; RCAHMS 1988); in both cases panels of complex rock art are found near to a major group of monuments.

Perhaps the simplest way of illustrating this relationship is by looking at the character of the rock art in relation to its distance from the edges of the basin (these figures are calculated not as straight lines on a map but as the distance along the local system of valleys and rivers). The simpler carvings are located well away from this area, whilst the more complex compositions are towards the limits of the Milfield plain. The number of concentric rings increases towards the monument complex (the figure for the number of rings is the mean of all the values falling within each distance band) (Table 19).

Another way of looking at the same problem is to consider the distinction between simple and complex rock art established in Chapter 5. Simple rock art in Northumberland included cups with either one or two rings; on sites with more

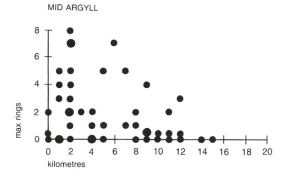

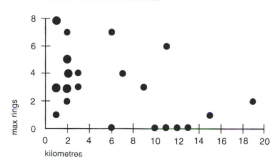

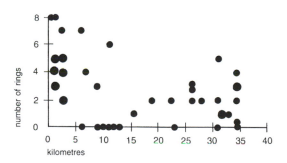

Figure 7.6 Scatter diagrams summarising the changing character of the circular motifs with distance from the edges of the monument complexes in Mid Argyll and north Northumberland

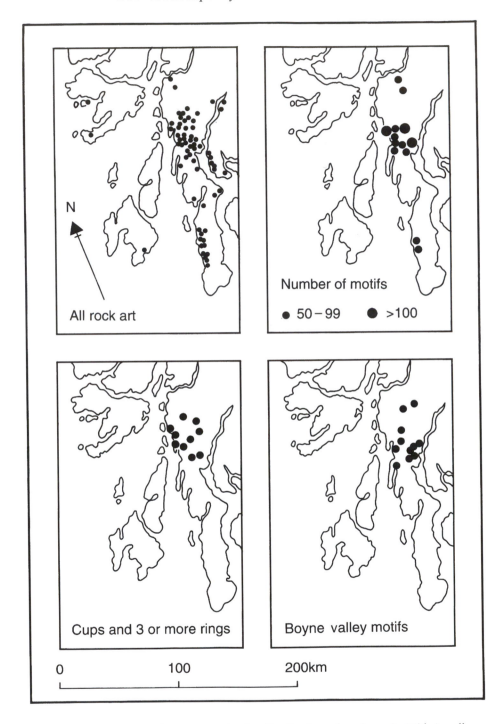

Figure 7.7 Contrasting patterns in the distribution of rock art in Mid Argyll (after Morris 1977)

Table 21 The character of prehistoric rock art in the Kilmartin complex and in other parts of Mid Argyll

	Cup marks	*Cups and rings*
Kilmartin complex	18	30
Other sites in Mid Argyll	38	16

complex art the maximum number of concentric rings was greater. The mean distance between the complex carvings and the edge of the Milfield basin was 9 km. Among the simple carvings the figure rose to 25 km. The same distinction is used in Table 20 which shows that the contrast between the two distributions is statistically significant. There is only a 5 per cent probability that these differences could have come about by chance.

Fig. 7.6 summarises this evidence, but it also shows that the complexity of the art may have increased towards the southern limits of its distribution. This is particularly interesting because it is here, around the Coquet valley, that a second group of monuments existed. Most of these were round cairns, but on the edge of this concentration at Alnham there was another small henge (Harding and Lee 1987, 213). The distance between the groups of more complex rock art is about 30 km. This compares with the mean spacing of henges or groups of henges in Britain which is between 40 and 60 km. The spacing of stone circles, however, is usually between 20 and 35 km (Barnatt 1989, chapter 5). Those figures are measured off maps and do not take the local topography into account. As the crow flies, the henges of the Milfield basin are 34 km from the centre of the rock art distribution in the Coquet valley. Such estimates are only approximations, but they may provide some basis for estimating the size of the region from which people came to visit these monuments.

Very much the same pattern can be seen in western Scotland where the rather more varied monument complex centred on Kilmartin seems to have exerted a similar influence. This is another fertile lowland area which contains a large number of Late Neolithic and Early Bronze Age monuments, in this case including a stone circle, several other settings of monoliths, a henge monument and a linear barrow cemetery (RCAHMS 1988). The limits of this area can be recognised in two different ways. Ronald Morris highlighted them by mapping the distribution of what he called 'Boyne' motifs in the local rock art: the rare examples of spirals, stars and lozenges and the rings without central cups (1977, 23). Despite the wide distribution of rock art in Argyll, all but one of these designs are located around the Kilmartin complex. The same is true of all the conventional carvings with more than two concentric rings (Fig. 7.7). But, having mapped this evidence, Morris did not discuss it.

We can also study this pattern along similar lines to the evidence from Northumberland. Again it is clear that cup-and-ring carvings are most often found in the Kilmartin area, whilst cup marks generally occur elsewhere in Mid Argyll. There is only a 1 per cent probability that this difference could have come about by chance (Table 21).

Table 22 The surfaces selected for carving in the Kilmartin complex and in other parts of Mid Argyll

	Boulder	Outcrop	Other
Kilmartin complex	11	24	13
Other sites in Mid Argyll	26	18	10

Table 23 The changing character of prehistoric rock art towards the edges of the Milfield basin and the Kilmartin complex

Distance to Milfield basin or Kilmartin complex	11–15 km	6–10 km	0–5 km
Mean number of rings (Kilmartin)	0.7	1.7	2.5
Number of sites (Kilmartin)	7	12	26
Mean number of rings (Northumberland)	1.4	2.8	4.4
Number of sites (Northumberland)	5	5	21

There is a corresponding contrast in the kinds of rock where the motifs are found. For the most part in the Kilmartin complex outcrops were preferred for carving, but elsewhere more boulders were selected. Again there is a 1 per cent probability that this difference could be due to chance (Table 22). This is consistent with the conclusion in Chapter 5 that the more complex art in this part of Scotland was usually placed on outcrops.

Fig. 7.6 also plots the distribution of rock carvings in relation to the edges of the Kilmartin complex. Again this diagram is based on distances along the valley system, and, as in Fig. 7.7, the carvings are recorded by the maximum number of rings found on any one site. There is a steady fall off in the complexity of the rock art, which reaches its lowest point at a distance of 15 km. Unlike Northumberland, there is no evidence that the complexity of the carvings picks up again, but it is still worth commenting that the distance over which this change occurs is exactly the same as that in northern England. It is also about half the mean distance between British stone circles. Again these figures may shed some light on the immediate hinterland of the monuments.

There is one further feature which is shared by these two regions. Not only does the rock art increase in complexity towards the monument complexes, it is also found more frequently. Table 23 illustrates both these patterns and compares the situation close to Kilmartin with that in north Northumberland. In this case the patterns are recorded on a larger scale. The distance columns have also been reversed so as to emphasise the process of travelling *towards* both groups of monuments.

It is hard to resist the conclusion that in these two cases the character of the rock art had been influenced by the special character of those two landscapes, for it was towards their limits that the rock carvings possessed the most specialised character. They may have imparted rather different information – more detailed, perhaps more sacred – than other places in the landscape.

There is reason to believe that comparable patterns may once have existed in other areas, but the evidence is limited. In the western suburbs of Glasgow, over-looking the Firth of Clyde, there is a major complex of rock carvings at Whitehill, including the famous Cochno Stone (Morris 1981, 85–90 and 123–37). That partic-ular rock has been covered over for its own protection but early records suggest that among the motifs there were spirals, cups with as many as five rings and draw-ings of human footprints. Nearby carvings include another nine sites with cups and rings and seven more with simple cup marks. They were ranged along the edge of the higher ground overlooking an area with a remarkable concentration of finds. This was the enigmatic site of Knappers Farm which has produced a variety of prehistoric material ranging from Neolithic pottery to Early Bronze Age graves (Ritchie and Adamson 1981). It was clearly a ceremonial complex of some kind, but it was destroyed with little record. From what does survive it seems as if it had contained a number of burials, one of them inside a decorated cist of Late Neolithic date, a timber circle and at least one feature associated with Grooved Ware. The full extent of this complex is unknown, but its topographical position recalls that of Neolithic monument complexes elsewhere in northern Britain. Further to the west at Bowling and Greenland there are other complex carvings (Morris 1981, 88–92 and 98–105), and again these stand out from the remaining petroglyphs in the same region.

A fourth area with rather similar evidence is near Dundalk in County Louth (Clarke 1982; Buckley and Sweetman 1991, 82–7). This is one of the few real concentrations of rock art in Ireland. It is situated a little over 30 km north of the Boyne valley and was a major source of the stones imported to Newgrange and Knowth (Mitchell 1992). The art itself is badly damaged and may be no more than a fraction of what once existed, but it seems to focus on the upper slopes of a shallow valley leading down to an estuary. Within the same area there are up to four earthworks that have been identified as henges and a now destroyed site at Killin which seems to have consisted of two megalithic tombs (Buckley and Sweetman 1991, 33 and 70–2). One of the stone-built monuments had originally been decorated. Two kilometres away at Carrickrobin there is also a menhir which is embellished with two passage-grave motifs: a spiral, and a cup-and-ring carving embellished with rays rather like that at Roughting Linn (ibid, 84–5). This may be a reused fragment from an older tomb.

It is hard to tell how the landscape had been organised, although the concen-tration of different sites is very striking indeed. Slieve Gullion, the highest passage grave in Ireland, overlooks the area from the north, whilst the distribution of simple undecorated tombs complements that of the rock carvings on the ground below. The most convincing henge monument seems to be located towards the eastern limit of this area, whilst the rock carvings are generally found further to the west, with the most complex example of all on the outer edge of their distribution. It may have been located close to one of the routes leading into the monument complex from the higher ground. If so, then its siting would have been very like that of Roughting Linn.

ENTRANCES AND EXITS

So far I have argued that sites like Roughting Linn are distributed around the areas containing concentrations of monuments, but I have not discussed their locations in more detail. Again the carved rock at Roughting Linn is typical of a wider pattern. It is located in the hills overlooking the head of the Milfield plain, beside a modern road leading into the lower ground. In fact it is really situated within a minor pass providing access through the ridge which closes off the basin on its northern side. From there the Northumberland coast is easily accessible.

The basin is defined by the Fell Sandstone on two sides, but to the south and west it is limited by rocks which may not have been suitable for carving. The main concentrations of petroglyphs overlook the north and east edges of this basin, but they are found in greatest numbers above the valleys leading into this area. Some of the sites, like the complex carvings on Chattonpark Hill, command views along the valley routes approaching the Milfield plain, but rather more are situated directly above the entrances to the lower ground, where the basin first opens out. Like those at Roughting Linn, the designs generally include complex circular motifs.

The same pattern is found in the Kilmartin complex, but in that case it is even more obvious. The edges of the lower ground are marked by a distribution of carvings – as in Northumberland, the number of carved rocks increases towards the limits of this area. Again the more complex carvings tend to be found on rock outcrops situated some way above the valley floor. We have already seen that these include most of the more elaborate designs in this region, but again their siting is distinctive. The more complex compositions overlook the ends of the valleys leading into the lowland basin where so many monuments were built. Where different valleys converge the carvings are still more ornate. If these valleys really had acted as routeways, this evidence might suggest a direct relationship between the character of the rock art and the number of people who may have seen it on their visits to the major monuments.

Mid-Argyll provides several examples of this process. Thus the great panels of carvings at Achnabreck overlook the end of a former loch but they do so close to a point where several different routes might have met (Pl. 21). The same applies to some of the carvings on the neighbouring hill at Cairnbaan, so that the petroglyphs on these two sites command both sides of a major valley near to the southern limit of the basin. At the same time, the local topography is all-important here. One of the main rocks at Cairnbaan faces the valley floor below Achnabreck, whilst the other, which is situated just a few metres away, commands a view northwards towards Kilmartin. These two carved surfaces at Cairnbaan contain different motifs from one another.

As we saw in Northumberland, not all the complex carvings were located around the edges of the area with the monuments. Again there were others distributed

Table 24 Intervisibility between individual sites in the Kilmartin complex

	Simple carving	Complex carving	Standing stone
Simple carving	20	13	6
Complex carving	11	18	9

Table 25 The distances between intervisible rock carvings in the Kilmartin complex

Mean distance between intervisible rock carvings	
Complex carvings to other complex carvings	1.8 km
Complex carvings to simple carvings	3.2 km
Simple carvings to other simple carvings	9.1 km

along the valleys leading towards those sites. This is one region in which it has been possible to study the patterns of intervisibility between the decorated rocks, using a digital elevation model (Gaffney, Stancic and Watson 1995). The results of this exercise are most revealing. We can consider the more complex carvings in Mid Argyll as those with three or more rings. We can also consider the visibility of standing stones. All the carved surfaces recorded by the Scottish Royal Commission (1988) are considered in this exercise. It shows that the sites with complex rock carvings tend to be found in places which are intervisible with other complex carvings; these also allow the menhirs to be seen. The sites with simpler rock art are more often in places with views of other simple carvings and are less often intervisible with standing stones. There is only a 10 per cent probability that this relationship could have come about by chance (Table 24). The strength of the relationship does not change if we distinguish between decorated and undecorated menhirs, and it remains the same even if the standing stones are left out of the analysis altogether.

There is also some patterning at a more detailed level. The connections between complex carvings extend over a shorter distance than those involving the simpler petroglyphs. On the ground the main chains of connections are between the sites located around two of the entrances to the lower ground (Fig. 7.8). One group of complex carvings is situated towards the southern limit of the study area and connects the decorated surfaces which overlook the route leading inland from the south-east with other carvings in the river valley. A few simpler carvings also contribute to this group, but none of these sites has any view of Kilmartin. The second group of sites is even smaller and is defined by three main sites. They are located up to 2 km apart and form a triangle which encloses a number of the major monuments in the area, including the southern end of a linear barrow cemetery. They also define the entrance to the Kilmartin valley and may once have been located close to an inlet of the sea.

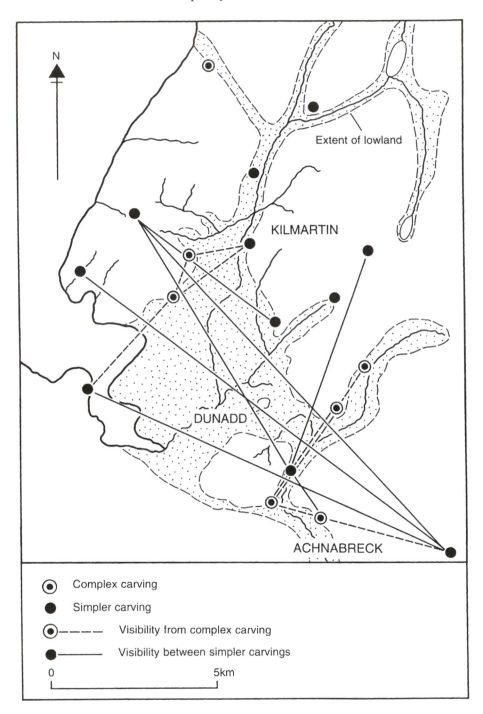

Figure 7.8 Patterns of intervisibility between carved rocks in the Kilmartin complex (partly based on computer analysis by Vince Gaffney and Helen Watson)

The evidence from Northumberland is very different, although there is the same emphasis on placing the rock carvings in locations that are visible from one another. As we saw in Chapter 5, this is an area in which the evidence has been examined in the field. Ruth Saunders' research has refined the basic pattern worked out from contour maps by showing a striking chain of connections extending between the rock carvings around the Milfield basin and other major sites in the valleys which lead into this area (R. Saunders pers. comm.). Once again these links seem to be highly specific. Only certain sites – generally the groups of more complex carvings – seem to have been linked together; many others do not conform to this pattern. Generally speaking, the visual links were between the hills rather than the carved rocks themselves, but this is hardly surprising since the average distance between intervisible carvings was about 6 km. The only area with a network of links over significantly shorter distances was around Dod Law (Pl. 22) which overlooks no fewer than three of the routes into the Milfield basin.

That sequence of intervisible rock carvings is important for another reason as it must surely shed light on the ways in which such sites were used. I have already argued that the monument complexes discussed in this chapter must have served the needs of a wider population. The carvings become more complex towards the areas with major monuments, and they also become more frequent. It is possible that people approaching the Milfield basin from the surrounding area passed along the routes marked by the various carvings and that those petroglyphs indicated important thresholds on the journey across country. Normally each of these locations could be identified from its predecessor so that the sequence of carved rocks ranged along the major valleys might have determined the paths which people were expected to follow (cf Tilley 1994, chapter 5). If so, then the changing configurations of the art might be explained in two ways. The complex compositions found closer to the main groups of monuments might have been addressed to an increasingly large and varied audience. At the same time, the messages that those images were intended to convey could have assumed a more and more specialised character. Where these routes entered the Milfield basin there were some of the most complex compositions of all.

The same argument applies to the rock art of Mid Argyll, but with one qualification. In Northumberland movement was entirely by land, but the location of the Kilmartin complex at the head of the Mull of Kintyre introduces another factor, for it lies astride an important land route between the inland lochs of western Scotland and the Irish Sea. This route extended overland for 15 km but it avoided sailing around the coastline for an additional 150 km. The strategic importance of this area would have made it a major focus for people from far afield. That may provide another reason why the local rock carvings had so much information to impart.

This interpretation has emphasised two important features of the more complex rock carvings in relation to the setting of ceremonial monuments. They were often located at 'entrances' in the natural terrain, and in order to reach them people may have needed to visit a whole sequence of other petroglyphs in their journeys across country. Those locations provided important thresholds along their route, and they were probably sited in places where the view over the country changed – that is why the sites with the complex rock art were not visible from a single location.

Both those features recall important characteristics of megalithic art in the Boyne valley. Here there are large stone monuments with a range of circular motifs defining their outer limit. The 'private' art of the interior could never have been seen by many people and it has little counterpart in open-air rock carvings. The major focus of activity was around the entrance to the passage tomb which could be marked, as it was at Newgrange, by particularly prominent circular motifs. These may be related to the motifs found on natural surfaces, but it is noticeable how the open-air sites tend to cluster around the entrances to those distinctive areas described as 'ritual landscapes'. We have seen how the passage tombs were sometimes replaced by 'open' monuments, and even by whole groups of enclosures. It seems as if the symbolic system recorded by megalithic art underwent a similar transformation. It may have opened out to embrace the landscape as a whole, so that the limits of those monument complexes echo the character of the megalithic kerb, and the concentration of rock art around the entrances to those areas reflects the importance that had once been attached to the entrance of the tomb. In effect the landscape became the ritual arena whereas formerly it was defined by the architecture of the individual site.

If that is so, it becomes easier to understand two other features. I have commented on the idea of thresholds along the paths leading to such areas. These thresholds were conspicuous hills or rock outcrops overlooking the river valleys and it was here that some of the most complex art was created. These sites have the distinctive feature that they often command a view of the next carved rock along that route but not of all the others, so that a visitor might need to consult each of these sites in sequence as he or she came nearer to the monument complex. Their siting meant that they could only be viewed in a prescribed order. Moreover each of these carvings was located at a point where the view over the surrounding country changed its character significantly.

Again this is a feature that characterises megalithic art, for many writers have commented that this is how the carvings in the largest tombs are organised. They emphasise significant thresholds in the course of the passage, at the opening of the main chamber or at the point where in turn it leads into a side chamber or recess. The siting of those images orchestrates the experience of moving in and out of the tomb, and it also emphasises the most significant points in the burial chamber (cf Thomas 1992). It seems as if the decorated stones within the settlement at Skara Brae might have played a similar role, highlighting important divisions of space in the area around the one exceptional building on the site (Richards 1991).

Significant places might have been marked in yet another way. For some years it has been recognised that carefully selected groups of artefacts are sometimes buried in the vicinity of henges and other monuments (Thomas 1991, chapter 4). Such pits often contain stone artefacts and animal bones as well as decorated pottery, and their contents are sometimes arranged with considerable formality. It is usually supposed that because this material was buried its position would have been lost, but this is an unnecessary assumption. Some of these pits were surrounded by wooden stakes (Barrett, Bradley and Green 1991, 83–4), and occasionally deposits of Late Neolithic artefacts were marked by cairns (Stone 1935), by a large undecorated boulder (Edwards and Bradley in press) or even perhaps by enclosing this material within a ditch (Shennan, Healy and Smith 1985). Although the objects themselves would not have remained visible, their locations might well have been apparent to later generations. The point is important because so much of that decorated pottery was Grooved Ware. Like the open-air rock carvings described in this chapter, it shares a number of design elements with megalithic art. Both groups of material could have been used to mark the importance of particular places.

One feature unites these characteristic patterns. I have argued that open-air rock art is closely related to the decoration of passage tombs and that their replacement by henges and other structures involved a more general change of perspective. The ritual arena opened out to embrace the wider landscape until the natural features in the surrounding area were treated in the same manner as the monuments themselves.

From the end of the Neolithic period the image of the circle was all-pervading. The henge monuments adopted this characteristic ground plan. For those who were allowed to venture inside these sites the near horizon would be marked by a circular perimeter. At the same time, their earthworks were often situated on low ground so that many of these enclosures would have been overlooked by a more distant horizon of hills. Some Neolithic monuments were aligned on cardinal points and others observed astronomical alignments (Burl 1976; Gibson 1994, 191–212), yet almost all were laid out according to the same principles as houses and burial mounds.

Such links may seem fortuitous, but it is worth considering whether they might have reflected the same conception of space. Tim Ingold (1993) has commented on the frequency with which different peoples see the world as a sequence of circles or spheres. This model has been discussed by students of comparative religions (Eliade 1989, chapters 1 and 2), but there is a practical reason why it should be so common. It reflects the perspective of a viewer in an open landscape whose immediate world is limited by the horizon. The characteristic plan of henges or similar structures encapsulates that experience, whilst the special treatment afforded to the edges of monument complexes extends the same idea across a larger area. The limits of those regions are treated like the monuments themselves, and in both cases their entrances are embellished with circular motifs. The cup and ring so typical of British and Irish rock art is such a powerful symbol because it can encapsulate so many different relationships. It might have developed as a reference to the tunnel imagery experienced in states of altered consciousness, but with the development of henges the same motif was extended to the landscape as a whole. By that stage the circular designs might have become the ideal representation of place.

I have now discussed the importance of a site like Roughting Linn on three different levels. I began by considering the decoration applied to megalithic tombs in Ireland and the conventions according to which it was deployed. I suggested a number of ways in which those protocols were echoed in the wider landscape long after the tombs themselves had gone out of use. I also discussed the ways in which rock carvings were drawn into the creation and use of another generation of field monuments until the ritual arena incorporated considerable areas of the landscape. Similar patterns can be recognised at an even larger scale, as they seem to have extended beyond the areas with monuments altogether, until they emphasised the significance of wholly natural landforms and a distinctive perception of the environment as a series of circular forms. At the same time, the structure of the carved surfaces themselves seems to have changed according to their position in the terrain. These are striking developments and even now their full significance eludes us. This account does not exhaust their interpretation, for the last two chapters have been confined to the evidence of settlements and monuments. The third feature to investigate is the treatment of the natural topography. That provides the subject matter of Chapter 8.

CHAPTER EIGHT

THE CIRCLE AND THE CRAG
The micro-topography of British and Irish rock art

—— ·✦· ——

INTRODUCTION

The last three chapters have had one feature in common. Although they were concerned with the rock art of different regions, the emphasis has been on the characteristics that unite those areas. The design grammar discussed in Chapter 5 was a very simple scheme which could be used in all the case studies. It depended on a straightforward distinction between 'simpler' and more 'complex' rock art. Similarly, Chapter 6 considered the relationship between rock carvings and the pattern of settlement in terms of those elements that were shared between different regions. In most cases the carvings seemed to vary according to elevation. To a large extent the contents of Chapter 7 took a similar course, but this time I discussed the relationship between rock carvings and the siting of ceremonial monuments. No doubt such basic comparisons do play a useful role in highlighting general patterns that cross-cut the distribution of these carvings, but to suspend analysis at this stage is to lose sight of some of the fine details that could illuminate our perception of this material.

Some contrasts have already been apparent. For example, the distinction between simple and complex rock art has to be defined in different ways in different regions. Thus this analytical distinction was not quite the same in Northumberland, Galloway and Strath Tay. That is not a weakness of these studies; rather, the decision to classify the compositions according to different criteria in each of these areas shows a sensitivity to important variations in the character of the art. The topographical distinctions which have played such a prominent part in this discussion also had to be qualified. In Galloway, for instance, the upland areas with the more complex rock art have proved to be extremely diverse, and many of the key relationships were with particular kinds of feature on the higher ground, in particular waterholes. In Strath Tay there a rather similar range of variation. For the most part the complex art was on the high ground, but a simple distinction between the floor and sides of the valley proved to be inadequate. Some of the complex art was related to a series of upland basins, whilst in two cases a major group of rock carvings was located above a gorge with a spectacular waterfall.

By structuring the last chapter around a discussion of Roughting Linn it was possible to break down some of the abstraction, and my account paid more attention to the immediate topography of the carvings. This is the appropriate point to take that approach even further and to consider the specific character of some of the carved rocks in relation to the interpretations that have been offered so far. This chapter has two distinct objectives. First, it re-examines the composition of some of the more complex carvings, emphasising the local distinctions that underlie the patterns analysed in earlier chapters. Second, it considers the significance of features that are lost to sight when we study the distribution of petroglyphs over an extensive area. In this case we need to investigate the influence exerted by natural landforms.

THE STRUCTURE OF COMPLEX ROCK CARVINGS

I have already identified a gradient in the composition of the rock carvings. The simplest element was the cup mark. This might be emphasised by one or more rings, and the largest and most elaborate motifs might be joined together. This pattern is found in practically every area, but that is not to say that the compositions always took a similar form. There is obviously a wide range of variation.

The carvings can normally be divided into two major groups and six subgroups (Fig. 8.1), although this scheme is not intended as a rigid typology. Instead it seeks to recreate the logic according to which such compositions were formed. Cup-and-ring carvings rarely occur in isolation, and when more than one of them is found they may be widely spaced across the surface of the rock (Type A). Such motifs might be left in isolation (Type A1) or they might be linked together (Type A2). Usually this happened when the radial lines leading to the centre of these images were connected in a more extensive composition.

The other case is where the cup-and-ring carvings were located close together (Type B). This might happen by filling in the spaces between existing motifs, or it could have been intended from the outset. In either instance, where this occurred decisions would have to be taken about how the composition was to develop. Those motifs might be left in complete isolation (Type B1) or they could be linked by a system of lines, often radiating from the central cup marks (Type B2). Sometimes that converted the distinct motifs into a larger and more unified design, but in other cases the rings themselves were separated by a series of enclosures (Type B3). The effect was to join some of these images together but at the same time to divide them from one another.

Where the circular motifs were close together, still more specific connections might have been formed. Sometimes new images abut the motifs that were already there (Type B4). Again those connections could be emphasised by joining some of the radial lines, but where one development created a space that was increasingly subdivided (Type B3), this procedure resulted in a distribution of images that was more and more clustered (Type B4).

Other schemes might have developed equally logically from these basic principles, but for the most part this did not happen. In fact Fig. 8.1 summarises nearly

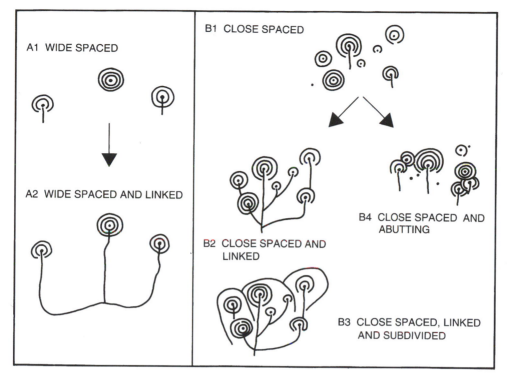

Figure 8.1 Alternative design grammars for British and Irish rock carvings

all the major variations in the organisation of complex rock art. This analysis might seem an intellectual exercise: a method that does little more than describe regional preferences in the organisation of the motifs. That is not the purpose of this discussion, for it seems likely that the structuring of the decorated surfaces was directly connected with the character of the surrounding landscape.

If we can offer a typology of rock art, we can also specify the range of topographical situations in which it is likely to occur. There are three main possibilities. In a landscape like Strath Tay there is a fairly simple dichotomy between the valley floor, with its evidence of settlement sites, and the higher ground where the more complex art is found. The topographical contrast is much the same along the entire length of the valley. In this case there are cup marks on the river terraces, whilst the cup-and-ring carvings are on the valley side and overlook these locations. The motifs are usually scattered across the carved surface (Type A1) and only rarely are they connected together to form a more elaborate design. The same arrangement is found at sites in Galloway where many of the carvings are made up of motifs that were left in isolation.

Contrast this situation with a landscape in which there is an expanse of upland territory surrounded by a large area of lower ground. This provides a context in which the uplands could have been used by several different communities. A good example is Ilkley Moor, which is the one extensive plateau between Wharfedale and Airedale (Ilkley Archaeology Group 1986). A comparable situation might be one where a pass channelled movement between two equally extensive regions. We have already seen this pattern towards the southern limit of the Fell Sandstone in Northumberland, where the rock carvings at Millstone Burn were concentrated on either side of a valley route leading from the coastal plain into the higher ground. In such cases it seems as if the motifs are crowded together on the surface of the rock (Type B1), and there are cases in which close-spaced designs abut one another (Type B4) or are connected up by lines (Type B2). In fact linear arrangements of carved motifs are particularly common around the edges of Ilkley Moor where they are generally found near to the valleys and streams providing access from the area below. It may be no accident that the axis of these compositions often follows their orientation.

The third situation is the one discussed in the previous chapter, where one region with a range of specialised monuments provides a focus for people coming from a wider area. In Northumberland we have already seen how the art changes its character towards the edges of these monument complexes. The motifs become more elaborate and they tend to be joined together in a more complex composition. But in this case the links take a most distinctive form, for whilst separate design elements are quite often connected by a network of lines (Types A2 and B2), the individual motifs may also be separated from one another by enclosures (Type B3). It seems as if motifs tended to accumulate, as they did at other sites, but in this case the links created between them were offset by a series of internal divisions. This does not reflect any obvious characteristic of the local physical environment, but it is extraordinarily reminiscent of the distribution of the henges and associated monuments in the Milfield basin. These are scattered over a considerable area, but each site also has an individual character. The 'ritual landscape' is subdivided between a number of different foci, and in this case there even seems to be evidence of Neolithic post or pit alignments separating some of these sites (Harding 1981; Miket 1981). There is the added complication that the pattern of connections between the different motifs is very selective indeed. Certain images were connected together to the exclusion of others, and often those links appear to be sequential: thus image A is linked to image B, image B is joined to image C, and so on. The effect is to create a hierarchy of designs, some of which are associated together, whilst others belong to less extensive networks or are excluded from the process altogether.

Does this mean that these rock carvings were conceived as maps, a view already considered in Chapter 3? This seems an unnecessary assumption simply because there is so little in common between the layout of the decorated surfaces and the distinctive features of the local topography. Surely the natural environment was important in quite another way. It provided opportunities for particular forms of land use and may have made others more difficult to achieve. Thus the upland sites in Strath Tay or in Galloway are linked fairly directly to lowlying settlement areas and the pattern of movement between them may have been reasonably straightforward. By contrast, the Millstone Burn complex or the uplands of Ilkley Moor were locations where for different reasons quite separate groups may have passed the rock carvings. Their relationships with one another would have been the subject of negotiation, especially if they were exploiting substantially the same natural resources. The carvings do not inform us about the spatial organisation of the upland landscape, but among other things they may provide an image of the social relationships that such practices entailed.

In the same way, the distinctive rock carvings close to Milfield do not 'represent' the layout of the basin, nor were they simply maps of the routes leading into this area. They may epitomise an essentially 'circular' perception of space but they also echo the distinctive organisation, not of subsistence resources, but of the specialised monuments which are the most striking feature of this area. They are not maps by which to plan a route across the landscape, but they may be statements of how the different people using that area were related to one another. That may also be why the connections between different images in the rock art were so selective.

By contrast, there is little order in the carvings around the other major ceremonial centre at Kilmartin, and here the main impression is that images were crowded onto the rock surface. Where motifs are linked, chiefly at Achnabreck, there is no evidence for subdivisions. What we do find at some of these sites are simple chains of connections which recall the 'hierarchical' organisation of some of the carvings around the Milfield basin. At Kilmartin the apparent lack of order may be explained partly by the long history of these carvings – there is a clear sequence of images at Achnabreck (RCAHMS 1988, 87–99) – and partly by the geography of the region. Most of the complex carvings in north Northumberland were created on or close to a small number of routes leading towards a major group of monuments, and many of them were quite near to one another. By contrast, the landscape around Kilmartin was much more diverse and the occupants of separate upland valleys may rarely have come into contact; indeed, there is every reason to suppose that some people must have visited this area by sea. Unlike those sites in north-east England, the monuments also appear to be located on a major long-distance route. The diversity in the organisation of the rock art may be one indication that the monuments of Mid Argyll served a more varied constituency than those in Northumberland.

I must end this section with a warning. The ethnographic evidence summarised in Chapter 1 shows very clearly that rock art can have several different layers of meaning. It is likely that the same was true in the past. If so, there is no reason to suppose that these arguments supply more than a very partial reading of the rock carvings in a few distinctive areas. This interpretation is most unlikely to exhaust their original significance. Nor is it wise to imagine that these ideas can be taken literally. Even supposing that the motifs do express a circular perception of space and that their organisation reflects certain aspects of social relations, that structure might well represent an ideal and could have little to do with the realities of everyday life. Indeed, the art might not refer to the present at all; it could have charted the relationships of people in the past, and in doing so it might have been tracing stories of a mythological character. The one point that can be maintained amidst so much uncertainty is that the layout of the carvings may have been influenced, however obliquely, by the character of the local topography.

ROCK ART AND NATURAL LAND FORMS

Sometimes that topography can be defined more precisely than I have done so far. Again there are a few basic features to consider: the relationship between the carvings and different rock formations, and their relationship to the routes leading through the wider landscape. Beyond those features we must also consider the placing of carved surfaces in relation to the sea and sky.

Once again Roughting Linn provides an ideal point of departure. I have already discussed the way in which the carvings are located beside a shallow pass; they are also within a short distance of a gorge. Like those in Strath Tay described in Chapter 6, this has an impressive waterfall. There is another distinctive feature which is not repeated on those other sites, for near to that waterfall there are a number of rock shelters, one of which is associated with fragments of burnt bone (Burgess 1972, 45–7).

The gorge at Roughting Linn is a little unusual because it lacks any decoration. In fact the sandstone is so eroded that no carvings could have survived, but this is not the case in three other instances: a cliff near the head of a gorge at Ballochmyle in Ayrshire (Stevenson 1993), and two other gorges at Hawthornden, south of Edinburgh (Morris 1981, 147–50), and at Morwick in Northumberland (Beckensall 1992a, 55–7). These sites have a striking feature in common, for they contain a remarkable series of images shared with megalithic art. At Ballochmyle there are a number of stars, whilst spirals feature prominently at the other sites, where they occupy positions which are quite difficult to reach today. Although Morwick and Ballochmyle are on or close to rivers with an abundant supply of fish, this may not be the only connection between these places. Very few major carvings are found on vertical surfaces in Britain, and the remarkable coincidence between gorges and such specialised motifs might be explained because these locations resembled the passages of megalithic tombs. The same might apply to the specialised carvings found on steeply sloping surfaces at Knock in Galloway (Van Hoek 1995, fig. 19) and Mevagh in County Donegal (Van Hoek 1988).

As we have seen, there are a number of caves or rock shelters close to Roughting Linn. Although none of these shows any evidence of decoration, this feature is found at seven sites in Northumberland. In only two cases were there any carvings inside the shelter itself, and in both instances these included cups and rings. More often the carvings are located on the surface immediately above the cave or shelter and there are no petroglyphs within the interior. These motifs are generally quite simple ones, and in two cases, at Dod Law and Millstone Burn, they are limited to cup marks. At Corby Crag the main feature is an enclosed basin and at Goatscrag there are cups and a series of arcs. The carvings above Cuddy's Cave (Pl. 23) have now disappeared, but a nineteenth-century drawing shows four cup marks, each with between one and four concentric rings (Tate 1865). There are few finds from any of these sites, but they do contain occasional pieces of flintwork, the earliest of them of Mesolithic date (Burgess 1972). An Early Bronze Age urned cremation is recorded from the rock shelter at Corby Crags, where the burial was in the floor beneath the carving on the overhanging surface of the rock (Beckensall 1992a, 52–3). Close to the decorated rock shelter at Goatscrag there was a similar site. This was without any evidence of carvings, but, like Corby Crag, it contained urned cremations (Burgess 1972).

It is worth emphasising the restrained character of so many of these carvings, for this may be related to a rather wider pattern in the distribution of British rock art. Although the more complex images are located on quite conspicuous outcrops, it is only rarely that they occur on the most spectacular exposures of all. For example, there is a most impressive series of caves at Caller Crag in Northumberland (Beckensall 1992a, 52–4). The site itself can be seen from a considerable distance, but the main group of carvings are well away from those features, on a vertical surface hidden behind the main outcrop. Nearly all the motifs are basins or simple cup marks. Similar evidence has been found at two sites in Derbyshire (Barnatt and Reeder 1982). At Rowtor Rocks there are simple circular motifs on the top of a prominent crag, but the only complex design is lower down. There is another simple carving on the crag at Robin Hood's Stride, but in this case it avoids the summit altogether.

In fact it was common practice to locate the more complex carvings some distance behind the edges of the higher ground. With the exception of a few simple motifs located directly above rock shelters, this applies to a series of prominent landmarks in Northumberland, including Goatscrag, Dod Law and Old Bewick. A variant of this pattern is found on Ilkley Moor, where some of the most conspicuous exposures, including the Doubler Stones and Pancake Rock (Pl. 24), have the most restrained decoration (Ilkley Archaeology Group 1986). These are flat-topped rocks perched on the edge of a crag, but the main decoration consists of cup marks, basins and grooves. Rocks which were set back from the break of slope could include a much wider range of motifs.

Occasionally these conventions extend over a considerable area. We have seen how the major petroglyphs in Mid Argyll focus on two of the entrances to the lowlying area around Kilmartin. The sites within each of these groups were visible from one another, but this was not the case with the main concentrations of rock art. The intervening area contains one especially conspicuous landmark, the isolated hill at Dunadd. It dominates the surrounding landscape and can be seen from many directions. It would have been an obvious landmark for anyone travelling towards Kilmartin, but again it was never a major focus for the creation of petroglyphs. There are quite a number of Neolithic and Early Bronze Age artefacts from the site, including a carved stone ball and a halberd, but the only prehistoric rock art found on the hill was a single cup and ring (RCAHMS 1988, 7 and 154). Perhaps the significance of such places was so well established that there was little need to emphasise their importance by adding carved designs.

Another preferred location for complex rock art was in mountain passes. The best example of this is at Derrynablaha in County Kerry (Anati 1963), where the sites have been restudied by Avril Purcell (1994). This is the only route across the high ground of the Iveragh peninsula and, as she has shown, some of the well-known carvings are carefully located so that the viewer's eye is directed towards the head of the pass. Other sites in the area command views into the lower ground, but it was sometimes necessary for the observer to turn the other way in order to see the carved surface. As a result the viewer would have been looking into the

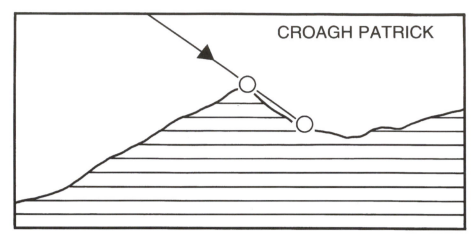

Figure 8.2 The view of the setting sun at Croagh Patrick as seen from the Boheh Stone
(after Bracken and Wayman 1992)

mountains. Derrynablaha has some features in common with Duncroisk in
Perthshire where a small valley to the west of Loch Tay is associated with a whole
group of rock carvings (Morris 1981, 53–8). In this case they are not located in a
pass but at the point where the road along the lower ground meets two other
routes leading into the mountains. Most of the art is quite restrained, but at the
centre of this complex, in the only place with uninterrupted views along the course
of the valley, is an outcrop with more complicated designs.

There are other cases where the art commands the sea rather than the land. Rock
carvings overlook a number of major estuaries, including the mouth of the Dee
near Kirkcudbright (Bradley, Harding and Mathews 1993), the former shoreline of
the Firth of Forth near Stirling (Morris 1981, 44–50), a section of the Cromarty
Firth below Swordale (D. Scott pers. comm.) and the Kyle of Tongue in Sutherland
(RCAHMS 1911, 186–7). The same happens in County Donegal where the most
complex carvings in the entire region, those at Mevagh, command a narrow channel
leading from the open sea to an extensive series of inland lakes (Pl. 25; Van Hoek
1988). The strategic location of these particular petroglyphs is emphasised by the
positioning of a beacon on the water's edge immediately below the site. A similar
interpretation may explain the concentration of rock art on Doagh Island, 30 km
away, where the images show a certain overlap with the tomb art of Loughcrew. In
this case the most complex carvings overlook the narrow channel separating the
southern shore of the island from the mountainous coastline of north Donegal
(Pl. 26; Van Hoek 1987). In other cases rock art may be associated with coastal
landing places. Knock illustrates this pattern in Scotland (Morris 1979, 127), whilst
a cup-marked rock at Tintagel suggests the same arrangement in Cornwall
(Hartgroves 1987, 83).

Carvings could also be located around inland lakes. Chapter 6 described a number
of sites where this happened in Galloway, and Avril Purcell's study of the rock art

of the Iveragh peninsula in south-west Ireland has identified further instances, among them some of the most complex designs in the region (1994). Rock art could also be directed towards the sky. The Boheh Stone in County Mayo is a particularly convincing example of this pattern (Fig. 8.2). The site is situated 7 km from Croagh Patrick, a place which has always been the focus of pilgrimage, and the viewer's eye is directed from the carvings towards its distinctive profile. Twice a year, the setting sun can be seen descending the northern face of the mountain. Together with the winter solstice, those occasions would have divided the year into three equal parts (Bracken and Wayman 1992). Such practices may have been quite common. In western Scotland decorated standing stones seem to have been orientated on the movements of the moon (Ruggles 1984), and the cup-marked rocks found in recumbent stone circles may well have emphasised a similar alignment (Ruggles and Burl 1985).

Such observations focus the viewer's attention on the skyline and quite often on the position of certain conspicuous hills. These may have no obvious archaeology of their own, but there are cases in which their flanks were lavishly decorated. At Traprain Law, an exposed surface was embellished with linear decoration not unlike the patterns found on Grooved Ware (Edwards 1935), and at Buttony in Northumberland a frieze of complex carvings follows a rock outcrop along the steep side of the hill, producing almost the same effect as a megalithic kerb (Pl. 27; Beckensall 1991, 22 and 30–2). At Lordenshaw, in the same county, the lower ground of a conspicuous hill contains a distribution of relatively complex carvings, whilst rather simpler designs are widely distributed across the higher ground. It seems as if the distribution of the more elaborate motifs defined the crest of the hill as somewhere special (Bradley and Mathews in prep.).

That situation may be more common than we suppose, and it is a feature that links this discussion to the contents of the following chapter. A number of burial cairns were constructed on the hilltop at Lordenshaw, and more can be found at other places discussed in this section. There are examples close to the rock outcrops at Goatscrag, Old Bewick, Dod Law and Caller Crag, and further examples are known on Ilkley Moor. As we have seen, burials are also associated with some of the decorated caves and rock shelters. The more we study the local setting of the rock art, the more its relationship with mortuary ritual requires investigation. The following chapter takes this question one stage further by reviewing the changing relationship between rock carvings and Early Bronze Age burials.

CHAPTER NINE

PUBLIC FACES
IN PRIVATE PLACES
Rock art and Early Bronze Age burials

—— •◆• ——

INTRODUCTION

For a long time the relationship between rock art and Early Bronze Age burials occupied a central place in British research. This was because here, and only here, pieces of carved stone could be found in direct association with easily dated artefacts. That evidence seemed to be vital in building a chronology, but, unfortunately, it was not always handled with care. The basic material was very limited and some of the written sources were unsatisfactory, yet the chronological arguments inspired by these finds dominated discussion so completely that very little was said about the role that rock carvings might have played in the funeral rite. This chapter acknowledges the poor quality of much of our evidence but attempts to redress the balance.

Carved rocks were not used in Bronze Age burials in every area. The decorated cists that once assumed such a prominent place in archaeological writing are hardly ever found in Ireland (Johnston 1989). There is an important concentration near to Kilmartin (RCAHMS 1988), but otherwise most examples are closer to the North Sea coast. Although there are many outliers, they are usually found between Perthshire and the East Moor of Derbyshire (Simpson and Thawley 1972). I shall refer to this group as the 'northern' tradition.

There is a second, more limited group of Bronze Age burials which are associated with decorated stones, but they are rarely considered in these discussions. These are found in Wales and western England and have been little studied because so many of the carvings are simple cup marks (Ashbee 1958, 189–93). Although they are easily overlooked, they provide some interesting evidence for different practices from those in northern Britain. I shall refer to these sites as the 'western' tradition.

Finally, there is a third, very small group of carved stones which spans this geographical division. For that reason it will be convenient to consider them now. These are the rare depictions of metalwork which are found both in western Scotland and in central southern England. In the north, the Kilmartin complex includes two of these sites, both of them cists decorated with drawings of axeheads (RCAHMS 1988, 68–70 and 72–4); there is a third 10 km to the north (ibid, 79).

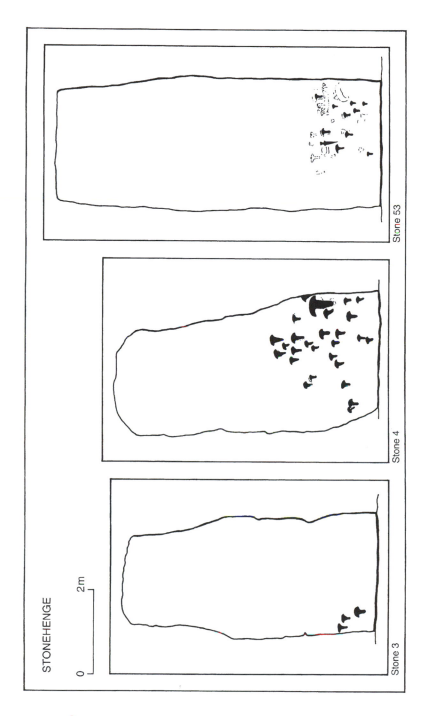

Figure 9.1 Carvings of Early Bronze Age artefacts at Stonehenge (after Cleal, Walker and Montague 1995)

In one case, at Nether Largie, these images appear to be superimposed on an earlier constellation of cup marks (Bradley 1993, 91–3). One feature of particular interest is that the axes are depicted without their hafts; they are shown simply as pieces of metal. This is especially striking as artefacts of this kind are unusual in Early Bronze Age graves but do occur in hoards.

The southern finds depict both axes and daggers, but these are not found on cists. At Badbury they were displayed on the outer kerb of a round cairn, buried when the monument was enlarged (Piggott 1939), and at Stonehenge one series of axes is carved on the outer circle of sarsens whilst the other is found in the central setting of trilithons (Crawford 1954). The latter group also includes the only convincing drawing of a dagger (Fig. 9.1). Again this association is rather revealing since daggers are among the principal artefacts found in local graves. The depiction of axes along with the dagger at Stonehenge is important in another way, for the richest of all the burials in the neighbourhood is the grave from Bush Barrow which includes the same combination of artefacts (Annable and Simpson 1964, 99 and 145–6). This is especially interesting in the light of a recent discovery from a barrow at Lockington in Leicestershire, where a cup-marked stone may have indicated the position of a shallow pit including two gold arm rings and a copper dagger (G. Hughes pers. comm.). In such cases it seems as if these carvings either recorded the deposition of metalwork or acted as the equivalent of metal deposits themselves.

The remaining carvings associated with Early Bronze Age burials are entirely abstract, and those in northern Britain have little in common with examples in the west. For that reason I shall consider both groups separately before I discuss their wider implications.

THE NORTHERN TRADITION

A useful starting point is provided by a recent excavation at Loanleven, 30 km south-east of the area studied in Strath Tay (Russell-White, Lowe and McCullagh 1992, 301). This site was the surviving segment of a ditched enclosure, which was being destroyed by quarrying. Inside this earthwork there were four cists, one of which included a series of carved designs.

The stone formed one of the long sides of the cist and had a series of circular motifs towards one end. It had been carved before the time of the burial because some of these designs would have been concealed by the end slab of the cist. The stone itself had been decorated by five distinct motifs, all of them circles without a central cup mark. The smallest of these was incomplete. This observation is especially important as it suggested to the excavator that the stone was being reused. The designs would have been located by the feet of the burial, an extended inhumation. The cist has a radiocarbon date of 1885–2170 BC.

This site is a recent discovery, but it has many features in common with earlier finds, extending back into the nineteenth century. There is rather similar evidence from a modern excavation at Balbirnie, 35 km away (Ritchie 1974). Here two fragments of carved stone were found during the excavation of a series of cists. These were among a number of burials inside a small stone circle which was later transformed into a cairn. One of the carved stones formed the side slab of Cist 1 and was decorated on its inner surface with cup marks and cups and rings. Again the excavator commented that it had been 'trimmed from a larger stone' (ibid, 21). There was a second decorated fragment in Cist 3, but in this case the decoration consisted entirely of cup marks. This was not one of the structural elements of the cist, but a packing stone. Cist 3 at Balbirnie contained a Food Vessel, so the burials on that site should be of about the same date as those at Loanleven.

Some readers might question the placing of the present chapter here, for they will consider northern British rock art to be entirely a Bronze Age phenomenon (Morris 1989). There are superficial attractions in this line of argument, for it is certainly true that discoveries like those just described associate panels of decorated stone with Early Bronze Age burials. But to leave the argument there is to ignore the fine print. Ever since such carvings were first recognised, during the nineteenth century, excavators have been aware of certain difficulties with this chronology. There were cases in which the motifs seemed rather weathered – this would be most unlikely if the stones were carved for use in the burial and covered over immediately. In other instances, which were more difficult to explain, the decoration had been truncated when the slab was built into the cist. Perhaps the burials indicated only a minimum age for the rock carvings (Simpson and Thawley 1972; Burgess 1990).

That was another view that was adopted too impetuously. Because many of the carvings were already old when they were reused in cists, all the northern rock art might seem to be of Neolithic date (Burgess 1990). That would certainly account for its occasional resemblance to passage-tomb motifs and for the designs that it shares with a few portable artefacts; these relationships were considered in Chapter 7. The case is perfectly logical but it is incomplete because it overlooks one vital observation. If pieces of already carved rock were built into Early Bronze Age burials in the north, this was not done haphazardly. The range of motifs found on the cist slabs is not a representative sample of the designs created on natural surfaces in the same area. Quite simply, cup marks are under-represented, whilst circular motifs occur more often in Bronze Age burials than they do in the surrounding landscape (Bradley 1992).

Having considered three examples in south-east Scotland, it is worth considering the evidence of carvings in the open air. A recently published survey in Perthshire brought to light roughly fifty sites (RCAHMS 1990 and 1994) yet three-quarters of these were decorated entirely with cup marks. That is very different from the proportion among the cist slabs of southern Scotland, about 70 per cent of which are decorated with circles or with cups and rings. The remainder include some cup marks but there are other designs as well (Morris 1981, 174–5). Those less standard motifs are also important here. The rare designs shared with passage-tomb art are over-represented in comparison with the carvings that occur on natural surfaces, whilst a few of the cist slabs include angular decoration with virtually no equivalent in the open air. Even if most of these carvings were already old when they were used in Bronze Age burials, people obviously respected the conventions according to which they had been composed.

Table 26 Rock art and Bronze Age burials in Northumberland

	Cups and rings	Cup marks only	Other designs
Carved stone in cists	12	1	3
Carved stones covering cremations	1	5	–

The cists at Loanleven and Balbirnie illustrate many of these points. At Loanleven the excavator suggested that the side slab was part of a reused menhir, whilst the cup-and-ring carving at Balbirnie may have been only a fragment from a larger decorated surface. Nor were the motifs selected at random. Those at Loanleven are quite unusual and are among the small group which seem to overlap with passage-grave art, yet the radiocarbon date excludes a Neolithic origin for the cist. It postdates the known history of passage tombs by a considerable period of time. The two decorated stones from Balbirnie reveal an interesting contrast. The more elaborate carving was reused as one of the side slabs in the cist, but the simpler cup-marked rock was not treated with the same formality and was relegated to a subsidiary role as one of the packing stones in a nearby grave. It seems as if a rather similar distinction was observed in Northumberland where nearly all the cists were embellished with circular designs. By contrast, the same area includes a number of simple cremation burials covered by a slab (Beckensall 1983). In almost every case those stones were decorated with cup marks (Table 26).

If fragments of already carved rock really were reused, it should be possible to work out their point of origin. Two new discoveries help to provide the all-important detail.

The most promising evidence comes from Greenland, close to Dumbarton, where it seems likely that the rock carvings are of two distinct phases (MacKie and Davis 1989). The older carvings, which show more signs of weathering, were truncated when some of the rock was quarried, but on the newly exposed surface there were similar motifs. These were obviously of later date and they were less eroded than the others. Although the excavator concluded that the stone was removed to build the rampart of a nearby hillfort, it seems much more likely that the carved fragments were incorporated in Early Bronze Age burials.

Similar evidence comes from Fowberry in Northumberland. In this case a much smaller outcrop is decorated with circular motifs, but it seems as if a single slab had been detached from the rock (Pl. 28). None of the existing carvings was affected, but again the newly exposed surface was decorated with a motif of exactly the same kind. This was in fresher condition than the others. Although the sequence is simpler than that at Greenland, it does have one advantage as there are a number of sites in the surrounding area where pieces of already carved stone were reused as cist slabs (Beckensall 1991). Similar evidence is lacking from the area around Dumbarton.

These are just two isolated cases and it remains to be seen whether other examples will come to light. They are important for two reasons. They supply welcome support for the idea that some of the cist slabs were taken from larger panels of

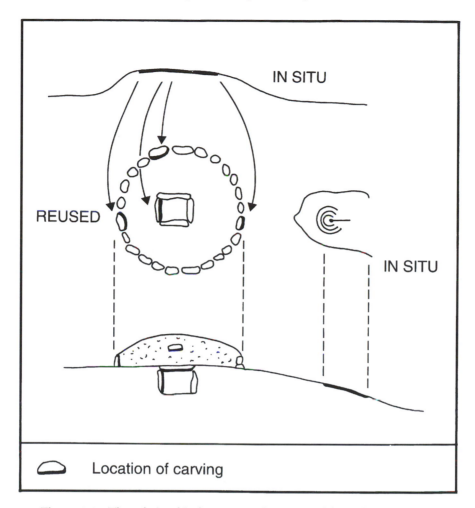

Figure 9.2 The relationship between rock art, cist slabs and burial cairns

rock art which had originally been located in the open air. At the same time, they provide vital dating evidence. In each case the outcrop continued to be carved after pieces of decorated stone had been removed. Assuming that those fragments were reused in burials, this provides a compelling argument that in northern Britain rock art was still being created during the Early Bronze Age. It is no longer possible to argue that it was exclusively Neolithic in date.

One of the objections to the view that pieces of carved rock were reused by chance is the way in which they were employed. As Ronald Morris pointed out (1989, 47), in the north these stones were almost invariably built into cists with the decorated surface on the inside. Where more than one surface had been carved, the more complex motifs were those within the cist. In the same way, where the covering slab had been decorated, as it was at Nether Largie, the motifs were usually located on the underside. Whatever the original setting of these designs, when they were reused they were directed towards the burial (Fig. 9.2; Bradley 1992).

At Loanleven the carving was located at the foot of the grave, but there are other sites where the position of the decoration within the cist may have influenced the organisation of the burial deposit so that a cremation or a ceramic vessel might be placed below the decorated stone. A further example comes from a chambered tomb at Cairnholy in Galloway (Piggott and Powell 1949, 118 and 123). In this case it seems as if the monument was reopened so that a decorated slab could be propped against the side wall of the inner chamber. In front of this stone was a deposit of Early Bronze Age pottery and cremated bone. A further decorated stone is located on the southern flank of the cairn and may be the remains of a cist slab. The surrounding area contains a whole series of rock carvings located on natural ourcrops around the upper limits of a valley (Bradley, Harding and Mathews 1993).

Not all the decorated pieces found in Early Bronze Age cairns were associated directly with the burials. There are other finds of isolated slabs of carved stone within the material of the monument. Although these have sometimes been interpreted as cist slabs, there is no support for this view. At Mount Pleasant in Yorkshire a decorated slab overlay a Beaker pot (Sockett 1971), but in most cases they occur in complete isolation. The important characteristic of these finds is that they were decorated on the underside. Where both faces of the stone carried carved motifs, it was the side with the more complex motifs that faced downwards (Bradley 1992). This is a feature that they seem to share with smaller fragments in the filling of the monument. A number of Early Bronze Age cairns have produced considerable quantities of cup-marked stones, and in north-east Yorkshire these are recorded from many locations around the edges of the moorland (Spratt ed 1993, 84–6; M. Smith 1994, 9). Others can still be found on the surface of monuments excavated in the nineteenth century. In two instances there is some evidence that, like the decorated slabs, these stones had been placed face downwards. This was certainly observed during excavation of a cairn on Weetwood Moor in Northumberland (Beckensall 1983, 119–21), and at Brotton in North Yorkshire the excavator commented that: 'eight of the stone heaps above the grave had "cup" markings, one with a "cup" both on the upper and lower surface. The "cup" was usually but not invariably downwards. If there were "cups" on more than one surface, the larger had the lower position' (Hornsby and Stanton 1917, 267). There were no diagnostic artefacts associated with this cairn, but two burials were discovered, one of them in a wooden coffin. In between these burials was a large flat stone decorated with cups and rings. Perhaps it is no surprise that the side with the carvings was placed on the old ground surface. This evidence is not unusual, for on a nearby site at Street House the position of an older post setting was marked by a packing of sandstone rubble including two cremations associated with Collared Urns and a number of cup-marked stones (Vyner 1988b).

Carved decoration also extended to the kerbs defining some of these cairns. Generally speaking, these designs were of simple cup marks and contrast with the decoration found inside the cists, but even here there are occasional anomalies. In at least two cases, at Glassonby in Cumbria and on Weetwood Moor in Northumberland (Pl. 29), it was the hidden inner surface of the kerbstone that was carved (Thornby 1902; Beckensall 1983, 119–21). At both these sites the decoration was unusually ornate, and at Glassonby it had features in common with passage-tomb art. Like many of the examples quoted in this section, these kerbstones may be reused fragments brought from other sites. Even though that cannot be proved, one common process underlies virtually all these cases. Where the rock carvings in the natural landscape often commanded a view over the surrounding area, those found inside these cairns were turned inwards towards the burial. The funeral rites required the inversion of normal procedures.

One reason for the large number of reused fragments in the cairns of northern England is that rock carvings and burial monuments tend to be found in the same areas as one another. But there are cases in which we must envisage an even closer relationship between them. At several sites in Northumberland recent fieldwork suggests that rock carvings and round cairns may have been used together to create a new component in the landscape (Bradley and Mathews in prep.), and there seems no reason why the same phenomenon should not be found elsewhere in the future.

There are cases in which cairns seem to have been constructed on top of already carved surfaces, and other sites at which the positions of the carvings may have reinforced the visual impact of the kerbstones (Fig. 9.2). It also seems likely that on certain sites the changing composition of the rock art emphasised the distinctive placing of these monuments in the landscape. The difficulty of interpreting these patterns is not because they lack clarity in the field; it is because it would only be possible to establish an unambiguous sequence through a complex programme of excavation. Until then, we can show that certain cairns had been superimposed on petroglyphs but cannot prove that those particular cairns were used for human burial. Conversely, where early excavation did find traces of a grave this work caused so much disturbance that the sequence of events can no longer be established with complete confidence (Bradley and Mathews in prep.).

There are at least three sites in Northumberland where a well-defined cairn overlies a decorated surface, and there are others where a steeply shelving rock just outside the monument was decorated, so that the motifs seem to reinforce the position of the kerb. An observer would need to stand downslope in order to view these particular carvings and this would have made the cairn appear more conspicuous. The carvings found in this setting were normally more complex than any others in the vicinity.

There is one site that combines all these features. This is a cairn at Fowberry which was excavated by Stan Beckensall (Fig. 9.3; 1983, 131–46; Bradley and Mathews in prep.). The site was located on the spine of a slight ridge with large areas of exposed rock. The monument was defined by a double wall containing a number of cup-marked stones, as well as a series of glacial erratics which had probably been chosen for their distinctive colour. The cairn also incorporated some cup-marked boulders, but many of these were displaced when it was damaged by quarrying. Even so, enough survived to allow us to interpolate the likely course

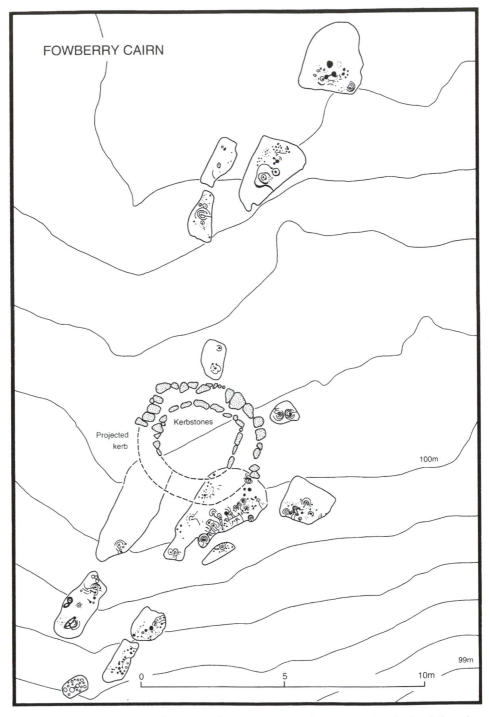

Figure 9.3 A kerb cairn and associated rock art at Fowberry, Northumberland (based on information provided by Stan Beckensall and field survey by Margaret Mathews)

of the kerbstones. This suggests that the cairn had been built on top of an outcrop decorated with a series of simple motifs: a cluster of cup marks, two of them linked by a groove, and possibly a small cup-and-ring carving. The same procedure reveals a dense distribution of more complex designs just beyond the edge of the cairn and at a rather lower level. These include cups with as many as three separate rings, a series of enclosures and a network of other lines. They would have been viewed from below the cairn, with the result that this composition would have appeared to enhance the boundary of the site. At a still broader level the cairn had been constructed towards the middle of the rock outcrop, and the changing character of the carved motifs appeared to reflect that feature. Towards either end of the ridge the carvings were relatively simple – mainly cup marks and basins – and they were at their most elaborate towards the position of the monument. It is impossible to say whether any of those carvings were created before the cairn was built. What matters is that they acted together to create a more striking effect (Bradley and Mathews in prep.).

Nearby there are other carvings that seem to reinforce some of the distinctive patterns found in northern British rock art. Only a short distance away there are two more sites, both of which have already featured in this chapter. One was a decorated outcrop from which a slab had been removed (Pl. 28), whilst the other was a cairn with a decorated kerbsone facing inwards (Pl. 29; Beckensall 1991, 37). This was also a site in which cup-marked stones were incorporated in the monument with the carved motifs on the underside. Another cairn 750 m from the site at Fowberry had been built against a decorated outcrop, and in this case the nineteenth-century excavation found evidence of a cist (I. Hewitt pers. comm.).

Many of these features form part of a series extending for some distance across Weetwood Moor (Beckensall 1991, 37–41). They have a very distinctive distribution. Complex carvings like those associated with the Fowberry cairn seem to be spaced at intervals and tend to be found in comparative isolation. The simpler motifs, on the other hand, usually occur in clusters in between these sites. There seems to have been a certain order in the way in which this area was used. Some of the larger rock surfaces were decorated with as many as five concentric circles which could be linked together in a more complex composition, whilst the simpler motifs generally consisted of cup marks and cups with only one ring. They respected the positions of the more elaborate carvings and to a large extent they avoided them. This echoes the distinctive arrangement at the Fowberry cairn which was located in the middle of a spine of carved rock with the most complex motifs close to its kerb and the simpler designs at the edges of the outcrop. It suggests that the cairn may have been built there because this was one of the focal points in a wider distribution of carvings.

This arrangement is not unique in northern England, and a rather similar pattern has been identified by Tim Laurie on Gayles Moor in North Yorkshire (pers. comm.). Here the rock carvings focus on a large unexcavated mound, which may be either a barrow or a natural moraine. There is a simple carving on top of this mound and a more complex design beside it, but the real importance of this feature is that it seems to have influenced the way in which rock carvings were organised in the surrounding area. The art is effectively 'zoned', with the more complex images at the centre of this group, whilst the simpler motifs, mainly cup marks, are located further from the mound on the edges of the distribution of carved rocks.

THE WESTERN TRADITION

There is much less to say about the western tradition of British rock art. Virtually all the carvings are of cup marks, with the result that it is very difficult to identify any significant variations in their distribution. At the same time, these images were often created on quite friable surfaces, and this has meant that they are best represented among the finds from burial monuments.

Because so few sites survive – or were created – in the open air, it is hard to tell whether the pieces found with Early Bronze Age burials were being reused. The earliest cup marks in this area may be those on the Neolithic entrance grave at Tregiffian (ApSimon 1973), a monument which was actually rebuilt during this period. There is more information from newly constructed mounds. One large slab incorporated in the inner kerb of the Tregulland barrow in Cornwall had been carved on both surfaces (Ashbee 1958, 189–93), and a cup-marked slab discovered below Simondston Cairn in south Wales had been truncated when a cist was built; again the decoration was on the inside (Fox 1937, 131–4).

Many more pieces of cup-marked stone were built into barrows in positions in which they could not have been seen. One of the cup-marked stones in the kerb of the round barrow at Crick would have been invisible once the mound was built (Savory 1940, 177–9), and the same applies to pieces incorporated in the kerbs of Early Bronze Age monuments in Cornwall, including those at Tregulland and Treligga (Ashbee 1958, 178; Christie 1985, 74–83). At Tregulland the excavator believed that one of the carved stones had originally been located over the central grave, and at Treligga Site 2 another loose fragment was found inside a burial cist. Where these sites were originally built as ring cairns, carved stones are commonly located within the material of the enclosure and others are found inside the monument itself. At Titchbarrow, also in Cornwall, a group of cupped and perforated stones were distributed outside the kerb of a round barrow (Trudgian 1976).

The dating evidence from these sites is limited but entirely consistent. Several of these monuments are associated with finds of Early Bronze Age Food Vessels, whilst Crick round barrow, which did not include any pottery, covered a grave containing a plano-convex knife which should be of similar date. A cup-marked stone from the cairn at Chysauster was associated with an amber bead (Christie 1986, 93), whilst the latest of these finds is probably from Treligga Site 2 which produced ceramics in the Trevisker style (Christie 1985, 82). This suggests that the chronology of rock carvings in the south-west may extend down to the Middle Bronze Age.

There is one other context with evidence of cup-marked stones, but once again it is uncertain whether these were being reused. A number of examples come from settlement sites. Like the find from Treligga, these are associated with pottery in

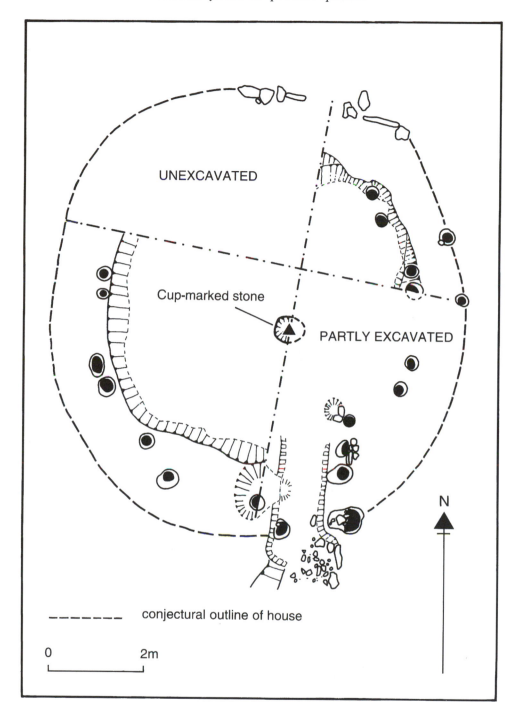

Figure 9.4 The position of the cup-marked stone in a Middle Bronze Age round house at Trethellan Farm, Newquay, Cornwall (after Nowakowski 1991)

the Trevisker style. Although the sample is small, these finds are not distributed haphazardly. Those associated with houses were sometimes deposited close to the hearth. At Nornour a stone with cup marks on the underside was located in this position inside House 9 (Butcher 1978, 94), whilst at Trethellan Farm a similar object was found in a pit near the central hearth of another house of Middle Bronze Age date (Fig. 9.4; Nowakowski 1991, 155). Further examples were found just outside the door of a building at Carn, and in a coastal midden at Lawrence's Brow belonging to the same period (Ashbee 1974, 155 and 166). Still more striking were two further finds from Trethellan Farm, each of which was deposited in a complex feature located outside the domestic buildings. These features are described by the excavator as 'ritual hollows' and were characterised by a series of pits, hearth bases and deposits rich in pottery, animal bones and organic material. These separate components were regularly renewed, and it seems unlikely that the decorated stones came to be there by accident (Nowakowski 1991, 86–96). It is more probable that artefacts that had been associated with the dead during the Early Bronze Age were increasingly deposited in a domestic context.

SUMMING UP

It was during the Early Bronze Age that important changes began to take place in the British landscape, although it was only in the following period that their effects were felt at all widely.

In southern England there is evidence for the start of cultivation close to older monuments beginning in the Early Bronze Age (Evans 1990), and in the Middle Bronze Age this was followed by the creation of field systems and by the appearance of enclosed settlements (Barrett, Bradley and Green 1991, chapter 5). The first land divisions were probably created soon afterwards (Bradley, Entwistle and Raymond 1994). In the north, the position is more confusing, but it seems possible that parts of the uplands witnessed small-scale agricultural activity during the Early Bronze Age. This would be consistent with the results of pollen analysis, and it may have been during this period that groups of houses were first established on the higher ground, accompanied by small field plots and clearance cairns. In every case the chronological evidence is limited, and at present there is a tendency to assume that the uplands became unsuitable for sustained exploitation during later periods (Burgess 1992). The argument depends on an environmental reconstruction which has been disputed (Grattan and Gilbertson 1994), and at the moment the clearest evidence from environmental archaeology comes from later phases of the Bronze Age (Wilson 1983; Fenton-Thomas 1992).

Funerary monuments also changed their character. In lowland Britain the Early Bronze Age saw the establishment of extensive barrow cemeteries, where a variety of different kinds of mound were built. These extended across large areas of the landscape and sometimes developed into great monument complexes in their own right. Far from representing a 'single grave' tradition, as is sometimes supposed, many of the individual barrows contained a whole sequence of burials, associated with a variety of different ways of treating the corpse and with a wide range of distinctive artefacts. John Barrett has suggested that this reflects a growing interest in classifying the dead (1990 and 1994, chapters 5–6). Such practices may have been connected with the growing importance of inheritance. Certainly it seems as if entire genealogies might be mapped by the careful placing of the mounds within these cemeteries and by the subtle ways in which successive burials were located in relation to those that were already there. These processes resulted in an elaborate topography of the dead in which social relations could be expressed by a highly structured use of space. Barrett suggests that it was in this identification between people and places that the organisation of the later prehistoric landscape had its roots (Barrett, Bradley and Green 1991, chapter 4).

If so, this is probably reflected in the changing location of the cemeteries. During the Early Bronze Age they had often been placed well away from the areas which provide the most convincing evidence of domestic occupation. In most regions of the British Isles, the mounds tended to cluster around the ceremonial monuments of earlier periods. In the Middle Bronze Age there was a significant change. In southern England the barrows became less conspicuous and now the dead were often buried just outside the settlement and its fields; their remains were deposited in clusters, some of them outside the mound altogether, and the link with the settlement area was made even more explicit by the practice of depositing the ashes in domestic pots (ibid, chapter 5). It is not clear whether a similar sequence took place in the north, but there certainly seems to have been a parallel development towards the creation of less conspicuous monuments, interpreted as cremation cemeteries. It is too soon to say where these were located in relation to settlement sites.

It seems possible that the changing use of rock art reflects something of those developments. It does so in two ways. First, it reflects a more general process by which elements from the past were appropriated by later generations. Just as timber circles could be replaced in stone, or barrow cemeteries developed around the earthworks of older monuments, the remains of existing rock carvings were pressed into service in a largely new social setting. Their symbolic significance was narrowed down to an emphasis on the dead. That link is made even more explicit by the rare depictions of metalwork that evoke the deposits of artefacts which are such a feature of the Early Bronze Age. In Wessex the carvings of daggers may refer to the artefacts buried with known individuals. Second, the reuse of rock art forges an increasingly direct link between particular people and particular places in the landscape. Fragments of carved rock were taken from locations with a well-established significance and they were reused in a completely different setting. Images that had once dominated tracts of the upland landscape were directed exclusively to the corpse. The conventions that applied in the world of the living were reversed by the fact of death.

These changes went even further. Not only were relics of particular places brought to the burial rite; sometimes the mound or cairn was erected in a place whose significance had already been established through the presence of rock carvings. At some sites in northern England this link was reinforced by the creation of further images on or outside the kerbstones. Again these practices established a closer identification between the significance of particular people in Early Bronze Age society and the importance of particular places in the terrain. Without that identification it would have been difficult to contemplate any significant changes of settlement and land use.

The evidence from the Later Bronze Age shows that such changes were effected, and for the most part they happened in a landscape where rock art no longer had any role to play. As we saw in Chapter 4, these developments sometimes resulted in the casual destruction of carvings that had fulfilled an important role in earlier periods. But the evidence from Cornwall suggests that the transition was not always quite so abrupt. This is another region in which carved stones seem to have played a significant role, both in the prehistoric landscape and in the burial rite. As we have seen, that role is most clearly evidenced at Early Bronze Age barrows. But just as there was a gradual shift in the siting of cemeteries, from prominent positions in the landscape to locations near to the settlement, symbols that had been associated with earlier funeral rites were transferred to a domestic setting. Here they might be deposited among the houses. The discovery of cup-marked stones beside the hearths in these buildings symbolises a much wider development. Ritual life and the everyday world had always been intimately linked. Now they were transformed.

CHAPTER TEN

IMAGINARY LANDSCAPES

—— •◦• ——

The title is not original. It was first used by the painter Paul Klee and recently it has been employed by the English composer Harrison Birtwistle to describe a number of his works. Among these is an orchestral piece, 'Silbury Air', whose character encapsulates many of the issues that have been considered here. This composition takes its name from Silbury Hill, one of the greatest monuments in prehistoric Europe, but it is not an evocation in the English pastoral tradition. In an interview the composer has said that he was attracted by the difficulty of coming to terms with its hidden structure; he was interested in the distinctive form of this monument (Hall 1984, 107–10). There is a concealed structure within the music too. Birtwistle expressed his conception in this way: 'I'm intrigued by games, where you can watch, not knowing the rules, but can see there is definite order nonetheless' (*Guardian*, 3 September 1992). That provides an analogy for how that piece of music works, and it is also our experience in contemplating prehistoric rock art.

This chapter is not so much a summary of the previous discussion as a series of reflections on its broader implications. It is not possible to recover the original meaning of these designs, but I have identified some of the hidden structures that governed its creation and its use. That allows me to ask a different question now. We may be able to describe the ways in which the material is organised, but what kind of phenomenon is it?

It is important to emphasise the connecting links between the separate studies provided in this section of the book. They can easily be misunderstood, for at first sight the argument seems to move between different theoretical positions, starting with a functionalist approach to the location of rock art and only later coming to terms with its symbolic dimension. At one point I commented on the distribution of prehistoric rock carvings in areas where the opportunities for settlement might have been curtailed. At another, I suggested that the placing of petroglyphs in the natural landscape might have been influenced by the organisation of the carved surfaces found in Irish tombs, and even by a more general 'circular' perception of the world. Is there a contradiction here?

I suggest that any contradiction is more apparent than real. The argument began rather cautiously, starting with easily tested propositions about the placing of carvings in relation to natural features. It ended with more speculative ideas about the relations between these sites and ritual monuments in the landscape, but from the outset its effect was intended to be cumulative. In this respect its structure is not unlike that of Australian rock art, which has several overlapping levels of significance. These do not cancel one another out, for they exist simultaneously. No one composition has a single meaning, so that even the most sacred designs may be found in places which are also important sources of food. Much depends on the contexts in which different people encounter them and on how much information they are allowed to know (Layton 1991; Morphy 1991). The more complex rock carvings in Britain might have been placed on the outer edges of the landscape because they marked a boundary. If so, then one interpretation is that they were addressed to strangers entering the area from outside. Another possibility is that these were special locations, set apart from the settlement area, where access could be restricted to certain people. As the motifs may have carried more than one level of meaning, both ideas may have something to commend them.

At the same time, the argument had a chronological component, although this is not to deny that the dating evidence leaves much to be desired. The origins of this style of rock art still remain obscure, and its relationship to the decoration found in megalithic tombs allows more than one possible sequence. Even so, two observations do seem to be securely based. A number of motifs that are shared with Irish passage graves occur on portable artefacts in contexts which are later than any of the decorated tombs; rock carvings with the same designs could have had just as long a history. Secondly, where carved stones were reused in Early Bronze Age burials, the choice of motifs was influenced by conventions that were already well established. That is why there seems no reason to suppose that the use of rock art was particularly short-lived. If that is true, then another implication follows. Just as those motifs may have changed their associations from one context to another, they may well have changed their meanings too. Such problems can only be addressed by taking a flexible approach.

Because the argument was intended to be cumulative, the text goes well beyond the functionalism of Chapters 5 and 6, but it does so, not by enumerating contradictory instances, but by identifying additional layers of significance in this material. The result is not to make the rock art less accessible. Far from obscuring the petroglyphs beneath a weight of commentary, it allows their distinctive character to emerge.

To say that British or Irish rock art was both sacred and secular is merely to perpetuate a division of experience found in contemporary society. That distinction would have been incomprehensible in prehistory. Motifs which had their closest counterparts on the walls of megalithic tombs might also be found around the limits of the settled landscape. The same designs could be shared between houses and tombs, and between stone circles and natural outcrops. Although open-air rock art may have coexisted with the art of the passage graves, its significance seems to have flowed from one medium into the other. One way of recasting the arguments in Chapters 5 and 6 is to say that, whilst rock art probably played a role in the definition of territory, it did so by investing certain key points in that territory with an added significance: a significance that could be understood through the use of similar motifs in monuments. Sognes (1994) has recently suggested that Norwegian rock carvings helped to define resources by imbuing them with special qualities, and Tacon (1994) has taken a similar approach to Australian art, arguing that painting and carving are among the ways in which a landscape can be 'socialised'. In Britain and Ireland too, the landscape was brought under control as its features were drawn into the ritual life of the community. As Mircea Eliade has commented, 'when possession is taken of a territory – that is, when its exploitation begins – rites are performed that symbolically repeat the act of Creation; the uncultivated zone is first "cosmicized", then inhabited' (1989, 9–10).

That is not to say that the process of carving natural surfaces imbued them with an entirely new importance in relation to the supernatural. The designs often utilise existing features of the rock that we know to be of geological origin. Basins that are the result of natural weathering were sometimes surrounded by rings, and cracks or grooves in the surface of the stone could be enlarged by pecking. On one site at Whitehill near to Glasgow the carvings are difficult to distinguish from the natural ripples on the same surface, and this may explain the choice of this particular rock for embellishment. In the past people may have believed that such features were the remains of older carvings, or these may have been aspects of the rock whose power had to be renewed. In either case the importance of such places may transcend the generations. Tacon emphasises the importance of stone as a medium for marking places, for it 'is associated with a sense of permanency. . . . It outlasts individuals and generations in a way that wood, bone or more fragile substances . . . never can' (1994, 126). If the significance of certain rocks was already established, the process of carving them made this process still more explicit. It may have done so by specifying their importance more precisely or it may have made it plain to an outside observer. In either case features of the existing landscape may have come under closer control as their significance was appropriated by particular people. The process is rather similar to the naming of places (Tilley 1994, 18–19).

Yet the carvings were never identical, even when they deployed a similar vocabulary of motifs. Nor were their locations. At one level they varied according to the physical properties of the rock – its size, its elevation, its visibility in the landscape – yet the organisation of the images on the decorated surface may also echo the organisation of communities in the surrounding area. The petroglyphs may not have been self-sufficient. They would have provided more information if they could be consulted in sequence, or if their contents could be compared with one another (Tilley 1994, chapters 1 and 2). This may explain the important relationship between paths and the locations of the rock art. At one level the practice of 'reading' these images in a prescribed sequence would have been rather like reading a narrative, and it is not inconceivable that some were intended to work in just this way (ibid, 32–3). But because these images marked stages in a journey that might have been followed many times, they would also have provided a reference point for more personal recollections: the narrative could have been one that was composed by the reader. The accumulation of images on the rocks was the accumulation of history itself, and an experienced observer might be able to interpret the way in which the passage of time had affected each composition. As we saw in Chapters

7, 8 and 9, the clearest sequences of carvings are found on the approach to specialised monuments, such as the henges of north Northumberland or the burial cairns in the same area.

In that particular region we also saw how the major carvings were intervisible over long distances, so that anyone approaching the henges of the Milfield basin might have moved between these images in a set order. Each site commanded a view extending as far as the next group of carvings. At that point the vista changed and yet another station along the route might appear in the distance. Such patterns can only make sense in terms of movement, but the petroglyphs themselves were more than signposts marking a path across unfamiliar terrain. They helped to determine the acceptable manner in which places were to be approached and understood – there is a precise analogy in the avenues leading towards monuments like Avebury and Stonehenge. At the same time, where the distribution of rock carvings extended along paths, these images would not only have established the relationships between different places in the landscape, they would also have influenced the relationships between the people who crossed those areas. As we saw in Chapter 8, that may be echoed in the organisation of the motifs on some of the carved surfaces.

At another level the existence of so many circular designs provides a theme that binds the rock carvings to the monuments and the monuments to the landscape as a whole. It is not just that these devices are shared between different contexts, the very form of the monuments expresses a similar conception of space. The setting of those monuments is also relevant to this point, for they were built in lowlying positions overlooked by a wide horizon. By its very simplicity a cup and ring, breached by a radial line, could mean many different things, and those meanings might well have changed during the currency of British and Irish rock art. Thus it could have reflected the tunnel imagery experienced in states of altered consciousness and might also symbolise the characteristic ground plan of a passage tomb. In a later phase the same motif might signify the organisation of a henge or a setting of monoliths. It could also stand for a 'circular' perception of space that referred to the landscape extending out from those sites. Alternatively, we could think of the monuments themselves as an embodiment of the wider world, as a metaphor for that landscape and a model of the cosmos. If so, then each of the carvings concentrated those same ideas into an image that could be deployed in many different settings.

Perhaps these arguments have been enough to show the potential of detailed studies of the topography of prehistoric rock art in Britain and Ireland. Not only have they suggested that there were certain common features which united the rock carvings in quite different areas, they have also exposed the emptiness of any attempt to distinguish between their role in practical affairs and their involvement in the transmission of more specialised knowledge. When such images were no longer created or maintained, more was at stake than a change in the pattern of settlement. The reorganisation of the landscape of the Later Bronze Age and Iron Age must have involved a fundamentally new conception of the relationship between people and the world.

It may be satisfying to have reduced so much material to a semblance of order, but these schemes have still to prove their usefulness over a wider area. As we saw in Chapter 3, the rock art of Britain and Ireland may form part of an international phenomenon. Whatever the superficial similarities between the rock carvings in different areas of Atlantic Europe, these links will only be of lasting interest if they can be investigated in the same ways. That is my objective in the final section of this book.

PART III

ROCK ART AND THE LANDSCAPE OF ATLANTIC EUROPE

——— ·•· ———

Still south we steered day after day
And only water lay around
As if the land had stolen away
Or sprawled upon the ocean ground . . . .
Sometimes in utter wonder lost
That loneliness like this could be
We stood and stared until almost
We saw no longer sky or sea . . . .
What thoughts came then! Sometimes it seemed
We long had passed the living by
On other seas and only dreamed
This sea, this journey and this sky.

from Edwin Muir (1946) 'The Voyage'

CHAPTER ELEVEN

IN COMPARISON
Rock art and the prehistoric landscape from Brittany to Portugal

— ·◆· —

INTRODUCTION

When Eóin MacWhite (1946) defined the characteristics of Atlantic rock art, he compared the various motifs found in different areas. That approach still commands considerable support today. Megalithic art is often analysed through the distribution of a range of distinctive designs, and some authors classify the images found in prehistoric petroglyphs across wide areas of Europe. Van Hoek, for example, has divided a single element – the rosette – into sixty-one distinct variants, extending from Scotland and Ireland into north-west Spain (1990).

This approach is very similar to the methods used to study portable artefacts. These are subdivided into different types on the basis of style and chronology and their distributions are mapped as evidence of cultural contacts, so that the drawings of weapons in prehistoric rock art are treated in exactly the same way as the objects that they depict. The end product is similar too, for in each case the process results in the identification of regional traditions.

Sometimes these studies pay more attention to the fine detail of the carvings. For example, they may seek to compile chronologies, using the evidence of those sites where different motifs overlap. Anati (1964) took this approach to Galician rock art, but his interpretation was too imaginative and has not been received with any enthusiasm. Other studies consider the pattern of association between the different designs, and these have been more productive. Sometimes the two methods converge, for different images may have been superimposed because those who created them intended to link different design elements with one another. As we saw in Chapter 4, a good example is the connection between circles and drawings of animals in Galician rock art. Again we can compare such studies with traditional approaches to material culture, where different kinds of artefact are organised in terms of their stratigraphy and associations.

Such approaches have often played a useful role in rock art research, but they have their limitations. Individual motifs are not really comparable with portable artefacts for they are normally combined with one another to create a decorated surface. Their 'association', therefore, follows certain rules and it may be more productive to compare different sites at this level: even when the same motifs were used, were they combined according to a similar logic? Nor is it particularly helpful to think of the carved surface as an 'assemblage' of design elements, similar to the contents of burials or hoards. It seems much more likely that the organisation and content of the carvings were related to their position in the landscape; similarly, the character of any one rock carving may have been influenced by the presence of other carvings in the vicinity. Whilst votive offerings do seem to change their composition according to the local environment – weapons, for example, are commonly deposited in water (Bradley 1990) – other groups of associated artefacts show less sensitivity to place. For that reason it is particularly misleading to compare the distribution of portable objects, which may have entered the archaeological record for many different reasons, with the distribution of petroglyphs which were purposefully located and only rarely moved from their original position.

In Part II of this book I began to explore the approach that I am advocating here. In Chapters 5 to 8 I sought to show how the character of British and Irish rock carvings changed according to their situation in relation to settlement areas, paths, monuments and natural landforms. In Chapter 8 I also argued that the layout of the carved surfaces showed still more local variation according to the ways in which people may have organised their use of the surrounding area. The patterns of association and distribution which have provided a focus for research were clearly influenced by the different roles that rock art played in the prehistoric landscape.

It remains to extend this approach to a wider region. My reason for considering MacWhite's contribution to rock art studies is that here is a case in which these different methods can be compared directly with one another. In Chapters 2 to 4 I argued that there were certain broad similarities in the pattern of settlement in different parts of Atlantic Europe and that those regions were apparently in contact with one another during the period in which the rock carvings were created. If that is true, it should be worth examining the petroglyphs of continental Europe along similar lines to my studies of sites in Britain and Ireland. This approach has two main objectives. First, it should shed additional light on the usefulness of integrating studies of petroglyphs with an investigation of the prehistoric landscape. And, second, by comparing the role played by a single 'style' of rock art in quite different patterns of settlement it could also help us to understand the character and significance of contacts along the coastline of western Europe. My objective is not to offer a single interpretation of the ancient landscape, but to assess the plausibility of my interpretation of British and Irish rock art by comparing it with what is known about the archaeology of other areas. As we shall see, this is not easy to achieve, and much of what follows results from a programme of fieldwork very similar to that undertaken in England and Scotland.

IN THE SOUTH

I have already considered the composition of Atlantic rock art from Brittany in the north as far as the Spanish/Portuguese border to the south. Not surprisingly,

Figure 11.1 Map of Atlantic Europe showing the areas with rock art discussed in the text

it has been most thoroughly researched in those areas where it includes the widest range of motifs. Less work has been carried out where the images consist of simple cup marks (Fig. 11.1). It is also true that in continental Europe more attention is paid to decorated tombs than to rock carvings in the open air. Understandably, the decoration associated with megalithic monuments has attracted far more attention than the rather intractable evidence of the other sites.

This is unfortunate as there are already indications that the full range of variation may have been underestimated. In Brittany, for instance, there are cup-marked rocks very much like those in western Britain (Briard 1984), and in Finistère these are commonly associated with Early Bronze Age cists and burial cairns (De Chatellier 1907; Burgess 1990). They may not reflect the entire repertoire of motifs, for once again circular designs have occasionally been noted (Gauthier 1939). Indeed, one Breton site has been compared directly with Roughting Linn in northeast England (Masille 1927) and a similar site has recently been identified at Sotteville-sur-Mer in Normandy (J. Briard pers. comm.). The same applies in northern Spain, where circular motifs, much like those in Britain and Ireland, are found in Leon, Castille, Cantabria, Salamanca and Zamora (Martin 1983; Grande 1987; Díaz Casado 1992; Gómez 1992 and 1993). These occur together with cup marks, but they are located within the general distribution of Schematic art which extends over large parts of the Iberian peninsula. A similar situation arises in the Pyrenees, where most of the more complex images are found in the eastern part of the mountains (Abélanet 1990). Again these share elements with Schematic art, but towards the western limits of the distribution of rock carvings simple cup marks predominate. Again there are occasional records of complex circular designs (Duhourcou 1972; Abélanet 1986, chapter 5).

In such cases it is difficult to discuss the organisation of the rock art in the prehistoric landscape. Either it has not been studied in sufficient detail, or the simple character of the carved motifs makes it difficult to identify any detailed spatial patterning. Fortunately, this is not true everywhere. In southern Brittany, in Loire-Atlantique, there is a notable concentration of cup-marked rocks close to the Vilaine. These are often found on rocks along the riverbank but there are other examples in the middle of the river itself. A number of these sites are covered at high water. Briard has made the important observation that such concentrations of decorated rocks may be found in the same areas as river finds of Early Bronze Age date (1984 and 1989, 65–6). This may be another case in which the creation of these designs recorded the deposition of artefacts in the neighbourhood.

In the Pyrenees the evidence is very different, for in this case the distribution of the rock art overlaps with that of megalithic tombs (Bahn 1984, 324–31). In a number of cases the capstones of these monuments are decorated with cup marks. Both groups of sites are closely associated with traditional transhumance routes leading to the high ground. In this respect it may be significant that the tradition of marking natural places seems to have continued into the historical period when the same motifs were used for cattle brands. One of the focal points in the distribution of rock carvings is a major upland lake. Unfortunately, these patterns are most obvious towards the Mediterranean, and cup-marked rocks are more common towards the Atlantic (Abélanet 1986, chapter 5; Abélanet 1990).

The evidence from north-central Spain is no more satisfactory. As we have seen, here the cup marks and circular motifs are found within the general distribution of Schematic art, and, as in Brittany, it seems as if some of these sites may have played a particularly specialised role in the prehistoric landscape. Schematic art itself has a lengthy history and seems to have originated early in the Neolithic period, although it was still being created in the Copper Age (Ripoll 1990). It occurs both as rock carvings and as painted decoration, and is found in a wide variety of settings, from open-air rock outcrops to cliffs, caves and rock shelters (Gómez 1992). In contrast to the sites considered earlier, many of these locations are dangerous and remote, and sometimes the carvings or paintings appear to have been hidden from view. The designs found at these sites have a very distinctive character and include a number of motifs that may have originated in entoptic imagery. They include dancing figures, hunting scenes and deer with exaggerated antlers, but there are also drawings of occuli (images resembling a pair of eyes), suns or stars, strange composite animals and human figures with flames or plumes radiating from their hair. Because these specialised images are found in such remote locations the sites have often been interpreted as sanctuaries (Grande 1987). A striking example is the rock fissure known as Cueva da Santa Cruz which had no fewer than 1,200 cup marks carved into its floor (Gómez 1993, 210). Like these sites, the open-air rock carvings found in Castille and Leon include drawings of animals, some of which are strikingly similar to those in Galicia (Martin 1983). A recent study of these sites by Gómez (1993) has a familiar ring. They may be found in valleys, passes, and in marginal areas that would be most suitable as grazing land. In such harsh conditions it is not surprising that he also observes that they are found near to water.

That also applies to the distinctive art of the Tagus valley in Portugal, which contains an equally idiosyncratic mixture of circular designs and drawings of animals (Baptista, Martins and Serrão 1978; Baptista 1981; Gomes 1990). Again these sites are located within the wider distribution of Schematic art. Rather like the rock carvings of the Vilaine in Brittany, these designs were carved on exposed rocks close to the water's edge. They have a most distinctive repertoire in which human figures and drawings of deer feature especially prominently. The animals are generally drawn in profile, but their bodies are subdivided as if to depict their internal organs. The more abstract motifs consist of circles, cup marks and spirals. They are not unlike those found in Atlantic rock art, but the style in which the human beings were depicted is similar to that of Schematic art. The size and complexity of the drawings of animals has suggested that these sites might have been connected with the practice of shamanism, and this idea might be supported by the way in which certain of the deer seem be emerging from natural cracks in the rock; I considered other examples of this characteristic pattern in Chapter 4. Unfortunately, little work has been carried out to place these sites in their contemporary landscape, although their presence almost exclusively on the banks of a major river suggests that they may have been created in a liminal situation. Nor is it clear precisely when they were made. There are several competing chronologies for the Tagus rock art. The longest envisages the intermittent creation of petroglyphs between the Upper Palaeolithic period and the Iron Age. The short

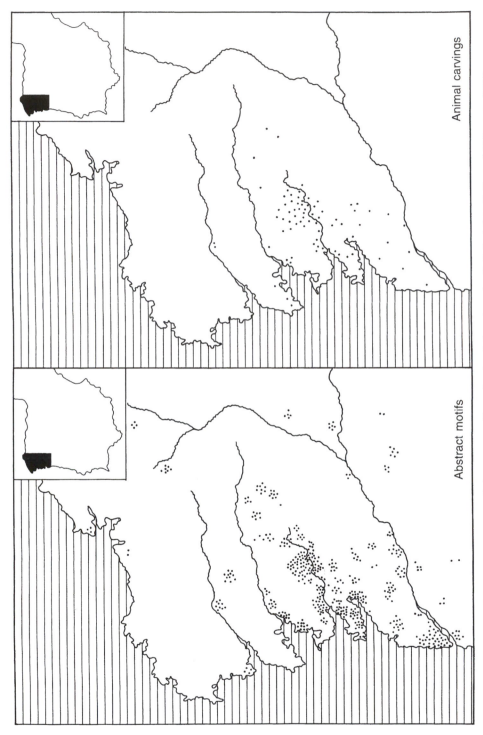

Abstract motifs

Animal carvings

Figure 11.2 The distribution of abstract motifs and animal drawings in Galicia (after Peña and Vázquez 1979)

chronology would involve an overlap with the other groups of carvings considered in this chapter (Baptista, Martins and Serrão 1978; Gomes 1990). It is hardly surprising that so little is known about the original contexts of these sites since many of them were lost when the level of the river was raised. We should be grateful that they were recorded at all. In any case the petroglyphs of the Tagus group have such a distinctive character and such a restricted distribution that they may not form an integral part of any wider tradition of rock carvings.

MacWhite was particularly concerned with the resemblance between British and Irish rock art and the petroglyphs found in the north-western part of the Iberian peninsula (1946; Beltrán 1995). Although most of these sites are in Galicia, some of the same motifs extend into northern Portugal. Further down the Atlantic coast circular motifs are less frequent and cup marks are found once again. In fact the Galician group of carvings appears strangely isolated. It is virtually confined to north-west Spain, and to the south and east its distribution is curtailed by the distribution of Schematic art (Gómez 1992). As we shall see, it is not found very widely and, apart from cup marks, the great majority of the carvings are within 60 km of the Atlantic coastline in the provinces of Pontevedra and La Coruña. The main distribution of sites extends along the coast for 120 km. The fact that their distribution is so restricted raises certain problems, for whilst the rock carvings are found on granite they do not extend across the entire area of this particular bedrock (García and Peña 1980, fig. 133). I shall return to this point in Chapter 12.

The distribution of Galician rock carvings can be divided into two groups, although they overlap to a considerable extent (Fig. 11.2). One includes a higher proportion of abstract motifs than the other, which combines the same repertoire of curvilinear designs with drawings of animals, mainly deer (Peña and Vázquez 1979). Further into the interior there is a distribution of cup-marked rocks not unlike that found in other parts of northern Spain or along the coast of Portugal (Costas and Novoa 1993). To the south, on either side of the Galician border, the motifs show a certain overlap with those found in Schematic art.

Until recently Galician rock art had been studied in a rather traditional manner. The main emphasis was on discovering and documenting the petroglyphs and on analysing these sites for their chronological and stylistic information. Thus there had been studies of the superimposition of different motifs and of their association with one another (Anati 1964 and 1968). Although these images have been drawn into discussions of prehistoric beliefs and ideology, this has usually taken place at a very general level, and has rarely considered the local setting of the sites themselves. Until recently, the rock carvings were important in local folklore (Aparicio 1989, 224–7; Vázquez Varela 1990, chapter 10) but had not assumed a significant role in studies of the prehistoric landscape.

That is not to say that the major publications overlooked this aspect of the sites entirely, but comments on their topographical setting always seem to have played a subordinate role. The best accounts of this material are by Antonio de la Peña, Javier Costas and their colleagues, who have always been aware of the distinctive siting of these images (García and Peña 1980; Costas and Novoa 1993). The least satisfactory is Anati's version which shows little sensitivity to the character of these sites and forces them into an ambitious cultural and chronological framework for which there is no justification (1968).

The Galician rock carvings are more varied than any of the others considered in this chapter, and for that reason they provide ideal material for a comparison with the rock art of Britain and Ireland. The commonest motifs are cup marks, followed in order of frequency by circles, deer, spirals and drawings of weapons (García and Peña 1980). Still rarer motifs include human figures, snakes, horses, animal tracks and idols. Approximately a fifth of the cup marks recorded in the province of Pontevedra occur in isolation, compared with just 2 per cent of the circular motifs. Among the major design elements found in that area, horses and humans do not appear on their own, and the proportion of isolated motifs is lowest among the circles (2 per cent) and spirals (4 per cent). Drawings of deer are more often associated with other motifs and only 16 per cent of these images occur in isolation. The remainder are less commonly found with other designs. Thus 21 per cent of the cup marks avoid any other motif, and among the depictions of weapons the proportion rises to 33 per cent. All but one of the drawings of snakes are found in isolation. Labyrinths and animal tracks are almost always associated with other images, and the same is true of the motifs interpreted as depictions of cylinder idols.

It is only recently that the first attempts have been made to study these designs in relation to the prehistoric landscape. This has been encouraged by several important developments. Field survey on the coastal peninsula of Morrazo, combined with the chance discovery of domestic sites, has begun to show a regular relationship between the distribution of the petroglyphs and the positions of settlements (Peña and Rey 1993). All too little is known about the character of these sites, although the associated pottery does suggest that their chronology would have overlapped with the use of the rock art. Generally speaking, they were spaced at intervals of about 2 km and the petroglyphs were located in between the occupied areas (Fig. 11.3). A number of the carved rocks were in valleys close to streams so that the settlements may have overlooked them from higher ground. In some cases these valleys might have provided the most efficient routes into the hills. Because the topography is so uneven, it may be more helpful to consider their relationship in terms of the time taken to walk between these two groups of sites. A few of the rock carvings are found within ten minutes' walk of the occupation sites, but more would have been reached in about half an hour. Others lie a little further away and may have been positioned outside or on the edges of the most intensively settled area. Further inland, a rather similar pattern has been observed in archaeological fieldwork during the construction of a gas pipeline across the main distribution of the rock carvings (Criado 1995). In this case it has been possible to predict the likely pattern of settlement before the sites had been revealed during topsoil stripping. In both areas the relationship between the two phenomena is so consistent that it helps to explain more isolated observations that had already been made in other areas.

There was rather less indication of variations in the siting of different motifs or combinations of motifs, but here again there has been some progress in recent years. It seems increasingly apparent that a rather different range of design elements

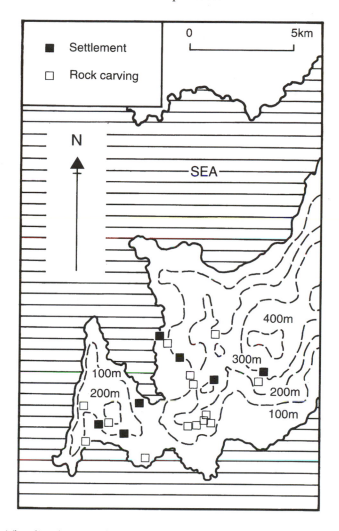

Figure 11.3 The distribution of rock carvings and settlement sites in Morrazo, Galicia
(after Peña and Rey 1993)

accompanied the settlement areas from those associated with groups of Copper
Age and Bronze Age barrows, whose distributions are sometimes accompanied by
finds of cup-marked rocks (Villoch 1995; Filgueiras and Rodriguez in press).
Although there is little overlap between Galician art and the decoration of megalithic tombs, this provides one indication that the simplest carvings may also be
related to the distribution of monuments in the landscape.

Such developments are most encouraging, for if we are to compare the results
of work in Britain and Ireland with those of rock art research in continental Europe,
the Galician material seems to offer the greatest potential. The petroglyphs are
widely distributed and well recorded, and they exhibit a considerable range of

variation. As we shall see, they are also found in a region with a varied topography and a complex ecological regime. This was perhaps the one area within the distribution of Atlantic rock art in which it seemed worthwhile to conduct similar studies to those discussed in the previous section of this book. For this reason Part III develops that framework by considering the prehistoric rock art of Galicia. It makes considerable use of the existing literature concerned with the archaeology of that area, but, in particular, it draws on the results of fieldwork in three distinct study areas conducted jointly with Felipe Criado and Ramón Fábregas (Bradley, Criado and Fábregas 1994a, 1994b, 1994c and 1995). The final section of this chapter introduces the prehistoric landscape of the study area before different aspects of the rock art and its interpretation are considered in Chapters 12 and 13.

ROCK ART AND THE MODERN LANDSCAPE OF GALICIA

Galician rock art is largely confined to the western part of the country where it is found in two contrasting areas: a series of three major peninsulas extending into the Atlantic, separated from one another by the long inlets known as rías; and a substantial tract of higher ground further to the east in between the heads of those rias and the mountains of the interior. It is in those mountains that the carvings revert to a series of simple cup marks.

Even today those areas have a very distinctive character (Alberti 1982). The most productive regions are probably the lowlying basins towards the coast. The rías are really drowned valleys, rather like Scottish lochs, and each of them supports an important fishing industry. In addition, large quantities of shellfish are collected along their shores. Intensive agriculture extends inland, principally along the river valleys. Here the soil is quite heavy and can be poorly drained, and for this reason the modern settlements avoid the valley floor and are usually located on rather higher ground.

At a still greater elevation the regime is more diverse. This is largely the result of changes in the nature of Galician agriculture since the seventeenth century. Before that time many areas were used for shifting cultivation, and in regions where the soil is affected by winter frosts this practice has continued to the present day. Despite the creation of field systems in these areas, any one plot of land may be cultivated only once every twelve years. Otherwise it provides rough grazing for cattle, sheep and horses. The warmer areas towards the southern borders of the country have seen much greater changes over the last few centuries and here the lower ground is often used more intensively. The uplands provide a supply of gorse which is cut and used as stable-bedding before it is spread on the cultivated land. An alternative tactic, favoured by rich peasant farmers, was to remove the field boundaries on the hills in order to stock more animals, and, as a result, these areas were no longer cultivated. Since the colonisation of the New World, the main crop has been maize. Although it is sometimes suggested that Galician agriculture employs a technology which has survived unchanged since the pre-Roman Iron Age, it is clear that many of the major developments, including the adoption of

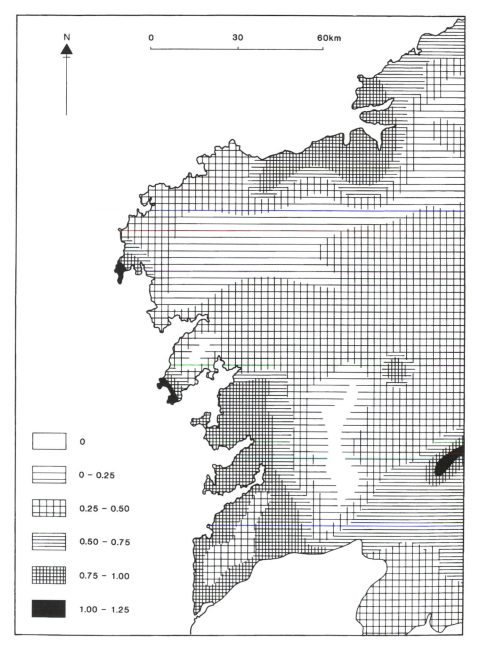

Figure 11.4 The extent of drought in Galicia during July. The lower values identify the areas with a moister climatic regime (after Carballeira et al 1983)

'Celtic' fields and raised granaries, actually took place during the post-medieval period.

Each of the peninsulas has a spine of hills which are used less intensively today and these areas are also covered with gorse and patches of heavily grazed grassland. Others have been planted with eucalyptus and pine. The same applies to the higher ground to the east of the rias, although in this case the uplands are far more extensive. On the coast, the peninsula of Barbanza has the largest extent of high ground, rising to a maximum of nearly 700 m, whilst the mountains of the inland area include an extensive plateau more than 600 m above sea level. Most of the rock carvings, however, are not much over 300 m in elevation.

These topographical differences result in major differences of ecology (Fig 11.4). Galicia can be roughly divided into three climatic zones (Carballeira et al 1983). The most favourable follows the Atlantic along the north and west coastline of the country and extends inland for between 30 and 55 km. This zone is widest over an area extending northwards for 100 km from the border with Portugal. This is precisely where the rock art is found. Most of the country has a less favourable climate, and along the eastern edge of Galicia, where the land rises to 2,000 m, conditions are especially severe. These distinctions are mirrored by the average temperatures across the course of the year. The warmest areas are along the coast and in the valley of the Rivers Miño and Sil. Again the zone with the highest average temperature includes the area with the majority of the rock carvings. Over most of the interior average temperatures are lower and they reach a minimum on the high ground near the border with Asturias, Zamora and Leon. The same geographical divisions are illustrated by potential crop production in Galicia, which is highest along the coast and in the two river valleys mentioned earlier and much lower on the high ground in the heart of the country.

On the other hand, the fertile coastal area experiences heavy rainfall in winter and drought during the summer months (ibid). This problem extends over a substantial area from the rias to the edge of the higher ground and particularly affects the south-west of Galicia where nearly all the rock art is concentrated. This produces the paradoxical situation that the very areas which are potentially the most productive are also those which can experience the most serious drought during the summer. This vitally affects the natural distribution of animals, particularly horses. Although each has an owner, they run free throughout the year, moving to the higher ground during the annual drought. They follow paths along the more shaded valleys and congregate in the shallow basins known as brañas, which are almost the only places to retain much moisture at the warmest time of year (Bradley, Criado and Fábregas 1995). They also gather in the lee of prominent rocks where they can obtain some shelter from the sun. To a smaller extent the same applies to the movement of cattle, although these do not range so extensively across the landscape. In some areas of Galicia the only breaks in the modern vegetation are created by these animals.

Does the present distribution of rock art reflect the situation in the past? One result of the expansion of rescue archaeology in Galicia has been to show that the heavier soils on the valley bottoms were not occupied before the Roman period, although some of them may have been exploited from the fortified sites known as castros, which, like the modern farms, overlook the edges of these areas (Criado ed 1991). Rather lower ground was occupied during the Late Neolithic period, but even these areas seem to have been abandoned in favour of more upland locations during the Beaker phase (ibid). After that the basic pattern of settlement remained unchanged until the first millennium BC. For this reason it seems unlikely that carved rocks were ever a significant feature of the valley floors: the present distribution of these sites should be representative of what was originally there. This is very fortunate as there has been much less clearance on the higher ground, although some areas contain networks of field walls half buried beneath the modern vegetation. Large expanses of exposed rock survive largely undamaged, including a series of distinctive granite outcrops which resemble the tors of south-west England (Pl. 30).

If the distribution of rock carvings differs from that of the castros, it does seem to reflect the areas with evidence of Early Bronze Age settlements. These are more extensively distributed than the fortified sites and generally avoid the heavier soils (ibid). The siting of the petroglyphs can also be compared with that of funerary monuments in the Galician landscape. These tend to be found on the higher ground and are often located along the paths followed by free-ranging animals to the present day (Infante, Vaquero and Criado 1992). There are major concentrations of these barrows along the principal watersheds and also where different paths converge. As all these sites have circular mounds it is rarely possible to date them without excavation. Some contain megalithic passage graves and date from the Neolithic period, whilst others were not constructed until the Early Bronze Age. Although cup-marked rocks can be found close to these monuments, they tend to lie beyond the upper limits of the more complex petroglyphs (Villoch 1995). Where the burial chambers had been decorated, often with painted designs, there is little evidence of an overlap with the contents of open-air rock art (Bueno and Balbín 1992). This does not necessarily imply a difference of age, for the two styles of art may have played quite different roles from one another.

In Galicia the open-air rock art is usually found on flat or gently sloping surfaces. As we have seen, the motifs divide into two main groups, based on the pattern of association between the different designs. The first of these is entirely abstract and includes panels of rock art which are based on the individual cup mark. These motifs may be embellished by the addition of one or more concentric rings and sometimes by a radial line. Different motifs may also be linked together and can be drawn into quite complex patterns. In addition, they may be embellished by further cup marks, either inside the circular motifs or elsewhere on the same surface.

The second group of carvings is mainly of animals. Although not all of them can be identified, it seems as if the majority show stags and hinds at different stages in their life cycle (García and Peña 1980; Costas and Novoa 1993). Occasionally they form part of hunting scenes. There are also drawings of horses, which are generally portrayed together with human figures, often riders. There are more occasional images of weapons, idols or other types of artefact.

These general patterns are crosscut by more local variations. The main concentration of animal art is on the higher ground to the east of the rías, where it is almost always accompanied by abstract designs (García and Peña 1980; Costas and

Novoa 1993). With only limited exceptions, depictions of animals are less common towards the coast, where the rock carvings consist mainly of circular motifs. These carvings exhibit another form of variation, as the same species of animals is depicted in at least two distinct styles (Soto and Rey 1994; Concheiro and Gil in press). It seems as if these were associated with different sections of the Atlantic coastline. On the peninsula of Barbanza, for example, the deer are drawn in a less naturalistic style than those found further to the south. There could be a comparable distinction around the Portuguese border where the carved surfaces show an admixture of abstract designs taken from Atlantic art and Schematic art (Costas 1984). Their proportions vary from one site to another, and there are cases in which nearby sites may be decorated in either of these styles. In northern Portugal it even seems as if motifs taken from the repertoire of Galician rock art were used in a new way. At Bouca do Colado a series of otherwise abstract motifs were linked together to portray a human figure not unlike the statues menhirs found in the same area (Baptista 1984 and 1985; Jorge and Jorge 1991).

SUMMING UP

I began this chapter with the suggestion that the best way of comparing the rock art of Britain and Ireland with the petroglyphs found in other areas was by conducting the enquiry at a very general level. It was potentially misleading to emphasise the distribution of individual motifs when it might be more informative to consider how those different motifs were articulated in the rock art of particular areas. Nor could the organisation of those compositions be divorced from their contexts in the local landscape. If the nature of prehistoric rock carvings was influenced by their position in the pattern of settlement, then the appropriate scale of comparison would be between entire landscapes.

That posed certain problems, for whilst the traditional approach to Atlantic rock art has identified certain similarities between the motifs employed in regions as far distant from one another as Ireland and Portugal, there are few areas in which we are able to consider its setting in the prehistoric landscape. Although there is promising evidence from Brittany, the Pyrenees, north-central Spain and the Tagus valley, in fact there is only one region in which all the criteria are met. As I have sought to show, Galician rock art is extensive and well recorded, and it is found in an area with a distinctive ecology and a rich archaeological record. Although landscape archaeology is a relatively recent development in north-west Spain, enough had already been achieved to indicate the potential for further work.

Having reviewed the rock art of Britain and Ireland, in the following chapters I shall consider the use of Atlantic rock art towards the opposite end of its distribution. Comparison between the use of rock carvings in these two regions may help to identify their potential for further studies of the ancient landscape.

CHAPTER TWELVE

THE CARNIVAL
OF THE ANIMALS
The distribution of Galician rock art

——— .•. ———

REGIONAL DISTRIBUTIONS

The feature that unites Atlantic rock art is the presence of circular motifs. What distinguishes Galician petroglyphs from those in Britain and Ireland is the practice of drawing animals as well. But both these areas have another characteristic in common, for they each include a variety of different designs which are unevenly distributed about the prehistoric landscape.

This account of Galician rock art takes a similar form to the earlier studies of rock carvings in the British Isles. In each case the starting point was an attempt to discuss the character of the compositions in relation to their place in the wider pattern of settlement. For this purpose we will consider the apparent complexity of different panels of rock art and will compare these sites from one part of the country to another. Once again this evidence may have light to shed on prehistoric exploitation of the landscape. But having considered the usefulness of the art as a source of information, this discussion will move one stage further, and Chapter 13 will extend that framework by considering the symbolic dimension that lies behind the creation of these images.

As we have seen, nearly all the Galician petroglyphs include complex circular motifs. The main exceptions are in those cases where cup marks are found in isolation. In Britain and Ireland, where the art is almost entirely abstract, it was necessary to consider this material in terms of a basic design grammar which distinguished the simpler panels of carved rock from those that were apparently more complex. In Galicia it is possible to recognise a broadly similar set of conventions at work. Peña's scale drawings of the rock carvings of Pontevedra show the familiar distinction between petroglyphs with few concentric circles and those with more elaborate motifs (García and Peña 1980). In this case some of the carvings are so fragmentary that they have had to be analysed one component at a time. This shows that just 54 per cent of the motifs with one or two concentric rings are joined to other designs. The figure rises to 81 per cent of the motifs with three or four rings and to 93 per cent of those with five or six. The figures are summarised in Table 27. There is a probability of one in a thousand that this contrast could have arisen by chance.

Table 27 The structure of prehistoric rock art in Pontevedra

Number of concentric rings:	*1 and 2*	*3 and 4*	*5 and 6*
Motifs linked to other designs	140	126	37
Motifs without links to other designs	120	29	3

Table 28 The distribution of circular motifs in two regions of Galicia

	1	*2*	*3*	*4*	*5*	*6*	*7 rings*
Pontevedra:							
Percentage of motifs	35	25	20	11	5	2	2%
Cumulative percentage	35	60	80	91	96	98	100%
Vigo:							
Percentage of motifs	52	27	15	5	0.5	0.5	–%
Cumulative percentage	52	79	94	99	99.5	100	–%

Table 29 The orientation of abstract designs in two regions of Galicia

	Easterly alignments *(0–180 degrees)*	*Westerly alignments* *(181–359 degrees)*
Pontevedra	48%	52%
Vigo	49%	51%

	Southerly alignments *(90–270 degrees)*	*Northerly alignments* *(271–89 degrees)*
Pontevedra	64%	36%
Vigo	55%	45%

At the same time, there is the tendency that I described in Chapter 3 for the motifs with most concentric rings to be connected to progressively simpler designs. This was clearly illustrated at Laxe dos Cebros, but Peña's illustrations reveal that it happens so frequently that it can be regarded as a general rule. As in Britain and Ireland, this hierarchy is reflected by the proportions in which the different motifs are represented. There is a continuous gradient from the simplest abstract designs to the most complex, but the more elaborate motifs appear progressively less often. This can be illustrated from both the basic corpora of Galician rock art, García's and Peña's study of Pontevedra (1980) and Costas' account of the sites south of the Ria de Vigo where the art is in a distinctive regional substyle (1984) (Table 28).

There is one other point of similarity with the British and Irish material, for once again the radial lines associated with the more complex motifs follow certain orientations more often than others, so that most of the motifs would have faced into the sun at different times of day. In this case the major emphasis is on the south and not the east; again the calculations consider individual motifs and are based on the published sites with detailed records (Table 29).

Unfortunately, there are certain difficulties with such schemes. Many of the abstract motifs are of kinds that would be considered as 'complex' in other parts of Europe, and in any case the 'simplest' designs are not always recorded in the field, although this is not a problem with the work of the particular authors whose results are summarised in these tables. A still more basic distinction is between carvings which are entirely abstract and those sites where the cup marks and circular motifs are supplemented by naturalistic designs. Normally, these are drawings of animals, but there are also depictions of a variety of artefacts. The usefulness of this distinction is shown by the fact that on a national scale these two groups of carvings have different distributions from one another. As we saw in Chapter 11, the abstract designs are more frequent near to the coast and drawings of animals are normally found further inland.

At the same time, it is not enough to compare the distributions of different groups of motifs. We must also consider the pattern of settlement during the period when the art was created. That is not a simple procedure. A number of occupation sites have been identified during recent fieldwork, but their true character remains elusive (Méndez 1994). There is pollen evidence to suggest the creation of more open conditions and possibly small-scale cultivation (Aira, Saa and Taboada 1988), but the structural evidence from these sites is very limited indeed. They consist of amorphous scatters of pottery and worked stone (usually quartz), and there are few identifiable structures or subsoil features. The density of artefacts is relatively low, but, to judge from the dated material, these locations seem to have been used for a long time, although not necessarily continuously. As Méndez (1994) has suggested, they may be places to which people returned over a lengthy period.

That is entirely consistent with their position in the landscape. With the exception of some of the sites on the coast, these locations seem to have had one feature in common. All are found near to the shallow basins known as brañas. These are the only areas to retain a significant amount of moisture at the warmest time of year. Many contain deposits of peat. This often began forming by the mid-Holocene, but for peat to have accumulated at all these basins would need to have been exceptionally well watered in the first place. The settlements are normally located around or alongside these brañas, and sometimes they overlook them from higher ground (Criado ed 1991; Méndez 1994). It seems likely that the inhabitants took advantage of the unusually favourable natural conditions in these places, and they may have moved from one area to another during the course of the year – we have already seen how the local climate encourages the annual migration of animals. On present evidence there is no real difference between the character of those sites found near to the coast and the settlements investigated on the higher ground. More important, there is no evidence of any enclosed settlements before the building of castros.

The rock art does not reflect the entire distribution of human activity in this part of Galicia. It seems to be closely related to the more favourable areas of the coastline and to the distribution of brañas in the hills further to the east. The petroglyphs are rarely found above 300 m, and, apart from cup-marked rocks, their distribution seldom extends into the main areas with burial mounds (Villoch 1995; Filgueiras and Rodríguez in press). The latter may have provided the main aggregation sites in the Galician landscape. The locations of these barrows are closely related to the tracks followed by free-ranging horses in the modern landscape and to the places where they can find shade and moisture in summer (Infante, Vaquero and Criado 1992; Criado, Fábregas and Vaquero 1991; Criado and Fábregas 1994). The presence of artefact scatters and rock shelters near to these monuments suggests that the full range of petroglyphs extended across only part of the area that might be visited in the course of a year (Criado ed 1991).

In Chapter 11 I argued that the distribution of rock art is not determined by geological factors. The sites were all on granite, which extends across much of the country, but it was only over a limited part of that area that any carvings were created. Instead the distribution of the rock art echoes certain general features of the Galician ecology. The main concentration of sites seems to have been near to the most productive land on the coast, and many of them are found in a restricted area where that zone is unusually extensive. Others occur around its edges, and here the most striking feature is the steep ecological gradient between the coastal area and its hinterland (Carballeira et al 1983). That region may have been unusually fertile, but it was also exposed to abrupt changes of climate and ground conditions. The same situation arises on the peninsula of Barbanza, but where similar variations are found in other parts of Galicia, the transition generally takes place over a greater distance (ibid).

The effect of these changes would have been especially marked within the restricted area that contains nearly all the rock art. The lower ground was potentially more productive than most parts of the country and for that reason it could have attracted an unusually high density of people and animals. It was also well suited to cultivation. But because of the magnitude of the changes that took place during the warmer months, the less productive uplands must have played a role in the settlement pattern, and it is here that other pressures might have been experienced. Only limited areas retained sufficient water during the annual drought and only certain parts of the landscape provided much shade at the hottest time of day (ibid; Alberti 1982; Torre, Pazo and Santos 1990). Even though there would have been large tracts of upland pasture near to the burial monuments, the intermediate area in between those cemeteries and the lower ground would have been subjected to particular pressures. They might have been concentrated in the vicinity of the brañas, where some of the settlements were established. Other critical points may have been along the paths leading through the more shaded valleys towards the main sources of water. It would have been in that intermediate zone, between the fertile lowlands and the more extensive tracts of upland pasture, that the greatest difficulties were experienced, and it was there that so much of the rock art was created.

This amounts to saying that the distribution of Galician petroglyphs cannot be explained by plotting them on soil maps. It shows a certain correlation with an unusually productive lowland area, but the equation is potentially misleading.

The density and complexity of the rock carvings is even greater towards the edges of that region, and this can only be interpreted if we take into account the ecological variations that affect those parts of the landscape every year. Such changes highlight the importance of the surrounding uplands, for those areas are capable of sustaining large numbers of animals at a time when the coast is affected by drought. Considered on a national scale, the distribution of Galician rock art was influenced less by the extent of the most productive land than it was by the magnitude of the ecological changes that might have taken place around its limits. These set the major constraints on the exploitation of resources. Galician petroglyphs appear in a region which combines an extensive area of productive lowland soils with major ecological variations during the course of the year. It is the volatile situation around the limits of the lowlands that may have been the decisive factor, so that the rock art is most abundant where the ecological gradient is steepest and is sparsely represented towards the limits of that area.

Regional patterning of this kind is consistent with the approach taken by Michael Casimir (1992). As we have seen, he argues that mobile populations are more likely to exert claims to specific territories when those areas are particularly productive and support an unusually dense population. It is under those circumstances that conflicts of interest can arise, and this process may easily result in closer controls over critical resources. In the opening chapter I argued that one way in which such claims might be exercised was by 'marking' important points in the landscape. Following a suggestion first made by Tim Ingold (1986), this process could alert mobile groups to those claims when they were unlikely to meet on a predictable basis. One such medium might have been provided by Galician rock art.

There is a further factor to consider, for in earlier chapters I have claimed that the character of British and Irish petroglyphs was influenced by the nature of the audience who would have viewed them. To some extent this was a question of numbers – there might be more information to impart where more people came into contact – but that was not the whole story. In certain circumstances designs that seem more complex to modern eyes may have had a very precise meaning in the past, whilst apparently simpler images could have carried several different levels of significance. To attempt any interpretation of the changing configuration of the rock art it is necessary to have some idea of who was intended to see it and the circumstances in which it was viewed.

LOCAL DISTRIBUTIONS

To assess any of these claims we need to consider the distribution of the petroglyphs at a larger scale and with more emphasis on the local micro-topography. Unfortunately, this raises serious problems, as landscape archaeology is a new development in Galicia. Until recently few of the petroglyphs had been recorded with these considerations in mind. There is another problem too. Because students of the local rock art have had a different agenda, some of their records are unsuited to this kind of research. They have analysed the characteristic imagery because that is what interests them, but they provide too little information about the topography of the rock itself or its setting in the local landscape. Because their main objective is to examine the designs for evidence of style and chronology, the relationships between nearby sites are of little relevance to their work. The same applies to the simpler carvings, such as cup-marked rocks, which are not recorded systematically because they have little to contribute to this kind of research.

That is not to deny that such work has its value; it simply has different objectives. But that does mean that the crucial information can only be collected by a programme of fieldwork. The remainder of this chapter summarises the principal findings of three field surveys undertaken jointly with Felipe Criado and Ramón Fábregas from 1992 to 1994. The full details of these are published elsewhere (Bradley, Criado and Fábregas 1994a, b and c and 1995).

It was essential to select study areas that could encapsulate the principal features of the rock art, and, in particular, the striking contrast between the petroglyphs on the coastline and the sites that lie further inland (Fig. 12.1). First of all, we needed to consider an area in which the art was relatively simple. The northern shoreline of the Ría de Muros was ideally suited for this purpose, since nearly all the published carvings were of abstract motifs. Our fieldwork focused on an area near to Muros itself, where we could examine two systems of valleys and basins which had already been the subject of a study by Eiroa and Rey (1984). Although that region seemed to typify the abstract carvings on the coast, there were some exceptional areas where the carvings depicted a significant proportion of animals. We chose a second study area at Rianxo where there is an exceptionally high density of these motifs, and here we were able to use the results of a new field survey by Bonilla, Parga and Torres (in press). Those carvings at Rianxo have much in common with the petroglyphs further inland, and so we selected an upland study area for comparison. Work took place in a series of valleys and basins near Campo Lameiro, where the results of earlier fieldwork were also available (García and Peña 1980; Peña 1981; Alvarez and Souto 1979; Alvarez 1986). The study area incorporated three well-known groups of carvings together with a substantial tract of ground in between them.

We can consider the information from these studies at two different levels. First, we should look at each of the areas in turn, investigating the exact relationship between the siting of the petroglyphs and the local topography. Then we can assess the similarities and differences between the rock carvings in these three regions.

The Muros study area contains two linked systems of basins and valleys on either side of a promontory (Fig. 12.2). One is a relatively narrow valley running northwards into the higher ground above San Francisco, whilst the other is a more extensive basin which runs westwards from Serres to meet it 2 km from the coast.

The San Francisco valley can be divided into two parts. Towards the sea there is a fertile basin, and this is linked by a steep-sided valley to an extensive braña with a spring (Pl. 31). The lower ground was clearly the main focus for settlement in the historical period, whilst the upper basin seems to have been used for pasture or shifting cultivation. That distinction is echoed by the evidence of the rock carvings. The edges of the San Francisco valley are marked by three of these, each of them comprising a cup mark embellished by concentric rings and a radial line.

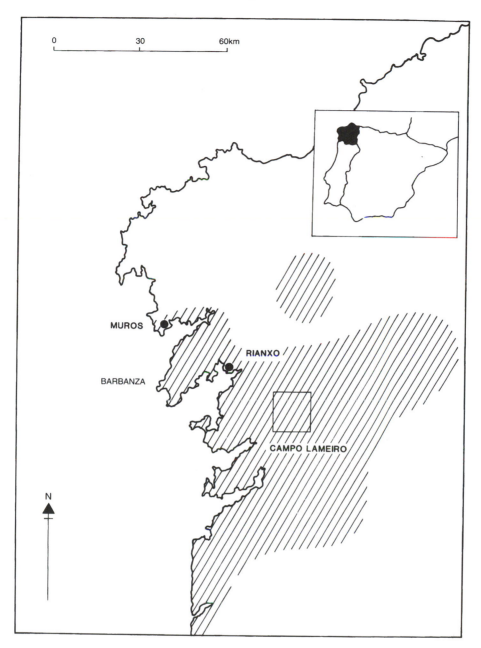

Figure 12.1 The distribution of Galician rock art and the positions of the three study areas

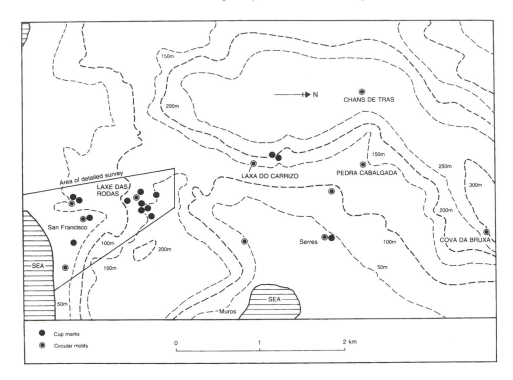

Figure 12.2 Map of the study area at Muros, showing the carved rocks
mentioned in the text

They command extensive views into the lower ground and follow the outer limits
of the area that would be suited to year-round settlement.

There are cup-marked rocks further up the slope. Again they overlook the lower
ground and one of these sites commands a view of the edge of the upland braña.
There are no carvings within the valley leading into the high ground, but around
the edges of that basin there are another eight rock carvings. Laxe das Rodas is
the pivotal point of this system (Pl. 32). It is the most complex rock carving in
this group and contains a range of circles, spirals and cup marks, as well as a
drawing of an animal (Eiroa and Rey 1984, 99–102). Although these occupy a quite
conspicuous outcrop, the rock is invisible from the low ground to the south but
can be seen everywhere in the braña, although the motifs themselves are invisible
from that area. They can only be viewed from the higher part of the rock, looking
towards the interior of the basin. There are isolated cup marks higher up the
outcrop than the circular designs, and more of these motifs occur on seven other
rocks distributed around the edges of the braña. Two decorated outcrops overlook
the heads of the valleys leading up from the coast, and another prominent rock,
bearing a single cup mark, is found where the basin merges with the valley extending
inland from Serres.

That valley is far larger and has been extensively cultivated (Pl. 33) so that many
sites could have been lost. On the other hand, it is overlooked by an extensive

plateau to the south where conditions are more suitable for fieldwork. Again the lower end of the valley is a focus for circular carvings, which command extensive views into and along the basin. In two cases these are located on prominent outcrops. The valley floor is overlooked by a complex curvilinear carving – Pedra do Carrizo – situated on the edge of the high ground (ibid, 114–15). There was just one cup-marked rock, located on the margin of the basin immediately upslope from one of the circular carvings.

Above the basin there are further sites. Two of the valleys which provide easy access to the plateau have petroglyphs on their flanks, and in each case these command extensive views in both directions. Two carvings are of cup marks and are located on quite prominent rocks, whilst a third – Pedra Cabalgada – occupies a still more conspicuous position and contains a distinctive mixture of cup marks and circular motifs (ibid, 116–18). This outcrop may well have been used as a rock shelter. Two more sites are outside the valley altogether. Chans de Tras is situated on top of the plateau and is found amidst a series of prominent outcrops beside a natural waterhole (ibid, 119–21). This area is quite moist and sheltered in summer and provides good grazing land. It is here that large numbers of horses congregate during hot weather. The second site – Cova da Bruxa – is quite different from all the rest (Formoso and Costa 1980; Eiroa and Rey 1984, 62–79). It overlooks the lower ground from a position on a steep scarp slope well outside the system of valleys and basins. It is the only rock carving to depict a large number of stags, some of them with prominent antlers. The same site includes a number of circular motifs and possibly a drawing of a dagger blade.

Thus the carvings at Muros were not distributed haphazardly and seem to have focused on two different environments, one of which would be suited to year-round occupation, whilst the other might be used less consistently. There is also some evidence that the routes leading into the higher ground might also have been marked by petroglyphs. The most important places in the landscape were apparently indicated by complex designs, and these were sometimes located on prominent outcrops. The circular carvings seem to have been overlooked by a less formal system of cup marks. At least nine of them were in conspicuous locations and for that reason they could have been added to places with an already established significance.

The other coastal study area was at Rianxo (Fig. 12.3). The main concentrations of rock carvings are found on the flanks of another basin leading into the uplands (Bonilla, Parga and Torres in press). Today the distribution of petroglyphs is divided between two groups, but this is probably the result of modern land use. The lower group of carvings is around a series of shallow valleys extending inland from the coast, whilst the other is on a low plateau. Beyond these two groups there are more isolated examples, most of which follow the shoreline to the east of the study area. Except for a few carvings on the edge of the main clusters, all these groups include drawings of animals, but beyond them the art is entirely abstract and has more in common with the petroglyphs at Muros. The one exception is found on the high ground at Leiro where a series of circular motifs is found together with depictions of halberds and daggers (Fig. 4.6; Calo and González 1980). Unlike the other sites, this carving commands an enormous view.

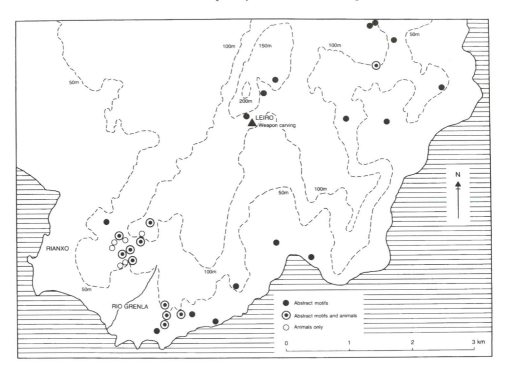

Figure 12.3 Map of the study area at Rianxo, emphasising the concentration of animal carvings

Nearly all the carvings at Rianxo are in two situations. They are either at the heads of shallow valleys or on their flanks a little below the highest ground. They seem to select rather conspicuous outcrops, and some of them enjoy views in all directions. Otherwise they command the interiors of the valleys at the expense of the surrounding area. They depict a large number of animals, mainly red deer (Pl. 34). These drawings share one predominant orientation and seem to be aligned along the contours. Because the study area is so disturbed, we cannot relate these images to long-established paths across the landscape. Otherwise there is little spatial patterning within either group of carvings. In the inland group the only depictions of weapons are on the higher ground, whilst the one site which depicts a human figure and stags with prominent antlers is the highest of them all.

The rock carvings at Rianxo were certainly located on a consistent basis. They overlook a series of sheltered valleys leading from the coast to the higher ground, and the animals are depicted moving along that axis. There are signs of spatial patterning at a broader level, for it is only in the main concentrations of petroglyphs that animals feature in the carvings at all. With just one exception, the motifs that have been recorded in the surrounding area are entirely abstract.

By contrast, Campo Lameiro is towards the centre of the inland distribution of rock art. Some of the carvings overlook a river valley which links this area to the

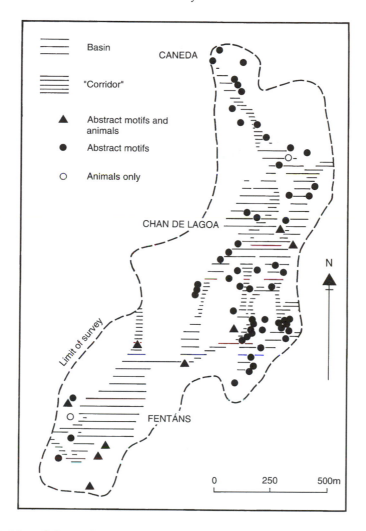

Figure 12.4 Map of the study area at Campo Lameiro emphasising the edges of the brañas and the sheltered valley routes or 'corridors' used by animals in the modern landscape

sea. The art has features in common with the carvings at Rianxo because, in addition to abstract motifs, it includes many drawings of animals (Peña, Costas and Rey 1993).

The valleys around Campo Lameiro are intensively farmed, but there is little evidence of cultivation on the higher ground, and horses move freely across the landscape. There is a series of brañas which provide excellent summer pasture, but otherwise the network of paths owes little to current patterns of land use and follows the routes along the valleys created by grazing animals. The study area (Figs 12.4 and 12.5) focused on two brañas with rock carvings, Fentáns (Pl. 35)

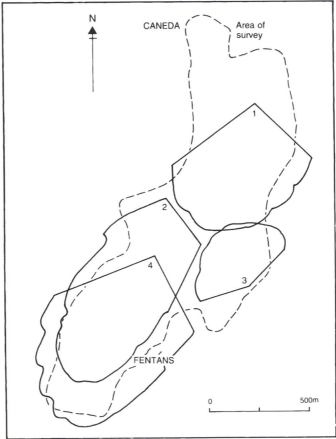

Figure 12.5 Three-dimensional sketches of the study area at Campo Lameiro showing the relationship between the siting of the petroglyphs and the routes followed by animals today

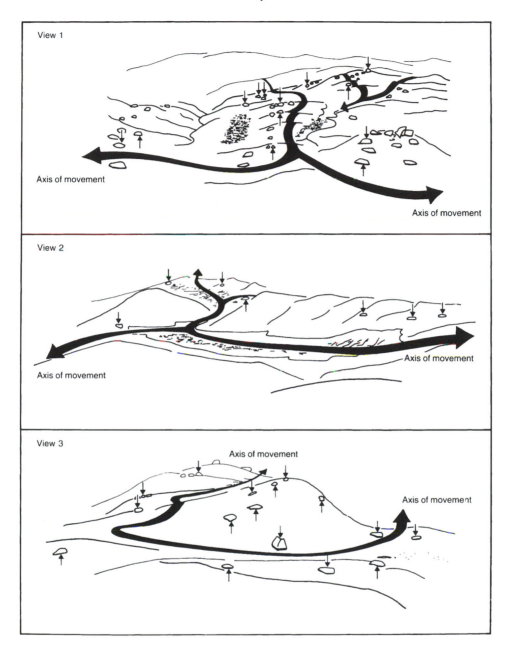

Figure 12.5 Continued

Table 30 The location of rock carvings at Campo Lameiro in relation to the edges of the brañas

	0–50 m	*51 m and above*
Rock carvings	63	5
Random sample	33	33

Table 31 The difference in height between the rock carvings at Campo Lameiro and the edges of the brañas

	0–5 m	*6 m and above*
Rock carvings	58	11
Random sample	32	33

and Chan de Lagoa and on the surrounding area and extended as far as two famous carvings of weapons, Caneda and Laxe das Ferraduras (García and Peña 1980, 30–4 and 55–7).

In contrast to Muros and Rianxo, rock carvings are extraordinarily abundant. The main concentrations are around the edges of the brañas and along the shallow valleys that communicate between them. There are few petroglyphs on the higher ground. This is confirmed by comparing the characteristics of these sites with a control sample of uncarved rocks selected by random sampling. The first test considered the distance between the rock art and the edges of both the brañas and the shallow valleys. There is only one chance in a thousand that the contrast between the two distributions could be fortuitous (Table 30).

The second test concerned the difference of elevation between the rocks in the random sample and the edges of the same basins and valleys. The contrast was significant at exactly the same level (Table 31).

The positioning of the carvings follows a consistent pattern. They are distributed along the sides of the valleys and the limits of the brañas and command views into these areas. For the most part they do not overlook the surrounding lowlands, although this would have been possible from locations only a short distance away. Few of the carvings are on particularly conspicuous rocks, although more prominent outcrops can usually be found nearby.

This may come about because the carvings are distributed along paths leading into and around these basins. The main concentrations are where the valleys provide access to the brañas or where different routes converge. The placing of the motifs on the rock surface suggests that they were intended to overlook particular parts of the landscape. At Fentáns, for example, a complex series of abstract and naturalistic carvings can only be seen by a viewer who is looking into the braña; as at Laxe das Rodas, the motifs are invisible from within that basin.

There are many drawings of horses and red deer. These are rarely found on their own, and where more than one animal is depicted on the same surface, they tend to face in one direction, as if they were crossing the landscape together. Moreover the orientation of the animals echoes the topography of the surrounding area and generally follows the same alignment as the nearby paths. As well as drawings of animals, there are numerous abstract motifs of the kind found at Muros. Generally speaking, abstract and naturalistic images occur together around the brañas, whilst purely abstract motifs are more frequent along the valleys that lead between them.

A few carvings are exceptional. These are located beyond the shallow valleys and basins and usually include a different range of motifs. There are isolated cup marks on the high ground above Caneda, but more striking are the occasional drawings of weapons and idols. The nearby sites at Paredes (García and Peña 1980, 24–7) and Laxe da Rotea do Mendo (ibid, 20–2) illustrate a further variation, for these include carvings of stags with a prominent display of antlers. Such sites can occupy conspicuous positions and overlook a considerable area of land.

Again the rock carvings adopt a consistent range of locations and seem to be closely associated with paths across the landscape. The animal carvings provide evidence that those same routes could have been important during the prehistoric period. Apart from the drawings of weapons and abnormally large stags, the petroglyphs are most densely distributed around a series of basins and shallow valleys which play an important role in the movement of horses today.

There are a number of striking similarities between our observations in these three study areas. The petroglyphs were located according to certain simple rules. They were usually placed at the mouths of productive basins, around their edges or along the flanks of the valleys that communicated between them. They were rarely located on prominent rock outcrops, and are seldom found on the highest ground in the area. They are frequently sited along the routes followed by free-ranging animals. Isolated cup marks tend to be higher up than the other motifs, and where animals are represented they normally follow a common axis which reflects the local topography.

There are two exceptions to these patterns. They are the depictions of weapons and those of outsize stags, which usually have prominent or exaggerated antlers. Both groups can be located beyond this system of valleys and basins, in places with a much more extensive view. Unlike the remaining motifs, the carvings of weapons are sometimes on steeply sloping surfaces which seem to confront the onlooker (Peña, Costas and Rey 1993).

There are also some contrasts between the study areas. On the edge of the rock art distribution at Muros there is a rather low density of petroglyphs, compared with the number of sites in the other two areas. At the same time, there seems to be a relationship between the density of petroglyphs in all three studies and the character of the rocks on which they were created. At Muros, and to some extent at Rianxo, the carvings are generally located on quite conspicuous rocks, whereas at Campo Lameiro, where petroglyphs are much more common, similar outcrops were avoided. Some of the rocks on the coastline may have had an established role in the way in which the landscape was organised.

In every case the key to the system seems to have been the sheltered, well-watered basins, and these still play a fundamental part in modern land use. They are also where settlements are being discovered. Unfortunately, we know very little about the character of these sites, and we have still to establish the nature of their subsistence economies. On the other hand, all three areas show a close relationship between the siting of the petroglyphs and the location of key resources in the landscape. All the carvings seem to be directed towards particular features of the terrain, and their siting follows a predictable pattern. That would have been essential if they had helped to define access to specific areas of the landscape in a mobile pattern of settlement.

At the same time, there is a very clear contrast between the rock art in these three areas. It is at its simplest at Muros, and more complex at Rianxo. The petroglyphs of Campo Lameiro are more complex still. That has to be explained.

Casimir (1992) suggested that mobile populations would be most likely to define their rights explicitly in areas of the landscape which are exceptionally productive but ecologically diverse. That may help to account for the overall distribution of the petroglyphs, but does it shed any light on the patterns identified at a local scale? If Galician rock art had acted as a territorial system, it ought to have a more complex structure in those areas where the greatest pressures were experienced. It is true that there are important contrasts between conditions in the foothills around Campo Lameiro and those experienced on the coast. What is perhaps less obvious is that exactly the same distinctions are found between the shoreline and the high ground of Barbanza, where the sharpest ecological gradient occurs in the area around Rianxo (Carballeira et al 1983; cf Fig. 11.4). It means that this region could have provided a focus for the migration of animals, whilst it also implies that different resources might have come under pressure at different times of year. Such local contrasts are not experienced at Muros, or anywhere else in the distribution of rock art along the coast. That may be why rock carvings are so common at Rianxo and why they have such a distinctive character.

I have chosen to present the results of these three surveys in some detail as they have been undertaken with exactly the same objectives in mind. They followed the same methodology and these surveys were undertaken with the aim of comparing the results directly. Other projects have followed a different methodology, but the basic system of rock carvings described at Muros, Rianxo and Campo Lameiro has been recognised more widely, and often during fieldwork which took place over the same period.

On the coastline the same broad patterns have been identified during a survey in Barbanza, one of the few coastal areas with a distinctive group of animal carvings (Concheiro and Gil in press). Like those described earlier, these petroglyphs seem to depict red deer moving along the paths leading into the hills. The same had been observed during a field survey close to Morana, Redondela and elsewhere at Campo Lameiro. In these areas there is a clear association between the rock carvings and the brañas, and this is repeated towards the southern limit of the distribution of Galician rock art on the coast at A Guardia (F. Criado pers. comm.).

The special importance of stags is also reflected in the results of other field projects and these are often depicted on high ground, in places that command an extensive view over the lowlands. It is not uncommon for the size of their antlers to be emphasised in these drawings. Such images have been found beside springs at Tourón (Peña 1987) and Porto do Son (Gil and Concheiro 1994). Elsewhere they overlook the heads of valleys with a different set of carvings, as they do at Paredes. The same is generally true of the drawings of weapons, and their number has increased as a result of recent fieldwork. Not only are there more of these carvings to consider, but Peña, Costas and Rey (1993) have pointed out that, like the occasional drawings of idols, these tend to favour vertical or steeply sloping rocks. This is consistent with our own observations and is quite different from the normal setting of other kinds of carving. Once again it seems as if the patterns described in the three study areas extend across a wider area.

This analysis of the distribution of Galician rock art has been conducted at two scales: the national and the local. It has been based on the distinctive ecology of Galicia and on comparisons between the organisation of the carvings in three different parts of the country. Although it seems to indicate that the petroglyphs provided a wider range of information where the audience was more varied, this approach can tell us nothing about the specific contents of these carvings. But that is not because such questions are entirely outside the limits of inference. In the following chapter I shall build on this simple outline by examining the symbolic dimension that was so important in this style of art.

CHAPTER THIRTEEN

THE MONARCH OF THE GLEN
The symbolic character of Galician rock art

———— •◆• ————

INTRODUCTION

Laxe das Ferraduras epitomises Galician rock art in the same way as Roughting Linn encapsulates many characteristics of the British sites. It is located on the edge of a steep-sided valley just outside the braña at Fentáns. It has attracted the attention of a number of scholars whose changing approaches to this site sum up many of the ways in which local petroglyphs have been studied (Anati 1964; García and Peña 1980, 55–7; Peña 1981). At the same time, its distinctive imagery raises questions which are fundamental to the interpretation of Galician rock art.

With the exception of two motifs which may be of medieval date, the rock is embellished with seven types of design: two circular devices; a series of animal hoofprints; two daggers; five human figures (four of them carrying objects of some kind); four cylinder idols; two daggers; and seven partially or wholly preserved drawings of animals (Fig. 13.1). One of these depicts a stag with a full set of antlers. Two of the idols are superimposed on one another and the outline of a third overlaps the antlers of the only stag. All the humans are portrayed by diminutive stick figures, but one seems to be touching the pommel of an enormous dagger.

The distribution of the images seems to reflect the topography of the rock (Vázquez 1995a). The circular motifs and the hoofprints are on its upper surface, whilst all the other motifs are distributed on its steeply sloping flank. The two groups of designs show virtually no areas of overlap, the only exceptions being two isolated hoofprints located on the side of the rock.

Laxe das Ferraduras featured in the first corpus of Galician rock art (Sobrino 1935), but it did not receive much attention in its own right until Anati published an analysis of the carvings in a volume of essays dedicated to the memory of the Abbé Breuil (Anati 1964). In this paper he postulated a complex sequence of images on the site. Although he quoted some evidence from other carvings, it was really on that basis that he devised a chronological scheme for Galician petroglyphs as a whole. This was later to feature in a book on the rock art of western Iberia (Anati 1968).

In Anati's view the carvings at Laxe das Ferraduras were created in four distinct phases. The oldest were the hoofprints. He considered that they were the most

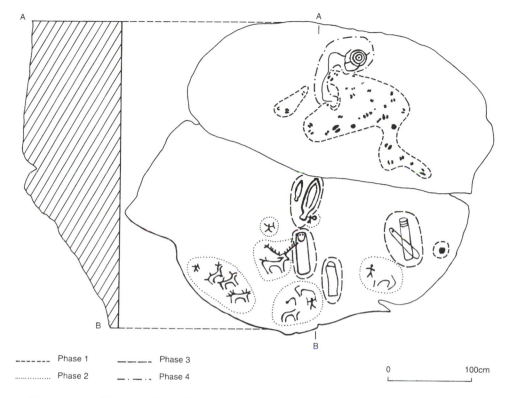

A   A

B   B

- - - - - - Phase 1   - - - - Phase 3

············ Phase 2   — · — · · Phase 4

0   100cm

Figure 13.1 The carved motifs at Laxe das Ferraduras, showing the different phases postulated by Anati (1964). Cross-section of the rock after Vázquez 1995a

eroded of the motifs and argued that they must have been created first because they adopted the most 'suitable' part of the outcrop: why this should be the case, he does not tell us. He suggested that these carvings of animal tracks could date from any time between the Upper Palaeolithic period and the Late Mesolithic.

The second phase was defined by the drawings of humans and animals which he interpreted as hunting scenes. These were earlier than the carvings of datable artefacts with which they overlap. He assigned the motifs belonging to his second phase to the Neolithic period, comparing them with elements found in Levantine art in southern Spain and with occasional animal drawings in the megalithic tombs of northern Portugal.

The third phase was defined by the drawings of daggers and idols, which, Anati argued, had been superimposed on the existing depictions of animals. These could be dated to the latest Neolithic period or to the Early Bronze Age. This estimate depended on comparing the representations of artefacts with excavated objects of the same types.

Lastly, the final phase of activity at Laxe das Ferraduras saw the carving of the circular motifs, which Anati considered to be less weathered than the other designs.

Although he allowed that these motifs may have been adopted elsewhere in Galicia during the currency of idols and daggers, he saw them as evidence of a new ideology entering the country during the Bronze Age.

There are many problems with this interpretation, and even with Anati's documentation of the motifs present on the site. Antonio de la Peña, who is responsible for a comprehensive study of the rock art of Pontevedra, has described Anati's scheme as subjective and artificial (Peña 1981). That sums up the situation admirably. There is no justification for creating an elaborate sequence on this site, and it is misleading to base any arguments on differences of weathering when the surface of the rock is so badly damaged. Some of the motifs recorded by Anati have never been seen since, and even the more reliable evidence of superimposition is very limited indeed. There is nothing to suggest that the motifs in question were carved at different times from one another. In fact superimposition is not common in Galician rock art and the evidence from Laxe das Ferraduras is quite distinctive. The drawing of the stag overlaps with that of one of the idols, but only to a very limited extent. Nearby, two cylinder idols are superimposed on one another, but for reasons that are never explained, Anati does not treat this relationship as evidence of sequence.

His arguments for a horizontal stratigraphy among the carvings at Laxe das Ferraduras are equally peculiar. He insists that the hoofprints must be the earliest motifs because they occupy the upper surface of the outcrop, but there seems no reason why we should accept his opinion that this was where the first carvings should have been made. In fact the distribution of the hoofprints centres on a cup mark with three concentric rings. Circular carvings of this kind are characteristically found on level or slightly sloping surfaces in Galicia, whilst drawings of weapons and idols are usually on rocks with a steeper incline (Peña, Costas and Rey 1993). Anati's approach is subjective, even fantastic, and, for all the confidence with which it is put forward, it is utterly insensitive to the topographical setting of the rock art. It illustrates only too well how rock carvings can be studied as if they are portable artefacts – and the limitations of that approach.

Peña (1981) has refuted Anati's claims for a lengthy sequence at Laxe das Ferraduras, but he has done more than that. In his commentary on Anati's interpretation he argued that the motifs at Laxe das Ferraduras are better treated as an integrated composition. He accepted that different motifs might be found on different parts of the rock but rejected the idea of a horizontal sequence on this site, arguing instead that the positioning of different designs might have been governed by convention. Such rules seem to have extended to other sites in Galicia. Thus drawings of animals are commonly found around the edges of panels of rock art, and curvilinear motifs are more often located towards their centre.

Peña's conclusions change the agenda entirely, for rather then dividing the decorated surface into so many separate design elements, he suggests that we should consider those compositions as a whole. In this chapter I shall follow that advice, examining different aspects of the rock art at Laxe das Ferraduras and investigating their implications for our understanding of Galician art as a whole.

THE SIGNIFICANCE OF PLACES

I would like to begin by recalling an observation that I made earlier. At Laxe das Ferraduras the animal track or tracks seem to focus on a single circular design. Indeed, some of the hoofprints seem to be restricted to one side of a carved line trailing from the edge of that motif (Fig. 13.2, C). There are very few depictions of animal tracks in Galician rock art, yet a similar arrangement is found at two of the other sites, Pedra do Outeiro da Mo (also at Fentáns) and Pedra Moura (Fig. 13.2; García and Peña 1980, 57; Costas 1984, 126–9). On the first of these the pattern is very straightforward: a single line of hoofprints leads directly to a cup-and-ring carving (Fig. 13.2, B). At Pedra dos Mouros (Fig. 13.2, A) the main axis of the carving is marked by a roughly straight line nearly 10 m in length which passes through the centre of a complex circular motif and divides the carvings into two groups. Some of the largest curvilinear motifs are restricted to one side of this line, and these include two very unusual features. In one case four concentric circles surround a motif normally found in Schematic art, and in the other a single ring surrounds an isolated hoofmark. There are also two motifs that may be human footprints; if so, they follow the same alignment. On the other side of this axis, there are at least ten more hoofmarks which share this orientation. Taken literally, they would suggest that the line running across the carved surface represented some kind of path.

The same possibility arises with many of the drawings of animals. The simplest example is probably Pedra do Lombo da Costa, the rock where a metal axe was found in a crack among the carvings (García and Peña 1980, 52–4). Again this is a site with one predominant axis, which in this case is indicated by two roughly parallel lines following the length of the carved surface amidst an array of circular designs. There are many carvings of deer or horses around the edges of this composition, but among the few convincing stags, identified by their prominent antlers, is an animal standing on one of the lines as if it depicted a ground surface. Most of the other animals, some 80 per cent of the total, share the same basic axis.

Support for this contention comes from an observation made during fieldwork at Rianxo and Campo Lameiro. In each case there were numerous drawings of animals, but these had one common characteristic. Whatever their species, the animals were viewed from the side but their outlines hardly ever overlapped. They tended to be depicted in line, as they would look if they were moving across the landscape together. With only limited exceptions, these animals followed a common orientation. That applied both to the drawings that show animals which we can identify as deer and to the much rarer representations of horses with riders. Either these horses seem to pursue the deer, or they confront them head on.

The topographical setting of these carvings is equally noteworthy, for the rocks which carry these images tend to be located beside the paths created by free-ranging animals in the landscape today. This is particularly true at Campo Lameiro. Not only do the carvings depict groups of animals crossing the landscape together; the paths that they appear to be following run in the same directions as those in the area now. Even at Rianxo, where the study area is heavily wooded, we could show that the axis of the animal carvings follows the contours and would be consistent

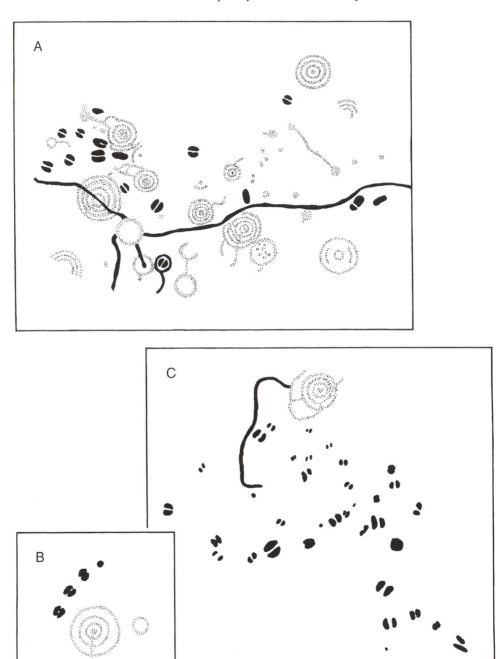

Figure 13.2 Animal tracks in Galician rock art. A: Pedra dos Mouros; B: Fentáns; C: Laxe das Ferraduras (after García and Peña 1980 and Costas 1984)

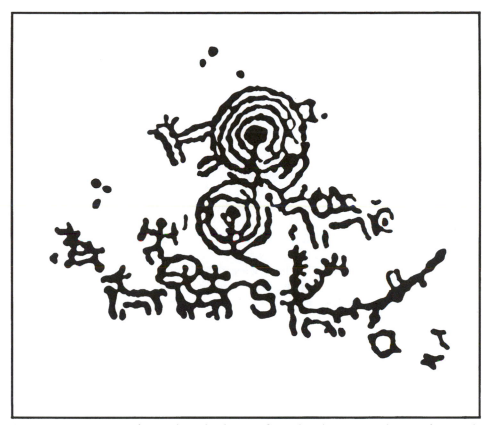

Figure 13.3 Drawings of animals and a human figure beside two circular motifs at Pedra do Pinal do Rei (after García and Peña 1980)

with the existence of routes leading between the coast and the hills. Again the carvings seem to emphasise the importance of trails, but they do so in topographical situations where the sites may have commanded real paths in prehistory (Pl. 36).

Those paths extend along the sheltered valleys leading through the higher ground, but they also extend around the edges of the brañas. That observation is most important, for there were exposed outcrops suitable for carving within those basins themselves. People must have made a deliberate decision not to use them. Instead, the carvings follow the limits of the brañas just as many of the paths do today, and the carvings of the animals seem to be laid out according to a similar axis.

In fact that over-simplifies the actual situation, as many of the drawings of animals are juxtaposed with abstract motifs. The distinctive pattern described at Pedra do Lombo da Costa is found at many other sites, although often in a simpler form. The basic arrangement is for the central area of the composition to be occupied by one or more circular motifs and for the drawings of animals to be located around their edges where they can adopt a single axis closely related to the local topography (Fig. 13.3). Where the petroglyphs were created on an uneven surface the major circular motif usually occupied the highest point. On the extraordinary site of Monte Tetón, the highest part of the rock was encircled by no fewer than sixteen concentric rings (Costas, Novoa and Albo 1991). This dominant motif was 3.5 m in diameter and its creation would have transformed the contours of the rock.

If the depictions of animal tracks suggest the importance of representing paths in Galician rock art, so do at least some of the drawings of animals. This would help to explain their distinctive siting in the landscape and might even account for the frequency with which the more complex circular motifs are linked together by a wider network of lines. More important, it seems as if the spatial relationship between the drawings of animals and the major circular motifs echoes actual features of the landscape. The animals file past the circular motifs just as the modern paths skirt the edges of the brañas, and the distribution of rock carvings follows those trails and avoids the interior of the basins. In the same way, it favours local view-points which command the interior of those brañas and ignores the higher ground which would have more extensive views. An excellent example is Laxe das Rodas (Eiroa and Rey 1984, 99–103), where we can look out across the largest circular motif and see the full extent of the basin opening at our feet.

That is not say that this evidence should be interpreted too literally. There is nowhere where we can form a precise equation between the distribution of circles and lines on a particular rock surface and the configuration of paths and basins in the surrounding area. It may be that the relationship was less literal and more metaphorical. The circular motifs could have stood for places of many different kinds – hills, trees and pools as well as basins – and, just as we saw in Britain and Ireland, they may epitomise a wider perception of the landscape that even extended to the layout of burial mounds. In the same way, the paths apparently depicted on these rocks may have been paths followed by people in the past, or by myth-ical beings whose movement across the landscape created a narrative that is lost today. These are imponderables; what matters is that the close relationship between petroglyphs and the local topography charted in Chapter 12 may have been echoed, however obliquely, in the ways in which those images were organised.

THE SIGNIFICANCE OF HUNTING

Because red deer are now extinct in Galicia, local archaeologists are more cautious in identifying these animals in the carvings than their British colleagues would be. The drawings of mature stags are quite unambiguous (Fig. 13.4), but it is not so clear how many of the other depictions of animals were intended to show hinds or young and how many were meant to represent horses. My own opinion is that

Figure 13.4 Drawings of stags in Galician rock art. A: Rotea de Mendo; B: Outeiro do Pio; C: Tourón; D: Os Carballos; E: Tourón; F: Chan de Carballeira; G: As Martizas; H: Porto do Son (after García and Peña 1980; Peña 1987; Peña, Costas and Rey 1993; and Gil and Concheiro 1994)

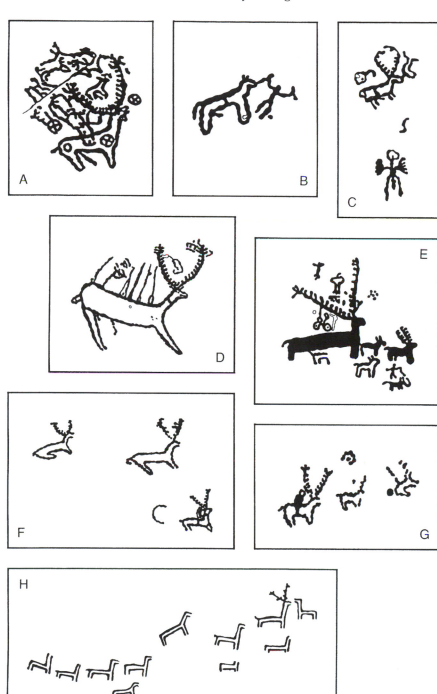

the characteristic posture of many of these animals identifies them as deer, but perhaps that is not so important, for, as we shall see, the overriding emphasis is on the stags. It is perfectly possible that those who created the carvings intended a certain ambiguity in the other cases. Whatever the answer, not many of the animals are depicted with riders (Pl. 36). It may be that few of the horses them-selves were thought of as domesticated animals.

At first sight these patterns are easy to explain. Surely this is hunters' art, empha-sising the importance of game. That would certainly account for the rather limited distribution of animal carvings, which are generally found away from the fertile coastal region, on the edges of the high ground (Peña and Vázquez 1979). It could also account for the distinctive siting of so many petroglyphs at the edges of shel-tered valleys and at the entrances to well-watered basins. We have already seen how these rocks do not command extensive views. Instead, they overlook specific areas of the landscape. They would have been well placed for observing the move-ment of animals. Some could have provided cover for anyone tracking red deer and would have been sited downwind of the animals themselves so that the people who were using those places would not have disturbed them. For the same reasons a number of these locations were well suited for ambushing game, especially if the animals were passing in the large numbers indicated by the petroglyphs.

There are some scenes that might support this interpretation (Fig. 13.4). At Laxe das Ferraduras (Fig. 13.1) two of the animals seem to have spikes sticking into their backs, very like the objects carried by the human figures in the same drawing; these artefacts could well have been spears (García and Peña 1980, fig. 61). That tentative interpretation is strengthened by a remarkable carving, Os Carballos at Paredes, which shows at least four carefully drawn spears piercing the body of a stag (Fig. 13.4, D; Peña 1985). In other cases hunting scenes could be identified by observing the relationship between the drawings of deer and those of horses with their riders. For example, at Pedra Outeiro do Cribo a figure on horseback appears to be following a small group of animals, one of which is a mature stag (García and Peña 1980, fig. 85).

Again there are obvious dangers in pursuing a literal interpretation of the rock art. If there are occasional drawings of horses with their riders, what are we to make of two other carvings which seem to show human figures riding on stags? At Chan da Carballeira three such stags are shown, all with a full set of antlers, crossing the landscape together (Fig. 13.4, F; Peña, Costas and Rey 1993, 11). One of these animals has a rider on his back and appears to have a halter around his neck (there is another around the neck of the stag at Os Carballos). Similarly, at As Martizas three animals cross the carved surface past a cup and ring (ibid, 26). Although the remains are fragmentary, the first two seem to be depicted in isola-tion but the third in line has another human figure on its back (Fig. 13.4, G). This animal is clearly a stag and again it has a full set of antlers. Without that distin-guishing characteristic it might well have been mistaken for a horse pursuing the other two animals, in which case we would interpret this composition as another hunting scene. Even if people had chosen to ride deer in preference to horses, it seems highly unlikely that they should have begun the experiment with the largest and fiercest individuals of all.

There are other anomalies that we should consider at this point. The choice of locations for carving often favoured fairly inconspicuous rocks, when more prominent outcrops were available nearby. The latter would have provided greater cover during hunting expeditions, whereas the rocks that were carved offer less opportunity for concealment. While the general location of these sites is consistent with their use in hunting, their specific location sometimes poses problems. In the Mesolithic period, when hunting was undoubtedly important, the distribution of artefacts focused on more substantial outcrops, as we see from the results of field survey at Bocelo (Criado ed 1991, chapter 4).

The contents of the drawings pose other problems, for they show such a restricted range of animals. Apart from very occasional snakes, they appear to be horses and deer, and there is no way of telling whether all the horses were considered as domesticates. In any case I would estimate that deer outnumber horses by as much as fifteen to one. There are no drawings which seem to show cattle, sheep and pigs despite the fact that they are the commonest animals among the faunal remains found at contemporary settlements in the Iberian peninsula (Harrison 1985); unfortunately, there are no comparative samples from Galicia. Nor does it seem at all probable that the uplands were employed exclusively for hunting when the settlements found there have the same character as those on more productive land. The pollen evidence raises further problems, for it suggests that there was small-scale agriculture near to some of the brañas (Aira, Saa and Taboada 1988). It is perfectly possible to combine hunting with farming, but it would be a strange economy indeed that placed its emphasis on cereal growing and ignored the potential of domestic animals in favour of the major predator that would have threatened the crops. This is particularly true if the brañas provided a focus for animal movements during the annual drought. Quite clearly, the contents of Galician rock art are very selective indeed.

This is only emphasised by a closer study of the drawings of deer. They seem to include various combinations of stags and hinds, but normally they appear in greater numbers than we would expect to encounter in a closed environment (Clutton-Brock, Guiness and Albon 1982). It seems most unlikely that they are portrayed exclusively in their role as game. Their age and sex distribution is quite different from the characteristic pattern found among the bones at hunting sites in other parts of Europe. We would usually expect an emphasis on the culling of surplus males and on the hunting of female animals who were too old to breed. This would ensure a continuous supply of meat and would guard against over-exploitation (Gamble 1986, 290–7). That is not the structure reflected in these drawings, where the females and/or young dominate many of the compositions.

In Pontevedra where I have attempted to identify the animals from the published drawings, approximately 60 per cent of them are likely to be hinds or young whilst 40 per cent can be identified as stags (the information is drawn from García and Peña 1980). Hinds or young appear with stags at approximately 44 per cent of the sites and are found on their own in a further 44 per cent of the illustrated carvings. At the remaining 12 per cent, stags are depicted in isolation. Where both sexes are shown together, the hinds and/or young animals normally predominate. That accounts for nearly 60 per cent of the petroglyphs. At another 30 per cent of the sites the proportions are roughly equal, whilst the males are apparently more common than females at the remaining 10 per cent of the rock carvings. There are severe limitations to this exercise, and these need to be stated clearly. Given the simple character of these drawings, it is not always possible to distinguish between horses and deer, nor is there a clear distinction between females and young. The latter point is of less importance as the does would remain with their mothers.

One explanation for these distinctive patterns may be that the deer are drawn at different stages in their annual cycle of movement about the landscape (Clutton-Brock, Guiness and Albon 1982; Putnam 1988). That is why less than half the carvings in Pontevedra seem to show stags and hinds together in the same locations. This is consistent with the behaviour of red deer where the mature stags occupy different parts of the landscape from the other animals for most of the year. It is only in the rutting season that their distributions overlap. This concern with illustrating the behaviour of the animals extends to occasional scenes of copulation, which are practically as common as depictions of the hunt (for a general account of the drawings of deer see Costas and Novoa 1993, 75–112).

In short the art depicts wild animals rather than domesticates but only rarely shows them being hunted and killed. It reveals a much more general interest in the life cycle of the red deer. That close identification with a single species calls for a more searching analysis.

THE SIGNIFICANCE OF STAGS

So far I have implied that the Galician rock carvings provide a rounded image of the social behaviour of the red deer, but that is not entirely true. At Laxe das Ferraduras there is a single stag with a conspicuous set of antlers which overlap with the most complex drawing of an idol. I do not consider that relationship to be fortuitous. Rather, by linking these two images, the people who created the carvings were making a deliberate point. That is even more obvious when we consider that elsewhere on the same surface two such idols were superimposed.

Another clue to the significance of stags is the presence of the human figures at Laxe das Ferraduras. These seem to have been hunting the deer. In this case they are shown in isolation, but at other sites they can be on horseback (Costas and Novoa 1993, 115–24). It is worth commenting that in nearly every instance where human beings are portrayed in Galician rock art there are stags in the same compositions (Fig. 13.4, B and C). The notable exception is Os Carballos where these figures are absent, but in this case the largest stag seems to have been pierced by a number of spears (Fig. 13.4, D; Peña 1985). At Outeiro do Pio Site 1 some of these connections are even more apparent (García and Peña 1980, fig. 109). In this drawing a human figure with what may be a spear in either hand confronts an animal which is either a stallion or a stag (Fig. 13.4, B); it is certainly identified as male by its exaggerated penis. On another site nearby a human figure is found on a small carving beside at least two other animals, one of them another stag with a conspicuous set of antlers (Peña 1987). This is not to suggest that in these drawings stags are being hunted to the exclusion of females, but given the significant number of rock carvings where hinds are depicted in isolation, it may indicate a special interest in taking the mature males.

That is not so surprising when we consider some other features of the drawings of stags. The most obvious is that their specifically male characteristics are often exaggerated. They can sport an extravagant display of antlers out of all proportion to the size of the body (Pl. 37). The penis can also be given special emphasis. Good examples are the large stags at Laxe da Rotea de Mendo (Fig. 13.4, A) and Outeiro do Cogoludo, each of which displays a fine set of antlers and has a penis which reaches almost to the ground (García and Peña 1980, figs. 8 and 11). Their posture also suggests that they are depicted in the act of bellowing. Although these features can be overemphasised in these drawings, they are less striking than a major difference in the scale at which some of the stags are depicted. Quite often the stags that share these characteristics are several times larger than any of the other animals. This even includes cases in which other stags are drawn at a smaller size.

A good example of this pattern is found at As Sombrinas, Tourón (Fig. 13.4, E; Peña 1987). The composition is a complicated one, with four major groups of abstract carvings radiating outwards from complex circular designs. Towards the edges of these clusters are at least fifteen depictions of animals, as well as a diminutive drawing of a human. Six of the animals are obviously stags and display a full set of antlers, but one of these animals is about three times the size of any of the others. Somewhat improbably, its antlers achieve the same length as its entire body. It is flanked on three sides by other drawings of animals, some of which are only a sixth of its size. In contrast to the normal method of depiction, the entire body of this stag has been carved in relief. That also applies to four of the other animals, three of which are beside this figure.

The locations of such drawings often have a feature in common. They tend to be found at a greater elevation than other petroglyphs in the vicinity and, unlike these, they may command considerable views. A good example is Cova da Bruxa above our study area at Muros (Formoso and Costa 1980). This overlooks a vast area of the surrounding landscape and is located part way up a mountainside, well beyond the characteristic pattern of paths and brañas associated with other petroglyphs in the area. Another example is found beside a spring at Porto do Son where nine deer, most probably hinds, are depicted climbing a steep hillside above the sea (Fig. 13.4, H; Pl. 38). They are led by a stag with clearly delineated antlers who confronts a tenth hind which is facing downhill (Gil and Concheiro 1994). In this case there are no other motifs on the site.

Again it is possible to link these observations with the characteristic behaviour of the red deer. I mentioned that the males and females occupy different areas for much of the year, but during the rutting season their distributions converge. It is then that the males engage in conspicuous displays and compete for dominance over the other animals. The older stags occupy the highest ground. They issue a challenge by bellowing and use their antlers to engage in combat with their rivals (Lowe 1966). Such aggressive displays may be precisely what is depicted in these drawings. The male characteristics of the stags are given special prominence, and a small number of stags, sometimes only one, are drawn at a much larger size than any of the other animals. The distinction is occasionally emphasised by the laborious procedure of depicting such animals in relief. The stags that are distinguished in this way often dominate a composition containing a significant proportion of hinds, and in certain cases the siting of these carvings on higher ground than any other petroglyphs evokes the stance adopted by the dominant males.

One of the key points in Anati's interpretation of Galician rock art was the idea that abstract motifs were a later development than the drawings of wild animals. His arguments may be flawed but the same opinions have been voiced by other scholars. For example, it is found again in discussion of the rock art in the Tagus valley (Baptista, Martins and Serrão 1978; Gomes 1990). This confusion probably arises because of a mistaken notion that wild animals, in particular red deer, lost their importance with the adoption of farming. Because they feature in Palaeolithic and Mesolithic paintings it is only too easy to suppose that hunting scenes must be among the earliest images found in other art styles (Anati 1993). This is a curiously naive perspective and, taken literally, it is flatly contradicted by the subject matter of European paintings from at least the Renaissance to the nineteenth century, among them the picture that gives this chapter its title. As the very existence of such paintings suggests, hunting scenes can be much more than illustrations of daily life.

In fact there are a number of points at which the depictions of deer in Galician rock art suggest a wider concern than the provision of meat. There seems to be an involvement in every stage in their life cycle, and where humans are portrayed as part of what may be hunting scenes they are tiny compared with some of the animals. On such sites there are nearly always drawings of stags. It is these creatures that seem to dominate the proceedings. Certain characteristics of the stags are exaggerated in these drawings and the very siting of some of the petroglyphs seems to have been influenced by the competitive displays engaged in by the dominant males.

Two small examples may help to illustrate this point. First, there are the scenes of people riding stags (Fig. 13.4, F and G). Perhaps these should be understood in terms of contests between humans and wild animals, in much the same sense as any of the hunting scenes. The second illustration is a remarkable image from Tourón (Fig. 13.4, C; Peña 1987). It shows virtually the only human figure who is depicted with a penis approaching a group of three animals, one of which is a stag with a massive set of antlers. The man has outstretched arms and, like his penis, his hands are out of proportion to the rest of his body. The fingers are widely spaced, so that the image resembles nothing so much as another stag with its antlers. This visual pun completes the identification between the man and the stag. Just as the hinds play a less conspicuous role in the rock art, the lives of women do not seem to figure in any of these drawings.

Images like that from Tourón may provide a clue to a better understanding of the art. Even if a whole range of animals, both wild and domesticated, were exploited on the higher ground, it was the deer that were assigned the greatest cultural significance, and among the deer the emphasis was most obviously on the behaviour of the older stags. These were the animals that would have presented the greatest challenge to the hunter. They also engaged in aggressive displays that might have provided a metaphor for comparable processes in human society.

This emphasis on fighting, hunting and the wild is what characterises the 'agrios' in Ian Hodder's terminology, and they are processes that assume a greater prominence in many parts of Europe during the later years of the Neolithic and the early part of the Bronze Age (Hodder 1990). The depictions of so many deer in Galician rock art may tell us little or nothing about the subsistence economy. They are primarily the expression of a distinctive ideology.

THE SIGNIFICANCE OF WEAPONS

There are two dagger carvings at Laxe das Ferraduras, located side by side towards the top of the sloping edge of the rock. One weapon, which is exactly twice the size of the other, is apparently held by a tiny human figure.

Such carvings occur throughout the distribution of Galician rock art, but they are much less frequent than the drawings of circles and animals that I have considered so far. The repertoire is very restricted. The main elements are daggers and halberds, although these are quite often found together with curious motifs interpreted either as shields or as some kind of vehicle (Costas and Novoa 1993, 157–81; Züchner 1992).

It is difficult to discuss the spatial organisation of these carvings as they can occur without the other motifs considered in this chapter. The main feature that these designs seem to share is a preference for sloping or vertical surfaces, and this makes them very different from the majority of the carvings found in Galicia. Their distinctive siting means that they may appear to confront the onlooker. Sometimes the effect can be very impressive indeed, as it is at Auga da Laxe where the principal carving includes no fewer than five halberds, eight 'shields' and nine daggers, the largest of which rises from the foot of the outcrop to a height of 2.5 m (Fig. 13.5; Costas 1984, 50–5).

Such collections of weaponry have two distinctive characteristics. Their arrangement on the rockface may show a certain formality and perhaps recalls the hoards in which similar combinations of artefacts are found. In Chapter 4 I commented on the close geographical relationship between the carvings of halberds and daggers at Leiro and the discovery of a nearby hoard containing the same types of artefact. The carvings of the daggers at O Ramallal are so closely packed together that they give the impression that these motifs might even have represented a real deposit of metalwork (Pl. 39; Peña, Costas and Rey 1993, 30).

The second characteristic of such collections is the way in which weapons seem to have been graded in terms of their importance, or perhaps the importance of their users. We have seen how one of the dagger carvings at Laxe das Ferraduras is twice the size of the other. Such basic distinctions are quite common in Galician rock art. At Auga da Laxe the one large dagger is almost exactly five times the size of the smallest example and is three times the length of some of the other weapons (Fig. 13.5). On another rock at this site two halberds are depicted side by side, and in this case one of these weapons is twice as large as its counterpart. At Castriño de Conxo exactly the same thing happens (Peña 1979), and at Dumbria, at the northern limit of Galician rock art, there are striking contrasts

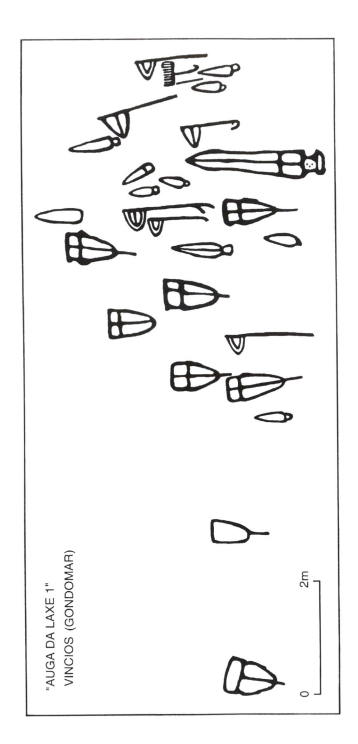

"AUGA DA LAXE 1"
VINCIOS (GONDOMAR)

0   2m

Figure 13.5 The weapon carvings at Auga da Laxe (after Costas 1984)

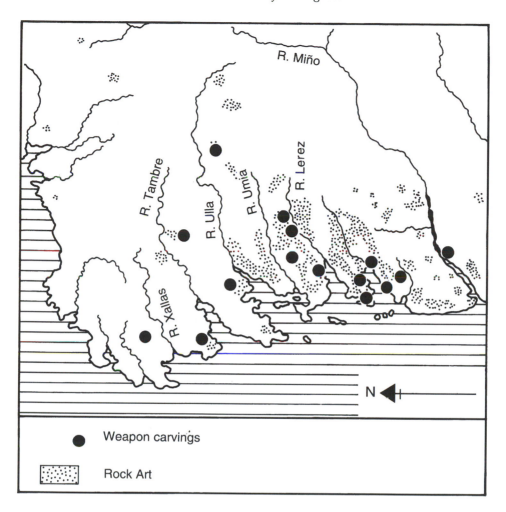

Figure 13.6 The distribution of weapon carvings in Galicia (after Costas and Novoa 1993). Note that the sea is shown at the bottom of the map in order to emphasise the coastal distribution of these images

in the sizes of the halberds and daggers (Costas and Novoa 1993, 163 and 166). It is not surprising that there should be some variations in the size of the weapon carvings. What is so striking is that the contrasts were often based on such obvious proportions.

The distribution of weapon carvings might appear to be rather unstructured, for they are found in small numbers throughout the area with rock art, but in fact this is rather deceptive (Fig. 13.6; Costas and Novoa 1993, 155–81). These motifs are generally located close to rivers or their estuaries and tend to be positioned towards the edges of the major concentrations of carvings; some, like those at Dumbria, are found some way beyond them. A number of the main sites with

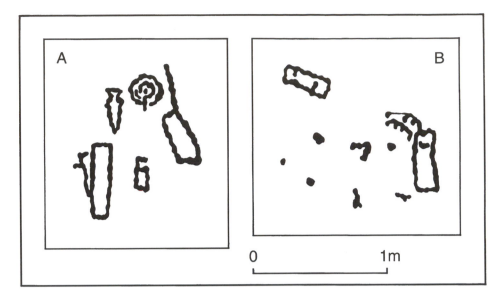

Figure 13.7 Drawings of weapons and idols in Galician rock art. A: Chan de Lagoa, group 6; B: Chan de Lagoa, group 1 (after García and Peña 1980 and Peña, Costas and Rey 1993)

drawings of weapons are near to the Ría de Pontevedra, above the Rio Lerez, close to the farthest limit of the peninsula of Morrazo and towards the southern edge of the Ría de Vigo. Not only were these carvings located towards the limits of the major concentrations of petroglyphs; they were normally placed on sloping rocks that commanded a considerable view (Pl. 40).

Laxe das Ferraduras is a good example of this arrangement. Despite the proximity of the carvings at Fentáns, this particular rock is located beyond the limits of the basin and commands a view in a quite different direction. It is situated on the edge of a steep slope, and before the area was planted with trees it would have overlooked a large area of the river valley below. The two drawings of daggers would have faced anyone passing the rock on the way from the valley floor to the basin at Fentáns. In the same way, the frieze of rock carvings at Conxo is located on the flank of a hill just outside the defences of a castro (Peña 1979). Although those earthworks are likely to be later in date, both features may have played a rather similar role in protecting the hilltop against intruders.

Only rarely are these motifs associated with other kinds of design, but some of these instances are revealing. Carvings of weapons can be found with drawings of stags of the kind discussed in the previous section of this chapter. This association is not particularly common, but a good example of this pattern occurs at Cova da Bruxa in our study area at Muros (Formoso and Costa 1980). More obviously, the carvings of weapons may be associated with depictions of idols, as they are at Laxe das Ferraduras. The form of these artefacts is so simple that they are difficult to identify in the petroglyphs, but it is worth observing that the association between idols and weapons is particularly common around Campo Lameiro where Galician rock art is at its most elaborate (Fig. 13.7; Vázquez Rozas 1995b).

It is in the same area that we also find the most convincing associations between weapons, idols and drawings of mature stags, but nowhere is the connection as explicit as it is at Laxe das Ferraduras, for here the images are confined to a limited area of the rock and two of them are directly linked. There may be a similar association between idols and stags at Chan de Lagoa where there is a remarkable carving which seems to show a pair of antlers growing from the head of a cylinder idol (Fig. 13.7, B; García and Peña 1980, fig. 18).

SUMMING UP

To sum up, I have already argued in some detail that Galician rock art had a profoundly ideological character, based on the importance of particular paths and places in the landscape and on the life cycle of the red deer. It emphasised the wild over the domestic, hunting over farming and placed a major emphasis on the activities or self-images of men. Whilst its distribution seems to be closely related to the early pattern of settlement, it cannot be used to illustrate the prehistoric way of life. The carvings of weapons and idols played an integral part in that ideology and their characteristics help to supplement some of the arguments that I put forward earlier. The weapon carvings show a similar preference for high places or places with extended views, and their siting in the natural terrain suggests that at one level they were meant to control access to certain areas of the landscape. Like the antlers of the stags, they present an image of male aggressiveness and could have supported similar claims to territory and position.

Those weapon carvings are sometimes located as if to look outside the local system of petroglyphs. That is why they were placed at prominent viewpoints above major valleys or close to the sea. That is only appropriate since those artefacts are of types that have their counterparts along considerable lengths of the Atlantic coastline. So on a more restricted scale do the cylinder idols, and, if the resemblances between the abstract motifs are to be believed, the same applies to the abstract designs in the repertoire of Galician rock art. Knowledge of the geographically remote is often a source of power (Helms 1988), and the same is also true of control over specialised knowledge. In this case that information could include the understanding of these images. This is the point at which to return to some of the broad issues introduced in the first part of the book and to compare the findings of our studies of Britain, Ireland and Galicia.

CHAPTER FOURTEEN

SIGN LANGUAGE
Rock art in the prehistory of Atlantic Europe

— •◆• —

Not many rock carvings are displayed to the British public, and when that does happen, the information boards adopt a defensive tone: we do not know why these images were made, and we cannot say what they meant. Visitors to Kilmartin are greeted in a more confident manner. The rock carvings, they are told, were created in the Early Bronze Age by people who came from north-west Spain. Imagine the delight of one of my Galician colleagues when he visited the area!

Of course that notice has been there for some years and at the time of writing it is to be replaced. But it does set out the issues in a particularly explicit manner. Even if we see it as a relic of an older way of thinking, it identifies the topics that need to be considered now. In concluding this study of Atlantic rock art I must go back over some of those issues.

There are two sets of questions to be asked. First, there are the kinds of issues that earlier workers would have recognised. How close was the relationship between the rock art of Scotland and Galicia? Was there really one tradition of rock carvings extending down the Atlantic shoreline from Britain and Ireland to Spain? And, even if the resemblances are close enough to be convincing, how are they to be understood? But behind these questions there are more important issues at stake. If we accept even parts of the traditional framework, how can that knowledge be brought to bear on the topics that are central to archaeology today? These include the investigation of prehistoric landscapes, social relations and ideology.

Some of the issues raised by the information boards at Kilmartin probably can be resolved. There is limited but consistent evidence for the emergence of certain of these images around 3000 BC or even before, and there are indications that rock carvings continued to be made into the early second millennium. We can no longer assign this material exclusively to the Early Bronze Age, but it is no more acceptable to relegate all but the carvings of metalwork to the Neolithic period. Part of the problem arises because of differences of terminology. Motifs that might be Neolithic in Britain and Ireland are Copper Age in the Iberian peninsula. The contrast is one of semantics, and not one of date. The opposite end of the sequence presents fewer problems. In both areas the history of these images was over by the Later Bronze Age and Iron Age when some of the rock carvings were reused in the fabric of hillforts and others were covered by their ramparts.

Such a chronology is particularly plausible because of growing evidence for a major division in the archaeology of Spain and Portugal. During the Copper Age and the Early Bronze Age there is an important distinction to be made between areas which were closely connected to the West Mediterranean and those with links along the Atlantic coastline. The first system relates the Copper Age settlements of Portugal to those in south-east Spain. The second suggests a network of contacts between north-west Spain, western France, Britain and Ireland. The boundary of those separate spheres is much the same as the modern frontier between Galicia and Portugal. In the past it might have been recognised as the distinction between the Schematic art of Iberia and the distinctive tradition of rock carvings in north-west Spain.

Long-distance contacts were certainly important in Galicia. Quite apart from the stylistic similarities between the metalwork in that area and finds from Brittany, Wessex and Ireland, the petroglyphs seem to depict certain objects that originally developed in other regions of Europe. If the depictions of cylinder idols draw on connections with areas further to the south, the weapons may well evoke sources as far afield as Ireland, where halberds are particularly frequent. The same process may have operated in the opposite direction, and George Eogan (1990) is surely right to emphasise the links between some of the stone and antler objects found in the Boyne valley and those in settlements and burial sites close to Lisbon. Cylinder idols belong in the same cultural context and, as we have seen, these are portrayed in Galician rock art.

What is the source of the other images? The notices at Kilmartin leave us in no doubt: abstract art of the kind found in western Scotland originated in Spain. That now seems very unlikely. Unless those images developed spontaneously from an origin in the human nervous system, we have to say that there is no precedent for most of the designs outside Ireland, Britain and possibly north-west France. Much the strongest claim comes from Ireland where the earlier designs found in the passage tombs may provide a source for this tradition, although we cannot exclude the possibility that megalithic art drew on a symbolic system whose importance was already established through its use on natural surfaces in the landscape. The other distinctive feature of Galician petroglyphs is the depiction of animals. This is a characteristic of all the major styles of rock art in the Iberian peninsula and occasionally it extends to the images found in megalithic tombs. It is likely that the animal drawings of Galicia are influenced by other, specifically Iberian traditions.

Such arguments establish the means, motives and opportunity for the connection suggested between Scotland and Spain. The means were there, because there were other cultural connections between Galicia and regions along the northern seaways – there is even a carving of a boat near the coast at Santa Maria de Oia (Fig. 14.1; Alonso 1995). The motives were there because prehistoric people in Galicia seem to have believed that it was important to demonstrate links with far-distant areas, and the opportunity was there because the chronological evidence from Atlantic Europe suggests that rock art was being created over very much the same period in several different regions.

Throughout this book I have insisted that we should compare the art styles of those areas, not on the basis of individual motifs, but according to the logic by

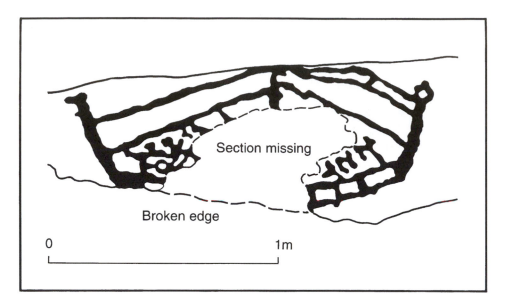

Figure 14.1 Drawing of a boat overlooking the coast at Santa Maria de Oia, Galicia (after Alonso 1995)

which they were brought together on any one surface. Naturally, there are problems where the motifs consist of simple geometric forms, but even here their use from one site to another may conform to simple rules. Because the open-air rock carvings of Atlantic France have not been extensively studied, it is necessary to confine our comparisons to Britain, Ireland and Galicia. In any case these are the only areas with a wide enough variety of motifs for this approach to be warranted.

Several elements stand out clearly in the organisation of these images. Many of them are based on a process of enclosing or embellishing the position of a simple cup mark; in other cases the same process takes place even though the enclosed space is left empty. Those circular motifs can consist of unbroken rings, but we are just as likely to discover that the central cup is joined to the exterior by a radial line. Sometimes the 'entrance' to that design may also be elaborated. The radial line can be extended until it connects with other motifs on the rock surface, but this is more likely to happen where the original motif is larger and more prominent than the others; this is normally because it is made up of several concentric rings. There is a simple hierarchy among these designs. Single rings are the most common, and multiple rings become steadily less frequent until occasional cup marks are enclosed by eight circles. Still more complex designs are altogether exceptional.

All these conventions are shared between the rock art of Ireland, Britain and Galicia. In the large sample of carvings from Northumberland motifs with more than two concentric rings are likely to be joined to one another by a network of lines. Precisely the same distinction is observed in Galicia. At both ends of the

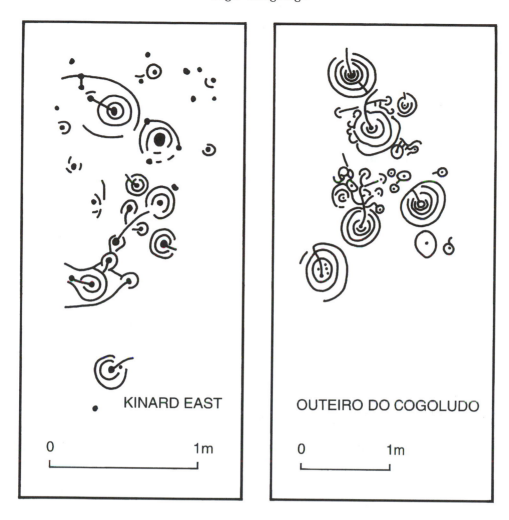

Figure 14.2 'Chains' of interlinked motifs at Kinard East, Dingle, Ireland and Outeiro do Cogoludo, Galicia (after Cuppage 1986 and García and Peña 1980)

distribution the radial line has one main orientation, although this conceals even more local preferences. Britain and Ireland favoured alignments towards the south and east; in Galicia there was more emphasis on the south. All these areas show the same tendency for more complex images to be linked to progressively simpler designs. We saw this process at work in our comparison between Old Bewick and Laxe dos Cebros, and it occurs very widely (Fig. 14.2). Still more striking, the different circular motifs appear in virtually the same proportions in both the areas with detailed records in Galicia, and in widely scattered regions of Britain and Ireland. Not only is there evidence for an obvious hierarchy of designs; the proportions in which these different elements appear are strikingly similar from one area

Table 32 The composition of prehistoric rock art in selected regions of Atlantic Europe

| | Cumulative percentage of motifs | | | | | | |
	1	2	3	4	5	6	7 and over
Galicia (all sites)	45	67	84	93	96	99	100%
Pontevedra	35	60	80	91	96	98	100%
Mid Argyll	43	67	81	93	97	99	100%
Vigo	52	79	94	99	99.5	100	– %
Galloway	51	72	86	93	97	99	100%
Donegal	50	77	94	97	100	–	– %
Northumberland	56	82	90	96	98	99	100%

to another. Table 32 illustrates this point, grouping different regions together for the purposes of comparison.

Table 32 also makes the point that within the conventions of Atlantic rock art there was considerable local variation. The greatest contrast is of course between areas in which all the carvings consist of abstract motifs and those regions where similar designs are found together with drawings of animals. But there were more subtle variations too. Even though the record is so patchy, it is clear that the purely abstract art was much more varied in Scotland, Ireland and northern England than it was in Wales, the south-west and in Brittany.

The rock art of the western Pyrenees seems to have an equally limited range. In Galicia, where the rock art is much more complex, there may be regional preferences in the ways in which animals were depicted between different peninsulas along the Atlantic coastline. South of Vigo, the abstract motifs are rather different from those close to Pontevedra, and in the interior of the country the rock carvings are almost entirely confined to simple cup marks.

There are more local distinctions to be made between different areas of Britain and Ireland. For example, the rock art of the Dingle peninsula has a more restricted repertoire than the carvings on the adjacent peninsula of Iveragh. In the same way, the rock art of Northumberland divides into a group of very complex carvings centred on the Milfield basin and a simpler group close to the Coquet valley. The limited body of carvings from Cumbria appears to be exceptionally elaborate, whilst those across the Pennines in West Yorkshire are generally rather simple. The same contrasts can be recognised between different groups of rock art in Scotland. The most complex art is found in Galloway and Mid Argyll, whilst there are much simpler designs in Strath Tay and in the north.

The uses made of rock art may have been rather different from one region to another. For example, there are only certain areas of Britain in which stone monuments were decorated in the same style as the natural surfaces in the landscape. These monuments include the menhirs and stone rows of Argyll, the cairns and stone circles of Cumbria, the Clava cairns of northern Scotland and the recumbent stone circles to which those sites are so closely related. For the most part the motifs used in such monuments are the same as those found in the local landscape, but the sites in Cumbria seem to be a special case and have rather more in common with the art of Irish passage tombs. Another example of regional patterning is the reuse of already carved stones in the Early Bronze Age burials discussed in Chapter 9. Here two different traditions may have been at work, yet both were restricted to specific parts of the distribution of British rock art. Thus the reuse of elaborately decorated fragments was more common on the east coast than on the west and was largely confined to the area between Perthshire and the Pennines. Within that region the use of cup-marked boulders in burial cairns and other monuments was most frequent from Northumberland to North Yorkshire. Another rather different tradition was found in Wales and the south-west, and there are hints that it may have extended into Finistère.

Why emphasise such local variations in a discussion which began by stressing the importance of long-distance contacts? It is because it provides a vital insight into the character of Atlantic rock art. Despite the striking similarities that we can recognise between areas that were considerable distances apart, rock art was really a *resource* that was available to be used by very different groups of people (Giddens 1979, 59–73; Bourdieu 1990, book 1, chapter 7). Its characteristic symbolism provided a spur for local inventiveness, and that is why so much of this account has been concerned with its role in quite specific contexts. If we knew more about its internal chronology, perhaps we would observe equally local changes in how it was used over time. That should not come as a surprise, for recent work has shown that other widespread developments were deployed in local ways, as part of the processes by which societies created and maintained their view of the world. The most obvious examples are the changing roles of Bell Beakers from one region of Europe to another (Harrison 1980), and the local traditions that determined how early metalwork was to be deposited (Bradley 1990). Both these examples refer to international phenomena which date from the same general period as the rock art. Because we are already aware of so much variation, they illustrate the argument effectively.

There is another level at which we can make this comparison. Bell Beakers could be used in settlements, but they might also be deposited in specialised contexts: in monuments or in graves. Nor did metal objects enter the archaeological record haphazardly, for there are striking local traditions in the ways in which this happened. Some items were buried with the dead, some appear in hoards and others were deposited singly in locations such as rivers, springs or lakes. But there is an important distinction between these contexts, for some were marked by the construction of a monument such as a burial mound, and others were entirely natural places to which a special significance was attached. That may be why depositing an item of metalwork and depicting that artefact in a petroglyph could have been thought of as rather similar processes.

It is because rock art is such an obvious way of assigning special significance to a place that it is best studied as part of landscape archaeology. But that involves certain difficulties. There is no reason to suppose that the importance of a particular rock was *created* by the addition of carvings; just as likely, these emphasised the meanings of somewhere that was already significant, in the same way as some of the burial mounds were built in places that had once been occupied by settlements.

Two features unite the evidence from all our study areas. In Britain, Ireland and Galicia, the rock art not only has a coherent structure which developed through the application of some very simple rules, there is also a consistent relationship between different kinds of design and their placing in the landscape. To some extent those variations may be due to differences in the character of the audience who would have seen them, but the main feature of all these areas is the special attention devoted to certain features of the local terrain. The character of the rock carvings changes from areas suited to sustained exploitation to those which might have been used intermittently, and very different compositions are encountered on the edges of the settled landscape from those found at its centre. That does not mean that different people made the same selection from the vocabulary of Atlantic rock art; the reality was much more volatile. Thus the more complex art in northern Britain was situated towards the higher ground and the simplest motifs of all were associated with the areas with settlements. In Galicia the same formal contrast was observed, but it was registered in the opposite way, so that the complex motifs are close to the occupied area and simple cup marks are distributed along the higher ground. Similarly, the contents of the rock art seem to be at their most complex close to ceremonial centres in Britain and Ireland, but in north-west Spain, where similar enclosures are absent, some of the major barrow cemeteries are accompanied by simple cup-marked rocks.

In other cases the emphasis was on the paths leading through the landscape and on certain significant places along their course. This might explain the chains of intervisible sites found near to the monument complexes in Northumberland and, possibly, Mid Argyll, whilst the careful siting of rock carvings in the Galician uplands reflects the movement of free-ranging animals across a region which provided few sources of shelter and moisture at the warmest time of year.

Our studies of the siting of rock art show how closely it was related to paths and places in the wider landscape and how it could have played a role in the organisation of land use. Its distribution suggests that it was associated with a mobile pattern of exploitation, for many of the rock carvings are at vantage points that overlook areas of grazing land, trails, springs and waterholes. It can also be found in places with an abundant supply of fish. Where a pattern of enclosed settlements had been established by the Copper Age, as seems to have happened in northern Portugal, this particular style of rock carvings had no role to play, nor did it retain its significance through the agricultural intensification of the Later Bronze Age and Iron Age. There are even cases in the north of England where older petroglyphs were slighted by the creation of early field systems. If we are to look behind the agricultural landscapes that are so familiar today, the study of prehistoric rock art provides one starting point.

That is where some accounts would end, but to do that would be weak-spirited, for the petroglyphs of Atlantic Europe were more than signposts or territorial markers. Their characteristic repertoire has much in common with the decoration found on specialised monuments and artefacts. Its imagery may have one of its sources in states of altered consciousness, and throughout its history, from its connection with Neolithic henges to its reuse in Bronze Age graves, it must have carried many levels of significance. We find only hints of that in the British and

Irish landscapes because the imagery is so difficult to interpret. Here we are forced to focus on its association with ceremonial centres. This suggests that the same concerns animated both the sacred space of the henges and the natural locations with rock carvings distributed across the wider landscape. The limited range of purely abstract motifs found in British and Irish rock art can be a source of frustration, but in fact there is something very distinctive about an art style that is virtually without any naturalistic imagery. In such cases the meanings of particular motifs and combinations of motifs would have had to be learned, and that information could be withheld.

On the other hand, in Galicia the abstract motifs that so limit the interpretation of British and Irish rock art are found in direct association with numerous drawings of animals. Although these have often been taken literally, as evidence of an economy based on hunting, a more detailed analysis of the carved surfaces suggests another interpretation. It indicates that some of the abstract motifs, particularly the rings and the lines, might refer to places in a landscape and the paths leading between them, but whether that was an actual landscape or a mythological world it is impossible to tell. What is clear is that different communities living in Atlantic Europe may have shared the same 'circular' perception of space. Moreover, certain details in the depiction of the animals suggest that these drawings were not concerned entirely with food production. They portrayed a highly specialised world: a world of men and red deer in which domesticated livestock were uncommon and women may have been excluded altogether. These images drew on the life cycle of the animals for a series of striking metaphors that seem to have emphasised fighting and the control of territory. The antlers of the rutting stag had the same significance as the drawings of weapons in Galician art. These were images of masculinity that remind us that the rock carvings are unlikely to depict the events of everyday life. They may have been carved on quite specific occasions and they may have been restricted to a quite specific audience. Perhaps that is why so many of them are found well away from the concentration of settlements near the coast.

If these ideas have anything to commend them, they should have two implications. The first is that we can use the evidence of rock art to expand our knowledge of the settlement pattern in that enigmatic period before the development of lasting settlements and land boundaries. That applies as much to the archaeology of Spain as it does to Britain and Ireland. It remains to be seen whether a similar approach might be helpful in other parts of Atlantic Europe where the archaeological sequence presents similar problems. But one effect of carrying out these studies has been to break down the conventional distinction between one kind of archaeology which is based on settlements and land use, and another with a greater interest in monuments and material culture. In Britain and Ireland it is clear that such a distinction cannot be maintained and that some of the images associated with ceremonial centres also extended to natural places in the landscape. The fact that the distribution of rock carvings also echoes the pattern of settlement does not alter the point. Rather, it lends weight to the observation that the distinction between the sacred and the secular is a product of our own experience that we have imposed on the past.

If that is clear from our studies of Britain and Ireland, it should be even more obvious from the rock art of Galicia. Here the petroglyphs are closely associated with the local ecology and with the pattern of movement through the landscape, yet the contents of the petroglyphs cannot be reduced to a simple equation between the depiction of animals and the source of the food supply. These drawings contain a much richer repertoire of images than is sometimes supposed. It is that richness that we must respect if we are to study them to any purpose. They could have had many different layers of meaning – meanings that might have been apparent to quite different people – but that was part of their role in ancient society. As archaeologists, we fall short of our ambition to talk about the past if we decide to portion our information in a similar way. All too often the prehistoric land-scape is studied for evidence of settlement and subsistence. This is the task of 'landscape archaeology'. Monuments associated with ritual and ceremonial are usually studied separately, and these are the province of a 'social archaeology'. Such a division of labour is faint-hearted, and ultimately it is impossible to maintain.

That is why my first encounter with rock art was so puzzling, even so shocking. It demanded a different response from other kinds of archaeological phenomena, and I began this project in order to discover what that response might be. In the end I have come to realise that my original ambition was misplaced. Rock art is just another component in the subject matter of archaeology, but for that very reason its implications are even more troubling than they seemed originally. In learning how to study it we must reconsider the very foundations of landscape archaeology.

BIBLIOGRAPHY

——— •*• ———

Abélanet, J. 1986. *Signes sans paroles*. Paris: Hachette.

Abélanet, J. 1990. *Les roches gravées nord catalanes*. Perpignan: Centre de recherches et d'études Catalanes.

Aira Rodriguez, M., Saa Otero, P. and Taboada Castro, T. 1988. *Estudios paleobotánicos y edafológicos en yaciaiemtos arqueológicos de Galicia*. Santiago de Compostela: Xunta de Galicia.

Alberti, A. P. 1982. *Xeografía de Galicia*, tomo 1. Coruña: Sálvora.

Almagro Gorbea, Ma. J. 1973. *Los ídolos del Bronce 1 hispánico*. Madrid: Biblioteca Praehistorica Hispana.

Alonso Romero, F. 1995. La embarcación del petroglifo Laxe Auga dos Cebros (Pedornes, Santa Maria de Oia, Pontevedra). *Actas del Congreso Nacional de Arqueología, Vigo*, vol 2, 137–45.

Alvarez Nuñez, A. 1986. Los petroglifos de Fentáns (Cotobade). *Pontevedra Arqueologica* 2, 97–125.

Alvarez Nuñez, A. and Souto Velasco, C. 1979. Nuevas insculturas en Campo Lameiro. *Gallaecia* 5, 17–61.

Anati, E. 1963. New petroglyphs at Derrynablaha, Co. Kerry, Ireland. *Journal of the Cork Historical and Archaeological Society* 68, 1–15.

Anati, E. 1964. The rock carvings of 'Pedra das Ferraduras' at Fentáns, Pontevedra. In E. Ripoll Perelló (ed), *Micelánea en homenaje al Abate Henri Breuil*, 123–35. Barcelona: Instituto de Prehistoria y Arqueología.

Anati, E. 1968. *Arte rupestre nelle regioni occidentali delle Peninsola Ibérica*. Brescia: Archivi di Arti Preistorica.

Anati, E. 1976. *Metodi di rivelamento e di analisis arte rupestre*. Capo di Ponte: Studi Camuni.

Anati, E. 1993. *Rock Art – The Primordial Language*. Capo di Ponte: Studi Camuni.

Anati, E. 1994. *Valcamonica Rock Art – A New History for Europe*. Capo di Ponte: Edizioni del Centro.

Annable, K. and Simpson, D. 1964. *Guide Catalogue of the Neolithic and Bronze Age Collections in Devizes Museum*. Devizes: Wiltshire Archaeological and Natural History Society.

Aparicio Casado, B. 1986. Sobre el supuesto ídolo calcolítico de A Caeira (Poio – Pontevedra). *Pontevedra Arqueologica* 2, 65–81.

Aparicio Casado, B. 1989. *Arqueología y antropología cultural de la margen derecha de Ría e Pontevedra*. Pontevedra: Diputacion Provincial de Pontevedra.

ApSimon, A. 1973. Tregiffian Barrow. *Archaeological Journal* 130, 241–3.

Armit, I. 1996. *The Archaeology of Skye and the Western Isles*. Edinburgh: Edinburgh University Press.

Ashbee, P. 1958. The excavation of Tregulland Burrow, Treneglos parish, Cornwall. *Antiquaries Journal* 38, 174–96.

Ashbee, P. 1974. *Ancient Scilly*. Newton Abbot: David and Charles.

Aubet, M. E. 1993. *The Phoenicians and the West*. Cambridge: Cambridge University Press.

Bahn, P. 1984. *Pyrenean Prehistory*. Warminster: Aris and Phillips.

Baptista, A. M. 1981. *A Rocha F-155 e a origem da arte do Vale do Tejo*. Porto: Grupo de Estudos Arqueológicos do Porto.

Baptista, A. M. 1984. Arte rupestre do norte de Portugal. Uma perspectiva. *Portugalia 4/5*, 71–86.

Baptista, A. M. 1985. A estátua-menhir da Ermida (Ponte de Barca, Portugal). *O Arqueólogo Português* 3, 7–44.

Baptista, A. M., Martins, M. and Serrão, E. 1978. Felskunst im Tejo-Tal, Sâo Simâo (Nisa, Portalegre), Portugal. *Madrider Mitteilungen* 19, 89–111.

Barker, G. 1985. *Prehistoric Farming in Europe*. Cambridge: Cambridge University Press.

Barnatt, J. 1989. *Stone Circles of Britain*. Oxford: British Archaeological Reports.

Barnatt, J. and Pierpoint, S. 1983. Stone circles: observations or ceremonial centres? *Scottish Archaeological Review* 2.2, 101–15.

Barnatt, J. and Reeder, P. 1982. Prehistoric rock art in the Peak District. *Derbyshire Archaeological Journal* 102, 33–44.

Barrett, J. 1990. The monumentality of death: the character of Early Bronze Age mortuary mounds in southern Britain. *World Archaeology* 22, 179–89.

Barrett, J. 1994. *Fragments from Antiquity*. Oxford: Blackwell.

Barrett, J., Bradley, R. and Green, M. 1991. *Landscape, Monuments and Society. The Prehistory of Cranborne Chase*. Cambridge: Cambridge University Press.

Barton, C., Clark, G. and Cohen, A. 1994. Art as information: Upper Palaeolithic art in western Europe. *World Archaeology* 26, 185–207.

Beckensall, S. 1983. *Northumberland's Prehistoric Rock Carvings*. Rothbury: Pendulum Press.

Beckensall, S. 1991. *Prehistoric Rock Motifs of Northumberland*, vol 1. Privately published.

Beckensall, S. 1992a. *Prehistoric Rock Motifs of Northumberland*, vol 2. Privately published.

Beckensall, S. 1992b. *Cumbrian Prehistoric Rock Art. Symbols, Monuments and Landscape*. Privately published.

Beltrán Martinez, A. 1995. Agunas consideraciones sobre el arte rupestre del noroeste de la Peninsula y las relaciones Atlanticas. *Actas del XXII Congreso Nacional Arqueología, Vigo*, vol 1, 19–24.

Bintliff, J. 1988. Site patterning: separating environmental, cultural and preservation factors. In J. Bintliff, D. Davidson and E. Grant (eds), *Conceptual Issues in Environmental Archaeology*, 129–44. Edinburgh: Edinburgh University Press.

Birks, H. 1975. Studies in the vegetation history of Scotland IV. *Philosophical Transactions of the Royal Society* B 270, 181–223.

Bonilla Rodríguez, A., Parga Castro, A. and Torres Alvaez, A. in press. Nueva zona de grabados rupestres in Galicia: prospección intensiva del ayuntamiento de Rianxo. *Boletin do Museo de Lugo.*

Boujot, C. and Cassen, S. 1992. Le développement des premières architectures funéraires monumentales en France occidentale. In C.-T. Le Roux (ed), *Paysans et bâtisseurs*, 195–211. *Revue Archéologique de l'Ouest*, supplément 5.

Bourdieu, P. 1990. *The Logic of Practice.* Oxford: Polity Press.

Bowen, E. 1977. *Saints, Seaways and Settlements in the Celtic Lands.* Second edition. Cardiff: University of Wales Press.

Bracken, G. and Wayman, P. 1992. A Neolithic or Bronze Age alignment for Croagh Patrick. *Journal of the Westport Historical Society* 19, 1–11.

Bradley, R. 1989a. Darkness and light in the design of megalithic tombs. *Oxford Journal of Archaeology* 8, 251–9.

Bradley, R. 1989b. Deaths and entrances: a contextual analysis of megalithic art. *Current Anthropology* 30, 68–75.

Bradley, R. 1990. *The Passage of Arms.* Cambridge: Cambridge University Press.

Bradley, R. 1992. Turning the world: rock carvings and the archaeology of death. In N. Sharples and A. Sheridan (eds), *Vessels for the Ancestors*, 168–76. Edinburgh: Edinburgh University Press.

Bradley, R. 1993. *Altering the Earth. The Origins of Monuments in Britain and Continental Europe.* Edinburgh: Society of Antiquaries of Scotland.

Bradley, R. 1995. Fieldwalking without flints: worked quartz as a clue to the character of prehistoric settlement. *Oxford Journal of Archaeology* 14, 13–22.

Bradley, R., Criado Boado, F. and Fábregas Valcarce, R. 1994a. Rock art research as landscape archaeology: a pilot study in Galicia, north-west Spain. *World Archaeology* 25, 374–90.

Bradley, R., Criado Boado, F. and Fábregas Valcarce, R. 1994b. Petroglifos en el paisaje: Neuvas perspectivas sobre el arte rupestre gallego. *Minius* 3, 17–28.

Bradley, R., Criado Boado, F. and Fábregas Valcarce, R. 1994c. Los petroglifos como forma de appropiación del espacio: algunos ejemplos gallegos. *Trabajos de Prehistoria* 51.2, 159–86.

Bradley, R., Criado Boado, F. and Fábregas Valcarce, R. 1995. Rock art and the prehistoric landscape of Galicia. *Proceedings of the Prehistoric Society* 61: 341–70.

Bradley, R. and Edmonds, M. 1993. *Interpreting the Axe Trade.* Cambridge: Cambridge University Press.

Bradley, R., Entwistle, R. and Raymond, F. 1994. *Prehistoric Land Divisions on Salisbury Plain.* London: English Heritage.

Bradley, R., Harding, J. and Mathews, M. 1993. The siting of prehistoric rock art in Galloway, south-west Scotland. *Proceedings of the Prehistoric Society* 59, 269–83.

Bradley, R., Harding, J., Mathews, M. and Rippon, S. 1993. A field method for investigating the distribution of rock art. *Oxford Journal of Archaeology* 12, 129–43.

Bradley, R. and Mathews, M. in prep. Rock carvings and round cairns on the Northumberland sandstone.

Breuil, H. 1921. *Roches gravées de la Péninsule Ibérique. Mémoires présentées au Congrès de Rouen, 1921*, 1–23. Rouen: Association Française pour l'avancement des sciences.

Breuil, H. 1934. Presidential address. *Proceedings of the Prehistoric Society of East Anglia* 7, 289–322.

Briard, J. 1984. *Les tumulus d'Armorique*. Paris: Picard.

Briard, J. 1985. Les relations maritimes à l'âge du bronze dans la zone Atlantique et ses annexes. In *Océan Atlantique et Péninsule Armoricaine*, 9–24. Paris: Editions du comité des travaux historiques et scientifiques.

Briard, J. 1987. Wessex et Armorique: une revision. In *Les relations entre le Continent et les Isles Britanniques à l'âge du bronze*, 77–87. Amiens: Revue Archéologique de Picardie.

Briard, J. 1989. Le culte des eaux à l'âge du bronze en Armorique. In *L'homme et l'eau au temps de la préhistoire*, 53–66. Paris: Editions du comité des travaux historiques et scientifiques.

Briard, J. 1991. Les premiers cuivres atlantiques en France. In J.-P. Mohen and C. Eluère (eds), *Découverte du métal*, 183–96. Paris: Picard.

Brun, P. 1988. L'entité 'Rhine–Suisse–France orientale': nature et evolution. In P. Brun and C. Mordant (eds), *Le groupe Rhine–Suisse–France orientale et la notion de civilisation des Champs d'Urnes*, 599–620. Nemours: Mémoires du Musée de Préhistoire d'Ile-de-France.

Brun, P. 1992. Le bronze Atlantique: essai de définition. In C. Chevellot and A. Coffyn (eds), *L'âge du bronze Atlantique*, 11–24. Beynac: Association des Musées de Sarladais.

Brun, P. 1993. East–west relations in the Paris Basin during the Late Bronze Age. In C. Scarre and F. Healy (eds), *Trade and Exchange in Prehistoric Europe*, 171–82. Oxford: Oxbow.

Buckley, V. and Sweetman, D. 1991. *Archaeological Survey of County Louth*. Dublin: Stationery Office.

Bueno Ramírez, P. and Balbín Behrmann, R. 1992. L'art mégalithique dans la péninsule Iberique: une vue d'ensemble. *L'Anthropologie* 96, 499–572.

Burgess, C. 1972. Goatscrag: a Bronze Age rock shelter cemetery in north Northumberland. With notes on other rock shelters and crag lines in the region. *Archaeologia Aeliana* 50, 15–69.

Burgess, C. 1976. Meldon Bridge – a Neolithic defended promontory complex near Peebles. In C. Burgess and R. Miket (eds), *Settlement and Economy in the Third and Second Millennia BC*, 151–79. Oxford: British Archaeological Reports.

Burgess, C. 1987. Les rapports entre la France et la Grande-Bretagne pendant l'âge du bronze – problèmes de poterie et d'habitats. In *Les relations entre le Continent et les Isles Britanniques à l'âge du bronze*, 307–18. Amiens: Revue Archéologique de Picardie.

Burgess, C. 1990. The chronology of cup and cup and ring marks in Atlantic Europe. *Revue Archéologique de l'Ouest*, supplément 2, 157–71.

Burgess, C. 1992. Discontinuity and dislocation in later prehistoric settlement: some evidence from Atlantic Europe. In C. Mordant and A. Richard (eds), *L'habitat et l'occupation du sol à l'âge du bronze en Europe*, 21–40. Paris: Editions du comité des travaux historiques et scientifiques.

Burl, A. 1976. *The Stone Circles of the British Isles*. New Haven: Yale University Press.

Burl, A. 1988. *Four-posters. Bronze Age Stone Circles of Western Europe*. Oxford: British Archaeological Reports.

Butcher, S. 1978. Excavations at Nornour, Isles of Scilly, 1969–73: the pre-Roman settlement. *Cornish Archaeology* 17, 29–112.

Calo Lourido, F. and González Reboredo, X. M. 1980. Estación de arte rupestre de Leiro (Rianxo – A Coruña). *Gallaecia* 6, 207–16.

Carballeira, A., Devesca, C., Retuerto, R., Santillán, E. and Ucieda, F. 1983. *Bioclimatología de Galicia*. Coruña: Fundación P. Barrie de la Maza.

Casimir, M. 1992. The determinants of rights to pasture: territorial organisation and ecological constraints. In M. Casimir and A. Rao (eds), *Mobility and Territoriality*, 153–203. Oxford: Berg.

Chapman, R. 1990. *Emerging Complexity*. Cambridge: Cambridge University Press.

Childe, V.G. 1957. *The Dawn of European Civilisation*. Sixth edition. London: Routledge and Kegan Paul.

Christie, P. 1985. Barrows on the north Cornwall coast: wartime excavations by C. K. Croft Andrew, 1939–44. *Cornish Archaeology* 24, 23–121.

Christie, P. 1986. Cornwall in the Bronze Age. *Cornish Archaeology* 25, 81–110.

Clarke, J. 1982. Prehistoric rock inscriptions near Dundalk, County Louth. *County Louth Archaeological and Historical Journal* 20.2, 106–16.

Cleal, R. 1991. Cranborne Chase: the earlier prehistoric pottery. In J. Barrett, R. Bradley and M. Hall (eds), *Papers on the Prehistoric Archaeology of Cranborne Chase*, 134–200. Oxford: Oxbow.

Cleal, R., Cooper, J. and Williams, D. 1994. Shells and sherds: identification of inclusions in Grooved Ware, with associated radiocarbon dates, from Amesbury, Wiltshire. *Proceedings of the Prehistoric Society* 60, 445–8.

Cleal, R., Walker, K. and Montague, R. 1995. *Stonehenge in Its Landscape: The twentieth century excavations*. London: English Heritage.

Clutton-Brock, T., Guiness, S. and Albon, S. 1982. *Red Deer: Behaviour and ecology of two sexes*. Edinburgh: Edinburgh University Press.

Coffyn, A. 1985. *Le bronze final Atlantique*. Paris: De Boccard.

Coffyn, A., Gomez, J. and Mohen, J.-P. 1981. *L'apogée de l'âge du bronze Atlantique: le depôt de Vénat*. Paris: Picard.

Coggins, D. 1986. *Upper Teesdale. The Archaeology of a North Pennine Valley*. Oxford: British Archaeological Reports.

Coles, J. 1964. New aspects of the Mesolithic settlement of south-west Scotland. *Transactions of the Dumfriesshire and Galloway Antiquarian Society* 41, 67–98.

Coles, J. and Simpson, D. 1965. The excavation of a Neolithic round barrow at Pitnacree, Perthshire, Scotland. *Proceedings of the Prehistoric Society* 31, 34–57.

Coles, J. and Simpson. D. 1990. Excavations at Grantully, Perthshire. *Proceedings of the Society of Antiquaries of Scotland* 120, 33–44.

Collins, P. and Waterman, D. 1955. *Millin Bay: A late Neolithic cairn in Co. Down*. Belfast: HMSO.

Concheiro Coello, A. and Gil Agra, L. in press. Una nueva zona de arte rupestre al aire libre en el NW: la peninsula de Barbanza. *Espacio, Tiempo y Forma* 7.

Conkey, M. 1980. The identification of prehistoric hunter gatherer aggregation sites: the case of Altamira. *Current Anthropology* 21, 609–30.

Conkey, M. 1989. The use of diversity in stylistic analysis. In R. Leonard and G. Jones (eds), *Quantifying Diversity in Archaeology*, 118–29. Cambridge: Cambridge University Press.

Costas Goberna, F. J. 1984. *Petroglifos del litoral sur de la Ría de Vigo*. Vigo: Publicaciones del Museo Municipal 'Quiñones de Leon'.

Costas Goberna, F. J. 1988. Consideracions sobre la posibilidad de aceramiento cronologico a los petroglifos del Castro de Santa Tecla. *Revista de Ciencias Historícas Universidade Portucalense Infante D. Henrique* 3, 39–55.

Costas Goberna, F. J. and Novoa Alvarez, P. 1993. *Los grabados rupestres de Galicia*. Coruña: Museu Arqueolóxico e Histórico.

Costas Goberna, F. J., Novoa Alvarez, P. and Albo Moran, J. M. 1991. Los gabados rupestres de Gagamala (Mondariz) y el Grupo IV del monte Tetón (Tomiño) provincia de Pontevedra. *Castrelos* 3–4, 85–116.

Cowling, E. 1946. *Rombald's Way: A prehistory of mid-Wharfedale*. Otley: Walker.

Crawford, O. G. S. 1954. The symbols carved on Stonehenge. *Antiquity* 28, 25–31.

Criado Boado, F. (ed) 1991. *Arqueología del paisaje. El área Bocelo-Furelos entre los tiempos paleoliticos y medievales*. Santiago de Compostela: Xunta de Galicia.

Criado Boado, F. 1995. El control arqueológico de obras de trazado lineal: plantamiento desde la arqueología del paisaje. *Actas del XXII Congreso Nacional de Arqueología, Vigo*, vol 1, 253–9.

Criado Boado, F. and Fábregas Valcarce, R. 1994. Regional patterning among the megaliths of Galicia (NW Spain). *Oxford Journal of Archaeology* 13, 33–47.

Criado Boado, F., Fábregas Valcarce, R. and Vaquero Lastres, X. 1991. Concentraciones de túmulos y vias naturales de acceso al interior de Galicia. *Portugalia* 12, 27–38.

Cunliffe, B. 1992. Le Câtel de Rozel, Jersey: the excavations of 1988–90. *Antiquaries Journal* 72, 18–53.

Cuppage, J. 1986. *Archaeological Survey of the Dingle Peninsula*. Ballyferriter: Oidreacht Chorca Dhuine.

Curran-Mulligan, P. 1994. Yes, but it *is* art. *Archaeology Ireland* 8.1, 14–15.

Darvill, T. 1987. *Prehistoric Britain*. London: Batsford.

Darvill, T. 1989. The circulation of Neolithic stone and flint axes: a case study from Wales and the mid-west of Britain. *Proceedings of the Prehistoric Society* 55, 27–43.

Davidson, J. and Henshall, A. 1989. *The Chambered Tombs of Orkney*. Edinburgh: Edinburgh University Press.

Davis, G. and Turner, J. 1979. Pollen diagrams from Northumberland. *New Phytologist* 82, 783–804.

De Chatellier, P. 1907. *Les époques préhistoriques dans la Finistère*. Quimper: Leprince.

De Jersey, P. 1993. The early chronology of Alet and its implications for Hengistbury Head and cross-channel trade in the late Iron Age. *Oxford Journal of Archaeology* 12, 321–35.

Delano Smith, C. 1990. Place or prayer? Maps in Italian rock art. *Accordia Research Papers* 1, 5–18.

De Lumley, H. 1995. *Le grandiose et le sacré. Gravures protohistoriques et historiques de la région du mont Bego*. Paris: Epona.

Díaz-Andreu, M. 1995. Complex societies in Copper and Bronze Age Iberia: a reappraisal. *Oxford Journal of Archaeology* 14, 23–39.

Díaz Casado, Y. 1992. *El arte rupestre esquemático en Cantabria*. Santander: Universidad de Cantabria.

Dronfield, J. 1995. Subjective vision and the source of Irish megalithic art. *Antiquity* 69, 539–49.

Duhourcou, J. 1972. Un sanctuaire mégalithique pyrenéen: le dolmen de Buzy, son petro-glyphe et sa pierre à légende. *Archéologia* 49, 72–7.

Edwards, A. 1935. Rock sculpturings on Traprain Law, East Lothian. *Proceedings of the Society of Antiquaries of Scotland* 69, 122–37.

Edwards, G. and Bradley, R. in press. Rock carvings and Neolithic artefacts on Ilkley Moor, West Yorkshire. In R. Cleal and A. MacSween (eds), *Grooved Ware in Context*. Oxford: Oxbow.

Eiroa, J. and Rey, J. 1984. *Guia de los petroglifos de Muros*. Muros: Concello de Muros.

Eliade, M. 1989. *The Myth of the Eternal Return*. Harmondsworth: Arkana.

Eogan, G. 1986. *Knowth and the Passage Tombs of Ireland*. London: Thames and Hudson.

Eogan, G. 1990. Irish megalithic tombs and Iberia. Comparisons and contrasts. *Probleme der Megalithgräberforschung*, 113–37. Berlin: De Gruyter.

Eogan, G. and Roche, H. 1994. A Grooved Ware wooden structure at Knowth, Boyne valley, Ireland. *Antiquity* 68, 322–30.

Evans, J. G. 1990. Notes on some Neolithic and Bronze Age events in long barrow ditches in southern and eastern England. *Proceedings of the Prehistoric Society* 56, 111–16.

Fábregas Valcarce, R. 1991. *Megalitismo del noroeste de la Península Ibérica. Tipología y secuencia de los materiales líticos*. Madrid: Universidad Nacional de Educación a Distancia.

Fábregas Valcarce, R. and Penedo Romero, R. 1994. Petroglifos e arte das cistas do noroeste. *Trebarvna* 3, 5–21.

Faull, M. and Moorhouse, S. (eds) 1981. *West Yorkshire: An archaeological survey to AD 1500*. Wakefield: West Yorkshire Metropolitan County Council.

Fenton-Thomas, C. 1992. Pollen analysis as an aid to the reconstruction of patterns of land use in the Tyne-Tees region during the first millennia BC and AD. *Durham Archaeological Journal* 8, 51–62.

Ferguson, C. 1895. On a tumulus at Old Parks, Kirkoswald. *Transactions of the Cumberland and Westmorland Antiquarian and Archaeological Society* 13, 389–99.

Filgueiras Rey, A. and Rodríguez Fernández, T. in press. Túmulos y petroglifos. La construccion de un espacio funerario. *Espacio, Tiempo y Forma* 7.

Formoso Romero, M. and Costa Calderon, J. 1980. Estación rupestre de Muros de San Pedro. *Brigantium* 1, 71–81.

Fox, C. 1932. *The Personality of Britain*. Cardiff: National Museum of Wales.

Fox, C. 1937. Two Bronze Age cairns in South Wales. *Archaeologia* 87, 129–80.

Fraser, D. 1988. The orientation of visibility from the chambered tombs of Eday. In C. Ruggles (ed), *Records in Stone*, 325–36. Cambridge: Cambridge University Press.

Friedrich, M. 1970. Design structure and social interaction. Archaeological implications of an ethnographic analysis. *American Antiquity* 35, 332–43.

Fulford, M. 1989. Byzantium and Britain: a Mediterranean perspective on post-Roman Mediterranean imports in western Britain and Ireland. *Medieval Archaeology* 33, 1–6.

Gaffney, V., Stancic, Z. and Watson, H. 1995. Moving from catchments to cognition: tentative steps towards a larger archaeological context. *Scottish Archaeological Review* 9/10, 41–64.

Gamble, C. 1986. *The Palaeolithic Settlement of Europe*. Cambridge: Cambridge University Press.

Gamble, C. 1991. The social context for European Palaeolithic art. *Proceedings of the Prehistoric Society* 57.1, 316.

García Alén, A. and Peña Santos, A. 1980. *Grabados rupestres de la Provincia de Pontevedra*. Pontevedra: Museo de Pontevedra.

Garwood, P. in press. Grooved Ware chronology. In R. Cleal, and A. MacSween (eds), *Grooved Ware in Context*. Oxford: Oxbow.

Gauthier, J. 1939. Le pierre de Méniscoul (Loire–Inférieure). *Bulletin de la société archéologique et historique de Nantes* 79, 105–8.

Gibson, A. 1994. Excavations at the Sarn-y-bryn-caled cursus complex, Welshpool, Powys, and the timber circles of Great Britain and Ireland. *Proceedings of the Prehistoric Society* 60, 143–223.

Giddens, A. 1979. *Central Problems in Social Theory*. London: Macmillan.

Gil Agra, D. and Concheiro Coello, A. 1994. A estación de grabados rupestres ao aire libre de 'Braña das Pozas' (Porto do Son, A Coruña). *Minius* 2–3, 7–15.

Gomes, M. 1990. A Rocha 49 de Fratel e os períodos estilizado-estático e estilizado-dinámico de arte do Vale do Tajo. *Homenagem a J. R. dos Santos Júnior*, vol 1, 151–77. Lisbon: Instituto de Investigação Científica Tropical.

Gómez Barrera, J. 1992. Manifestaciones de la facies esquemática en el centro y norte de la Península Ibérica. *Espacio, Tiempo y Forma* 5, 231–64.

Gómez Barrera, J. 1993. *Arte rupestre prehistórico en la Meseta Castelano-Leonsa*. Valladolid: Junta de Castilla y Léon.

Gonzalez Anta, R. and Tejera Gaspar, A. 1990. *Los aborígenes Canarios*. Madrid: Ediciones Istmo.

Grande del Brio, R. 1987. *La pintura esquematica en el centro-oeste de Espana (Salamanca y Zamora)*. Salamanca: Ediciones de la Diputación de Salamanca.

Grattan, J. and Gilbertson, D. 1994. Acid-loading from Icelandic tephra falling on acidified ecosystems as a key to understanding archaeological and environmental stress in northern and western Britain. *Journal of Archaeological Science* 21, 851–9.

Hadingham, E. 1974. *Ancient Carvings in Britain: A mystery*. London: Garnstone Press.

Hagen, A. 1990. *Helleristninger i Noreg*. Oslo: Norske Samlaget.

Hall, M. 1984. *Harrison Birtwistle*. London: Robson Books.

Harbison, P. 1967. Mediterranean and Atlantic elements in the Early Bronze Age of northern Portugal and Galicia. *Madrider Mitteilungen* 8, 100–22.

Harding, A. 1981. Excavations in the prehistoric ritual complex near Milfield, Northumberland. *Proceedings of the Prehistoric Society* 47, 87–135.

Harding, A. and Lee, G. 1987. *Henge Monuments and Related Sites of Great Britain*. Oxford: British Archaeological Reports.

Harrison, R. 1974. Ireland and Spain in the Early Bronze Age. *Journal of the Royal Society of Antiquaries of Ireland* 104, 52–73.

Harrison, R. 1980. *The Beaker Folk*. London: Thames and Hudson.

Harrison, R. 1985. The 'polyculturo ganadero' or the secondary products revolution in Spanish agriculture 5000–1000 BC. *Proceedings of the Prehistoric Society* 51, 75–102.

Harrison, R. and Gilman, A. 1977. Trade in the second and third millennia BC between the Maghreb and Iberia. In V. Markotic (ed), *Ancient Europe and the Mediterranean*, 90–104. Warminster: Aris and Phillips.

Hartgroves, S. 1987. The cup-marked stones of Stithians Reservoir. *Cornish Archaeology* 26, 69–84.

Hartley, R. 1992. *Rock Art on the North Colorado Plateau*. Aldershot: Avebury.

Hawkes, C. 1940. *The Prehistoric Foundations of Europe to the Mycenean Age*. London: Methuen.

Hawkes, C. 1977. *Pytheas: Europe and the Greek explorers*. Oxford: Blackwell.

Helms, M. 1988. *Ulysses' Sail*. Princeton: Princeton University Press.

Hicks, S. 1972. The impact of man on the East Moor of Derbyshire from Mesolithic times. *Archaeological Journal* 129, 1–21.

Hodder, I. 1990. *The Domestication of Europe*. Oxford: Blackwell.

Hodder, I. 1992. Symbolism, meaning and context. In I. Hodder, *Theory and Practice in Archaeology*, 11–23. London: Routledge.

Hood, B. 1988. Sacred rocks: ideological and social space in the north Norwegian Stone Age. *Norwegian Archaeological Review* 21, 65–84.

Hornsby, W. and Stanton, R. 1917. British barrows near Brotton. *Yorkshire Archaeological Journal* 24, 263–8.

Ilkley Archaeology Group 1986. *The Carved Rocks on Rombalds Moor*. Wakefield: West Yorkshire Metropolitan County Council.

Infante Roura, F., Vaquero Lastres, J. and Criado Boado, F. 1992. Vacas, caballos, abrigos y túmulos: definición de una geografia del movimiento para el estudio arqueológico. *Cuadernos de Estudios Gallegos* 40, 21–39.

Ingold, T. 1986. Territoriality and tenure: the appropriation of space in hunting and gathering societies. In T. Ingold, *The Appropriation of Nature*, 130–64. Manchester: Manchester University Press.

Ingold, T. 1993. Globes and spheres: the topology of environmentalism. In K. Milton (ed), *Environmentalism: The view from anthropology*, 31–42. London: Routledge.

Jackson, P. 1995. A continuing belief system? Irish passage grave art and the cup and ring engravings of the British Isles and Eire. In K. Helsgog and B. Olsen (eds), *Perceiving Rock Art: social and political perspectives*, 396–406. Oslo: Novus.

Johnston, S. 1989. *Prehistoric Irish Petroglyphs: Their analysis and interpretation in anthropological context*. Ann Arbor: University Microfilms.

Johnston, S. 1991. Distributional aspects of prehistoric Irish petroglyphs. In P. Bahn (ed), *Rock Art and Prehistory*, 86–95. Oxford: Oxbow.

Johnston, S. 1993. The relationship between prehistoric Irish rock art and Irish passage tomb art. *Oxford Journal of Archaeology* 12, 257–79.

Jorge, S. O. 1994. Cólonias fortifiçöes, lugares monumentalizados. Trajectória das concepçiönes sobre um tema do calcolitico peninsular. *Revista da Facultade de Letras* 11, 447–546.

Jorge, V. O. and Jorge, S. O. 1991. Figurations humaines préhistoriques du Portugal. Dolmens ornés, abris peints, rochers gravés, statues-menhirs. *Revista da Facultade de Letras* 8, 341–84.

Kayser, O. 1986. Les amas coquilliers d'Armorique. *Archéologia* 218, 68–74.

Kinnes, I. and Longworth, I. 1985. *Catalogue of the Excavated Prehistoric and Romano-British Material in the Greenwell Collection*. London: British Museum Publications.

Laurie, T. 1985. Early land divisions and settlement in Swaledale and the eastern approaches to the Stainmore Pass. In C. Burgess and D. Spratt (eds), *Upland Settlement in Britain*, 135–62. Oxford: British Archaeological Reports.

Layton, R. 1986. Political and territorial structure among hunter gatherers. *Man* 21, 18–33.

Layton, R. 1991. *The Anthropology of Art*. Second edition. Cambridge: Cambridge University Press.

Layton, R. 1992. *Australian Rock Art: A new synthesis*. Cambridge: Cambridge University Press.

Le Roux, C.-T. 1990. Le petro-archéologie des haches polies armoricaines, 40 ans après. *Revue Archéologique de l'Ouest*, supplément 2, 345–53.

Le Roux, C.-T. 1992. The art of Gavrinis presented in its Armorican context and in comparison with Ireland. *Journal of the Royal Society of Antiquaries of Ireland* 122, 79–108.

Lewis-Williams, J. D. 1987. A dream of eland: an unexplored component of San shamanism and rock art. *World Archaeology* 19, 165–77.

Lewis-Williams, J. D. and Dowson, T. 1988. The signs of all times: entoptic phenomena in Upper Palaeolithic art. *Current Anthropology* 29, 201–45.

Lewis-Williams, J. D. and Dowson, T. 1990. Through the veil: San rock paintings and the rock face. *South African Archaeological Bulletin* 45, 5–16.

Lewis-Williams, J. D. and Dowson, T. 1993. On vision and power in the Neolithic; evidence from the decorated monuments. *Current Anthropology* 34, 55–65.

L'Helgouac'h, J. 1976. The tumulus de Dissignac, Saint-Nazaire (Loire–Atlantique) et les problèmes du contact entre le phénomène megalithique et les sociétés à l'industrie microlithique. In S. de Laet (ed), *Acculturation and Continuity in Atlantic Europe*, 142–9. Bruges: De Tempel.

L'Helgouac'h, J. 1983. Les idoles qu'on abat. *Bulletin de la Société Polymathique du Morbihan*, 57–68.

Lowe, E. 1966. Observations on the dispersal of red deer on Rhum. *Symposia of the Zoological Society of London* 18, 211–28.

Lubell, D., Jackes, M., Schwarcz, H., Knyf, M. and Meikeljohn, C. 1994. The Mesolithic–Neolithic transition in Portugal: isotopic and dental evidence of diet. *Journal of Archaeological Science* 21, 201–16.

Lynch, F. 1976. Towards a chronology of megalithic tombs in Wales. In G. Boon and J. Lewis (eds), *Welsh Antiquity*, 63–79. Cardiff: National Museum of Wales.

McGrail, S. 1987. *Ancient Boats in North-west Europe*. Harlow: Longman.

McGrail, S. 1993. Prehistoric seafaring in the Channel. In C. Scarre and F. Healy (eds), *Trade and Exchange in Prehistoric Europe*, 199–210. Oxford: Oxbow.

MacKie, E. and Davis, A. 1989. New light on Neolithic rock carvings: the petroglyphs at Greenland (Auchentorlie) Dumbartonshire. *Glasgow Archaeological Journal* 15, 125–55.

MacWhite, E. 1946. A new view on Irish Bronze Age rock-scribings. *Journal of the Royal Society of Antiquaries of Ireland* 76, 59–80.

MacWhite, E. 1951. *Estudios sobre las relaciones Atlánticas de le peninsula Hispánica en la Edad del Bronce*. Madrid: Publicaciones del Seminario de historia primitiva del hombre.

Malmer, M. 1981. *A Chorological Study of North European Rock Art*. Stockholm: Amqvist and Wiksell.

Mann, L. M. 1915. *Archaic Sculpturings. Notes on art, philosophy and religion in Britain, 2000 BC to 900 AD*. Edinburgh: Hodges.

Marguerie, D. 1992. *Evolution de la végétation sous l'impact humain en Armorique du Néolithique aux périodes historiques*. Rennes: Université de Rennes.

Martin Valls, R. 1983. Las insculturas del castro de Yecla de Yelta y sus relacíones con los petroglifos gallegos. *Zephyrus* 36, 217–31.

Masille, L. 1927. Le pierre à cercles et à cupules de Pleucadec (Morbihan). *Bulletin de la société polymathique du Morbihan*, 99–104.

Masset, C. 1993. *Les dolmens. Sociétés néolithiques et pratiques funéraires*. Paris: Errance.

Meijide Cameselle, G. 1989. Un importante conjunto del Bronce Inicial en Galicia: el depósito de Leiro (Rianxo, A Coruña). *Gallaecia* 11, 151–64.

Mellars, P. 1987. *Excavations on Oronsay*. Edinburgh: Edinburgh University Press.

Méndez Fernández, F. 1994. La domesticación del paisaje durante la Edad del Bronce gallego. *Trabajos de Prehistoria* 51.1, 77–94.

Mercer, R. 1988. Sketewan, Balnaguard, Perthshire. University of Edinburgh, *Department of Archaeology Annual Report* 34, 26–7.

Miket, R. 1981. Pit alignments in the Milfield basin and the excavation of Ewart 1. *Proceedings of the Prehistoric Society* 47, 137–46.

Mitchell, F. 1992. Notes on some non-local cobbles at the entrance to the passage graves at Newgrange and Knowth, County Meath. *Journal of the Royal Society of Antiquaries of Ireland* 122, 128–45.

Mitchell, M. and Young, A. 1939. Report on excavations at Monzie, Perthshire. *Proceedings of the Society of Antiquaries of Scotland* 73, 62–71.

Mitchiner, M. 1986. *Medieval Pilgrim and Secular Badges*. Sanderstead: Hawkins Publications.

Moar, N. 1969. Late Weichsellian and Flandrian pollen diagrams from south-west Scotland. *New Phytologist* 68, 433–67.

Moffatt, J. 1885. Prehistoric grave from the Lilburn Hill Farm on the Lilburn Tower Estate. *Archaeologia Aeliana* 10, 220–2.

Mommsen, H., Diehl, U., Lambrecht, D., Panternburg, G. and Weber, J. 1990. Eine mykenische Scherbe in Spanien. *Prähistorische Zeitschrift* 65, 59–61.

Monteagudo, L. 1977. *Die Beile auf der Iberischen Halbinsel*. Munich: C. H. Beck.

Morales, M. and Arnaud, J. 1990. Recent research on the Mesolithic in the Iberian Peninsula: problems and perspectives. In P. Vermeersch and P. Van Peer (eds), *Contributions to the Mesolithic in Europe*, 451–61. Leuven: Leuven University Press.

Morphy, H. 1989. Introduction. In H. Morphy (ed), *Animals into Art*, 1–17. London: Unwin Hyman.

Morphy, H. 1991. *Ancestral Connections*. Chicago: Chicago University Press.

Morris, R. 1977. *The Prehistoric Rock Art of Argyll*. Poole: Dolphin Press.

Morris, R. 1979. *The Prehistoric Rock Art of Galloway and the Isle of Man*. Poole: Blandford Press.

Morris, R. 1981. *The Prehistoric Rock Art of Southern Scotland*. Oxford: British Archaeological Reports.

Morris, R. 1989. The prehistoric rock art of Great Britain: a survey of all sites bearing motifs more complex than simple cup marks. *Proceedings of the Prehistoric Society* 55, 45–88.

Muckelroy, K. 1980. Two Bronze Age cargoes in British waters. *Antiquity* 54, 100–9.

Munn, N. 1973. *Walbiri Iconography*. Ithaca: Cornell University Press.

Northover, P. 1982. The exploration of long-distance movement of bronze in Bronze and Early Iron Age Europe. *Bulletin of the University of London Institute of Archaeology* 19, 45–72.

Nowakowski, J. 1991. Trethellan Farm, Newquay: the excavation of a lowland Bronze Age settlement and Iron Age cemetery. *Cornish Archaeology* 30, 5–242.

Obermaier, H. 1925. Die Bronzezeitlichen Felsfravierungen von Nordwestspanien (Galizien). *Jahrbuch für Prähistorische und Etnographische Kunst* 1, 51–9.

Odak, O. 1989. Figurative and schematic rock art of Kenya: animal representation and tentative interpretation. In H. Morphy (ed), *Animals into Art*, 161–78. London: Unwin Hyman.

O'Kelly, M. 1982. *Newgrange. Archaeology, Art and Legend*. London: Thames and Hudson.

O'Sullivan, A. and Sheehan, J. 1993. Prospection and outlook. Aspects of rock art on the Iveragh Peninsula, Co. Kerry. In E. Shee Twohig and M. Ronayne (eds), *Past Perceptions: The prehistoric archaeology of south-west Ireland*, 75–84. Cork: University of Cork Press.

O'Sullivan, M. 1986. Approaches to passage tomb art. *Journal of the Royal Society of Antiquaries of Ireland* 116, 68–83.

O'Sullivan, M. 1989. A stylistic revolution in the megalithic art of the Boyne valley. *Archaeology Ireland* 3.4, 138–42.

Peña Santos, A. 1976. Asociaciones entre antropomorfos y circulares o espirales: datos para una iconografía do los grabados rupestres gallegos. *Gallaecia* 2, 96–116.

Peña Santos, A. 1979. Notas para una revisión de los grabados rupestres de 'O Castriño' en Conxo. *El Museo de Pontevedra* 33, 3–32.

Peña Santos, A. 1980. Las representaciones de alabardas en los grabados rupestres gallegos. *Zephyrus* 31, 115–29.

Peña Santos, A. 1981. Comentario a 'La Pedra de Ferraduras (Fentáns, Galicia, Espana)' de Cesare Giulio Borgna. *El Museo de Pontevedra* 35, 3–8.

Peña Santos, A. 1985. Excavación de un complejo de grabados rupestres en Campo Lameiro (Pontevedra). *Ars Praehistorica* 3/4, 285–90.

Peña Santos, A. 1987. Cuatro conjuntos de grabados rupestres en la feligresía de Tourón (Pontevedra). *Cuadernos de Estudios Gallegos* 37, 7–30.

Peña Santos, A., Costas Goberna, F. and Rey García, J. 1993. *El arte rupestre en Campo Lameiro*. Santiago de Compostela: Xunta de Galicia.

Peña Santos, A. and Rey García, J. 1993. El espacio de la representación. El arte rupestre galaico desde una perspectiva territorial. *Revista de Estudios Provinciais* 10, 11–50.

Peña Santos, A. and Vázquez Varela, X. M. 1979. *Los petroglifos gallegos*. Coruna: O Castro.

Péquart, M., Péquart, S.-J. and Le Rouzic, Z. 1927. *Corpus des signes gravés des monuments mégalithiques du Morbihan*. Paris: Picard.

Piggott, S. 1939. The Badbury Barrow, Dorset and its carved stone. *Antiquaries Journal* 19, 291–9.

Piggott, S. 1972. Excavation of the Dalladies long barrow, Fettercairn, Kincardineshire. *Proceedings of the Society of Antiquaries of Scotland* 103, 23–47.

Piggott, S. and Powell, T. 1949. The excavation of three chambered tombs in Galloway. *Proceedings of the Society of Antiquaries of Scotland* 83, 103–61.

Piggott, S. and Simpson, D. 1971. Excavation of a stone circle at Croft Moraig, Perthshire, Scotland. *Proceedings of the Prehistoric Society* 37, 1–15.

Purcell, A. 1994. Carved landscapes: the rock art of the Iveragh peninsula. MA thesis, University College, Cork.

Putnam, R. 1988. *The Natural History of Deer*. Bromley: Helm.

RCAHMS 1911. *Second Report and Inventory of Monuments and Constructions in the County of Sutherland*. Edinburgh: HMSO.

RCAHMS 1971. *Argyll*, vol 1. Edinburgh: HMSO.

RCAHMS 1988. *Argyll*, vol 6. Edinburgh HMSO.

RCAHMS 1990. *North-east Perth. An archaeological landscape*. Edinburgh: HMSO.

RCAHMS 1994. *South-east Perth. An archaeological landscape*. Edinburgh: HMSO.

Renfrew, C. 1976, Megaliths, territories and populations. In S. de Laet (ed), *Acculturation and Continuity in Atlantic Europe*, 198–220. Bruges: De Tempel.

Renfrew, C. 1979. *Investigations in Orkney*. London: Society of Antiquaries.

Renfrew, C. 1993. Trade beyond the material. In C. Scarre and F. Healy (eds), *Trade and Exchange in Prehistoric Europe*, 5–16. Oxford: Oxbow.

Rhoads, J. 1992. Significant sites and non-site archaeology: a case study from south-east Australia. *World Archaeology* 24, 198–217.

Richards, C. 1991. Skara Brae: revisiting a Neolithic village in Orkney. In W. Hanson and E. Slater (eds), *Scottish Archaeology: New perceptions*, 24–43. Aberdeen: Aberdeen University Press.

Ricq-de Bouard, M. 1993. Trade in Neolithic jadeite axes from the Alps. In C. Scarre and F. Healy (eds), *Trade and Exchange in Prehistoric Europe*, 61–7. Oxford: Oxbow.

Ripoll Perelló, E. 1990. Acerca de algunos problemas del arte rupestre postpaleolitico en la Peninsula Ibérica. *Espacio, Tiempo y Forma* 3, 71–104.

Ritchie, J. N. G. 1974. Excavation of the stone circle and cairn at Balbirnie, Fife. *Archaeological Journal* 131, 1–32.

Ritchie, J. N. G. and Adamson, H. 1981. Knappers, Dumbartonshire: a reassessment. *Proceedings of the Society of Antiquaries of Scotland* 111, 172–204.

Root, D. 1983. Information exchange and the spatial configuration of egalitarian societies. In J. Moore and A. Keene (eds), *Archaeological Hammers and Theories*. New York: Academic Press.

Ruggles, C. 1984. *Megalithic Astronomy. A new archaeological and statistical study of 300 western Scottish sites*. Oxford: British Archaeological Reports.

Ruggles, C. and Burl, A. 1985. A new study of the Aberdeenshire recumbent stone circles (2): interpretation. *Archaeoastronomy* 8, 25–60.

Ruggles, C., Martlew, R. and Hinge, P. 1991. The North Mull Project (2): the wider astronomical significance of the sites. *Archaeoastronomy* 16, 51–75.

Ruiz-Gálvez, M. 1978. El tesoro de Caldas de Reyes. *Trabajos de Prehistoria* 35, 173–86.

Ruiz-Gálvez, M. 1987. Bronce Atlántico y 'cultura' del Bronce Atlántico en Peninsula Iberica. *Trabajos de Prehistoria* 44, 251–64.

Ruiz-Gálvez, M. 1991. Songs of a wayfaring lad. Late Bronze Age Atlantic exchange and the building of regional identity in the west Iberian peninsula. *Oxford Journal of Archaeology* 10, 277–306.

Ruiz-Gálvez, M. 1995. *Ritos de paso y puntos de paso: la Ria de Huelva en el mundo del Bronce Final Europeo*. Madrid: Complutum extra 5.

Russell-White, C., Lowe, C. and McCullagh, R. 1992. Excavations at three Early Bronze Age burial monuments in Scotland. *Proceedings of the Prehistoric Society* 58, 285–322.

Savory, H. 1940. A Middle Bronze Age barrow at Crick, Monmouthshire. *Archaeologia Cambrensis* 95, 169–91.

Scarre, C. 1992. The Early Neolithic of western France and megalithic origins in Atlantic Europe. *Oxford Journal of Archaeology* 11, 121–54.

Scott, J. 1989. The stone circles at Temple Wood, Kilmartin, Argyll. *Glasgow Archaeological Journal* 15, 53–124.

Sharples, N. 1985. Individual and community: the changing role of megaliths in the Orcadian Neolithic. *Proceedings of the Prehistoric Society* 51, 59–74.

Shee Twohig, E. 1981. *The Megalithic Art of Western Europe*. Oxford: Clarendon Press.

Shee Twohig, E. 1988. The rock carvings at Roughting Linn, Northumberland. *Archaeologia Aeliana* 16, 37–46.

Shee Twohig, E. 1993. Megalithic tombs and megalithic art in Atlantic Europe. In C. Scarre and F. Healy (eds), *Trade and Exchange in Prehistoric Europe*, 87–99. Oxford: Oxbow.

Shennan, S., Healy, F. and Smith, I. 1985. The excavation of a ring ditch at Tye Field, Lawford, Essex. *Archaeological Journal* 142, 150–215.

Sheridan, A. 1987. Megaliths and megalomania. An account, and interpretation, of the development of passage tombs in Ireland. *Journal of Irish Archaeology* 2, 229–65.

Sherratt, A. 1990. The genesis of megaliths: ethnicity and social complexity in Neolithic north-west Europe. *World Archaeology* 22, 147–67.

Sherratt, A. 1991. Sacred and profane substances: the ritual use of narcotics in later Neolithic Europe. In P. Garwood, D. Jennings, R. Skeates and J. Toms (eds), *Sacred and Profane*, 50–64. Oxford: Oxford University Committee for Archaeology.

Simpson, D. 1988. The stone maceheads of Ireland. *Journal of the Royal Society of Antiquaries of Ireland* 118, 27–52.

Simpson, D. and Thawley, J. 1972. Single grave art in Britain. *Scottish Archaeological Forum* 4, 81–104.

Simpson, J. 1867. *Archaic Sculpturings of Cups, Circles etc upon Stones and Rocks in Scotland, England etc and other Countries*. Edinburgh: Edmonston and Douglas.

Smith, C. 1989. Excavations at Dod Law West hillfort, Northumberland. *Northern Archaeology* 9, 1–55.

Smith, C. 1992. The use of ethnography in interpreting rock art: a comparative study of Arnhem Land and the Western Desert of Australia. In M. Morwood and D. Hobbs (eds), *Rock Art and Ethnography*, 39–45. Melbourne: Australian Association for Rock Art Research.

Smith, M. 1994. *Excavated Bronze Age Burial Mounds of North-east Yorkshire*. Durham: Architectural and Archaeological Society of Durham and Northumberland.

Sobrino Buhigas, R. 1935. *Corpus petroglyphorum Gallaeciae*. Santiago de Compostela: Seminario de Estudios Gallegos.

Sockett, E. 1971. A Bronze Age barrow at Mount Pleasant, near Normanby, North Riding. *Yorkshire Archaeological Journal* 43, 33–9.

Sognes, K. 1994. Ritual landscapes: towards a reinterpretation of Stone Age rock art at Trøndelag, Norway. *Norwegian Archaeological Review* 27.1, 29–50.

Soto Barreiro, M. J. and Rey Castineiras, P. 1994. Unha metodoloxiía de estudio para petroglifos: resultado en Laxe da Sartana. *Braña* 4, 49–72.

Spratt, D. (ed) 1993. *Prehistoric and Roman Archaeology of North-east Yorkshire*. Second edition. York: Council for British Archaeology.

Stanley, J. 1954. An Iron Age fort at Ball Cross Farm, Bakewell. *Derbyshire Archaeological Journal* 74, 85–99.

Stevenson, J. 1993. Cup and ring markings at Ballochmyle, Ayrshire. *Glasgow Archaeological Journal* 11, 33–40.

Stewart, M. 1958. Strath Tay in the second millennium BC – a field survey. *Proceedings of the Society of Antiquaries of Scotland* 92, 71–84.

Stewart, M. 1966. The excavation of a setting of standing stones at Lundin Farm, near Aberfeldy. *Proceedings of the Society of Antiquaries of Scotland* 98, 126–49.

Stone, J. F. S. 1935. Some discoveries at Ratfyn, Amesbury, and their bearing on the date of Woodhenge. *Wiltshire Archaeological Magazine* 47, 58–67.

Stopford, J. 1994. Some approaches to the archaeology of Christian pilgrimage. *World Archaeology* 26, 57–72.

Stout, G. 1991. Embanked enclosures of the Boyne region. *Proceedings of the Royal Irish Academy* 54 C, 37–74.

Tacon, P. 1994. Socialising landscapes: the long-term implications of signs, symbols and marks on the land. *Archaeology in Oceania* 29, 117–29.

Tate, G. 1865. *The Ancient British Sculptured Rocks of Northumberland and the Eastern Borders*. Alnwick: Hunter Blair.

Thomas, J. 1990. Monuments from the inside: the case of the Irish megalithic tombs. *World Archaeology* 22, 168–78.

Thomas, J. 1991. *Rethinking the Neolithic*. Cambridge: Cambridge University Press.

Thomas, J. 1992. Monuments, movement and the context of megalithic art. In N. Sharples and A. Sheridan (eds), *Vessels for the Ancestors*, 143–55. Edinburgh: Edinburgh University Press.

Thornby, C. 1902. Ring-marked stones at Glassonby and Maughanby. *Transactions of the Cumberland and Westmorland Antiquarian and Archaeological Society* 2, 380–3.

Tilley, C. 1991. *Material Culture and Text: The art of ambiguity*. London: Routledge.

Tilley, C. 1994. *A Phenomenology of Landscape*. Oxford: Berg.

Tipping, R. 1992. The determination of cause in the generation of major prehistoric valley fills in the Cheviot Hills, Anglo-Scottish border. In S. Needham and M. Macklin (eds), *Alluvial Archaeology in Britain*, 111–21. Oxford: Oxbow.

Topping, P. 1992. The Penrith henges: a survey by the Royal Commission on the Historical Monuments of England. *Proceedings of the Prehistoric Society* 58, 249–64.

Torre Luna, M. P., Pazo Labrador, A. and Santos Solla, J. M. 1990. *Galicia, rexión de contrastes xeográficos*. Santiago de Compostela: Biblioteca de Divulgación.

Trudgian, P. 1976. Observations and excavation at Titchbarrow, Davidstow. *Cornish Archaeology* 15, 31–47.

Tylecote, R. 1987. *The Early History of Metallurgy in Europe*. Harlow: Longman.

Van Hoek, M. 1987. The prehistoric rock art of County Donegal (part 1). *Ulster Journal of Archaeology* 50, 23–46.

Van Hoek, M. 1988. The prehistoric rock art of County Donegal (part 2). *Ulster Journal of Archaeology* 51, 21–47.

Van Hoek, M. 1990. The rosette in British and Irish rock art. *Glasgow Archaeological Journal* 16, 39–54.

Van Hoek, M. 1993. The spiral in British and Irish rock art. *Glasgow Archaeological Journal* 18, 11–32.

Van Hoek, M. 1995. *Morris' Prehistoric Rock Art of Galloway*. Privately published.

Vázquez Rozas, P. 1995a. Los petroglifos gallegos: selección de su emplazamiento en las rocas grabadas. *Actas del XXII Congreso Nacional de Arqueología, Vigo*, vol 1, 69–76.

Vázquez Rozas, P. 1995b. El tema de la caza y el cilindro antropomorfo en los petroglifos gallegos. *Actas de XXII Congreso Nacional de Arqueología, Vigo*, vol 1, 77–81.

Vázquez Varela, X. M. 1990. *Petroglifos de Galicia*. Santiago de Compostela: Biblioteca de Divulgación.

Vázquez Varela, X. M. 1993. Alucinaciones y arte prehistórico; teoría y realidad en el noroeste de la Península Ibérica. *Pyrenae* 24, 87–91.

Villoch Vázquez, V. 1995. Monumentos y petroglifos: la construcción del espacio en las sociedades constructoras de túmulos del noroeste peninsular. *Trabajos de Prehistoria* 52.1, 50–70.

Vyner, B. 1984. The excavation of a Neolithic cairn at Street House, Loftus, Cleveland. *Proceedings of the Prehistoric Society* 50, 151–91.

Vyner, B. 1988a. The hillfort on Eston Nab, Eston, Cleveland. *Archaeological Journal* 145, 60–98.

Vyner, B. 1988b. The Street House Wossit: the excavation of a Late Neolithic and Early Bronze Age ritual monument at Street House, Loftus, Cleveland. *Proceedings of the Prehistoric Society* 54, 173–202.

Wainwright, G. and Longworth, I. 1971. *Durrington Walls: Excavations 1966–1968*. London: Society of Antiquaries.

Walker, M. 1977. 'Schematised' rock markings as archaeological evidence. In P. Ucko (ed), *Form in Indigenous Art*, 452–69. Canberra: Australian Institute of Aboriginal Studies.

Whittle, A. 1977. *The Earlier Neolithic of Southern England and Its Continental Background*. Oxford: British Archaeological Reports.

Williams, J. 1970. Neolithic axes in Dumfries and Galloway. *Transactions of the Dumfries and Galloway Antiquarian Society* 47, 111–22.

Wilson, D. 1983. Pollen analysis and settlement archaeology of the first millennium BC in north-east England. In J. Chapman and H. Mytum (eds), *Settlement in North Britain, 1000 BC to 1000 AD*, 29–54. Oxford: British Archaeological Reports.

Wilson, P. 1988. *The Domestication of the Human Species*. New Haven: Yale University Press.

Wobst, H. M. 1977. Stylistic behaviour and information exchange. In C. Cleland (ed), *For the Director: Research essays in honour of J. B. Griffin*, 317–42. Ann Arbor: University of Michigan Museum of Anthropology.

Woodman, P. and O'Brien, M. 1993. Excavations at Ferriter's Cove, Co. Kerry: an interim statement. In E. Shee Twohig and M. Ronayne (eds), *Past Perceptions. The prehistoric archaeology of south-west Ireland*, 25–34. Cork: Cork University Press.

Zilhão, J. 1993. The spread of agro-pastoral economies across Mediterranean Europe: a view from the far west. *Journal of Mediterranean Archaeology* 6, 5–63.

Zindel, C. 1970. Incisioni rupestri a Carschenna. *Valcamonica Symposium, 1965*, 135–42. Capo di Ponte: Edizioni del Centro.

Züchner, C. 1989. Haıser, Felder und Wege in der galischen Felsbildkunst. *Madrider Mitteilungen* 30, 55–75.

Züchner, C. 1992. Idol, Schild oder Wagon? Zur Deutung einer Gravierung vom Castro de Conjo bei Santiago de Compostela. *Madrider Mitteilungen* 33, 1–5.

INDEX

—•◆•—